IMAGES
of America

GRANDVILLE

On the Cover: Pictured in 1900, girls play volleyball in the schoolyard of Grandville Union High School, located at Wedgwood Court and Prairie Street. Note the large bows in their hair. The dresses and shoes most likely got in the way of playing ball. (Courtesy of the Grandville Historical Commission.)

IMAGES
of America

GRANDVILLE

Grandville Historical Commission

ARCADIA
PUBLISHING

ISBN 978-0-7385-8406-5

Published by Arcadia Publishing
Charleston, South Carolina

Printed in the United States of America

Library of Congress Control Number: 2009943859

For all general information, please contact Arcadia Publishing:
Telephone 843-853-2070
Fax 843-853-0044
E-mail sales@arcadiapublishing.com
For customer service and orders:
Toll-Free 1-888-313-2665

Visit us on the Internet at www.arcadiapublishing.com

We dedicate this book to William Winglar, who was a part of our team when we started this project. We know how you wanted to finish this with us. Rest in peace, dear friend!

Contents

Acknowledgments

Joined by our mutual passion for history, Bill Dudas, Bill Winglar, and myself, Joyce Cole, started this journey with the blessing of the Grandville Historical Commission. Bill Winglar passed away at the start of this project, so we finished this for him. We wish to thank the commission for its support, the local community for donating photographs, and all the people who shared their stories with us.

A great big thank-you goes out to Grandville–Jenison Lions Club member Margaret Timmer, who donated her time and much-needed computer skills. We could not have done it without you! And a special thanks is given to Grandville High School student Shea Cole, who spent his Saturdays organizing photographs on the computer.

INTRODUCTION

Owashtanong River . . . ever hear of it? Oakestown . . . is that another name you could be familiar with? Hopewell Indian mounds . . . does that ring a bell? No? Well, let me tell you a story of "once upon a time in the history of Grandville, Michigan." Flash back a moment to a deep forest, a clear flowing river, and a beautiful prairie. Ottawa Indians paddle down the mighty Owashtanong River, which means "far away waters" in their native tongue. They pass burial mounds that line the river of the ancient and long-gone Hopewell Indian tribe. In 1832, white men paddled that same river, which they renamed the Grand River for the mighty rapids a few miles upstream that could not be passed.

Fur traders were the first to come, then hunters, then pioneers. It was a wild, unsettled area, known for mosquitoes and malaria. Most people just passed on through, but Charles Oakes stayed for a while. He opened up a fur-trading post and took an Indian wife. There was a nice sandy bend in the river, an easy place to come onshore where trees thinned out revealing a beautiful prairie. The Indians called the area Little Prairie. Oakes called it Oakestown, while others knew it as "that little village on the Grand River." Hence, it became known as Grandville.

A tide of immigration came to Grandville. The 1850 census shows people coming from places such as England, Holland, Ireland, Canada, Germany, and most of the New England states, including Vermont, Maine, and New York. The *Grand Rapids Enquirer* reported, "During the past week our streets have been taken by the Dutch." The Hollanders resorted here in uncommon numbers, and the ox teams took over in caravans. Most moved on to VanRaaltes religious colony in Holland, and the rest spread throughout the county.

Grandville kept up the pace with Grand Rapids, most people expecting Grandville to become the larger city, as business was doing well there. It boasted more sawmills and plaster mines and employed many more people. Many letters were written asking to send men from back East, as the enterprises did not have enough hands for all the work. By 1870, Grandville boasted five dry goods and grocery stores, two churches, two drugstores, two blacksmith shops, one boot store, one shoe store, and a harness shop.

Steamboats made it easier to transport goods. They also shortened travel time from Grandville to Grand Rapids, formerly accessed by Indian trails. The *Olive Branch* was described as a floating palace in its day. She was propelled by a 24-foot-wide paddle wheeler and was the fastest on the river, with the best accommodations. Despite marine regulations about racing steamboats, the *Empire*, another paddle wheeler, challenged the *Olive Branch* and was defeated. She lost both heads out of her cylinders and did not ply the river for that whole summer; the captain was fired. It was said that the *Olive Branch* was blameless. Was it because she won the race?

For those who enjoyed racing horses, there was always a group that would race from Grandville to Jenison along the river. One might have wanted to stop by Albert Medemar's house on the way. At one time, he owned most of the land in Grandville, and he was employed by the steamer *Daniel Ball* going from Grand Haven to the Rapids. He helped build the school in Grandville and helped Platt the city streets with John Ball (of John Ball Zoo fame). He was also superintendant of the plaster mills. One could go and talk to some interesting people at McCoys General Store. Sitting around the pot-bellied stove, tales of the 1898 Spanish-American War or talk local politics could be heard. The local city ordinances were tacked to the wall in Caldwell's market. They instructed one man to build a pen for his hogs, a hotel was given a liquor license, and others warned that tramps were not to be sheltered at the village's expense and absence from a village meeting would result in a fine (if an excuse proved insufficient). Life was good for the little river town of Grandville in those days. It had good churches and one of the finest of schools. It had boats, trains, and eventually automobiles. Yes, industry abounded.

Grandville was founded in 1832 and incorporated in 1933. It is one of the oldest suburbs of Grand Rapids, Michigan. Today, the city has come into its own. There are numerous churches, schools, and businesses, including a new destination mall called Rivertown Crossings, which has brought more jobs and more people. The western border of the city is also the border of Kent County, marked by Kenowa Avenue, where Georgetown Township begins. To the east and south of Grandville is the city of Wyoming, and the city of Walker/Standale is to the north.

Grandville is forever growing and changing. As of the census in 2000, the city boasted 16,263 people, and the median income was $55,047. Main roads through town are Twenty-eighth Street, Chicago Drive, Wilson Avenue, I-196, and Rivertown (Forty-fourth) Street. Welcome to Grandville, we are glad to see you!

One

Schools and Churches

Going to school in the 1800s and early 1900s in Grandville was not easy, and education was not always considered that important. Children were needed at home on the farm to do chores or to take care of siblings. It was deemed important to be able to write one's name in case a signature was needed, and it was important to know arithmetic to avoid being cheated at the market when buying or selling livestock or produce. To know anything more was considered a luxury.

Children faced a very long walk to school; some would ride a horse. If a child was late, the doors would be locked until recess. In bad weather, many students would not go to school. For a boy, punishment was usually chopping wood for the stove that heated the schoolhouse. For a girl, sweeping was a typical penalty. The dunce cap was also used, and ridicule was accepted punishment. Teachers were allowed to strike the children, either by hand or a switch made from a tree.

Students were not allowed to sit together: one side of the room for boys and the other for girls. If a child spoke in class, he or she had to rise and address the teacher as "ma'am" or "sir." In that era, penmanship was more important than spelling, and memorization of long poems or readings was the norm. In the Grandville No. 10 one-room schoolhouse, kindergarten through the eighth grade was taught together. School often lasted 10 months, excluding the month of October for the local potato harvest, and ended by the eighth grade; a big graduation ceremony was then held.

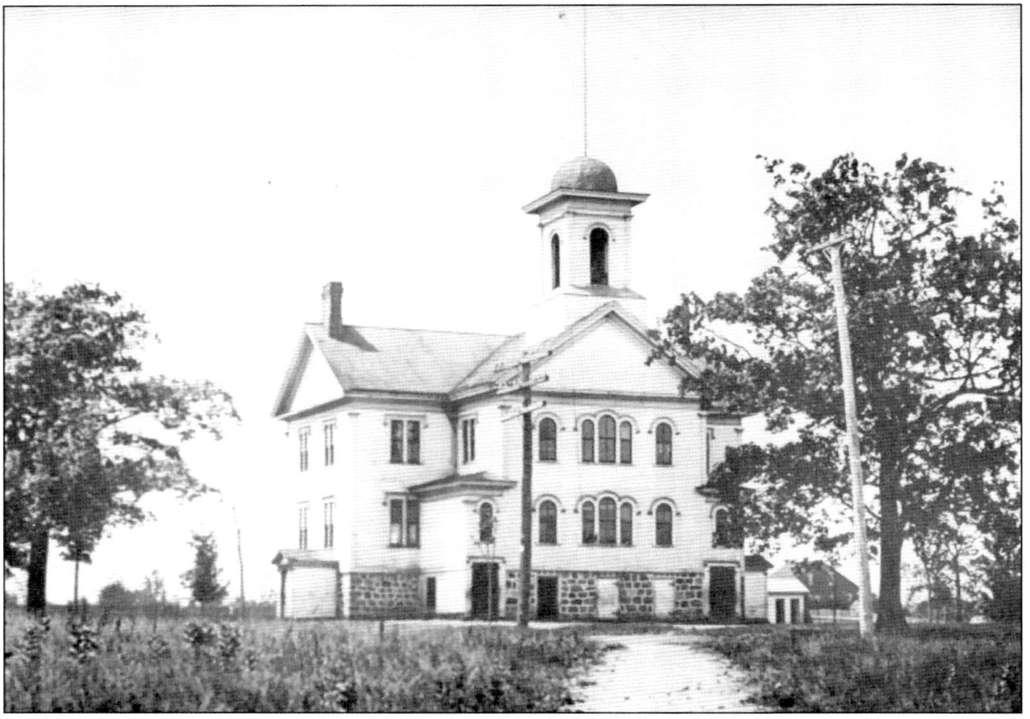

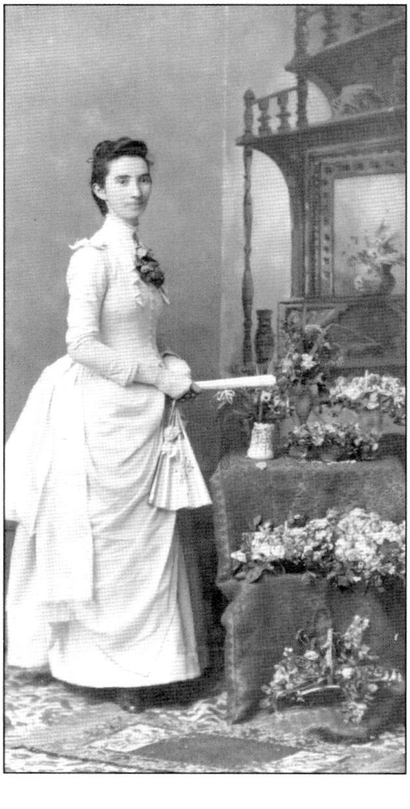

Grandville Union School was located at Wedgwood Court and Prairie Street from 1867 to 1910. It cost $10,000 to purchase the lot and construct the building. The school housed kindergarten through 12th grade. It was described by a local paper as "elegant, the finest schoolhouse in the country." It was a two-story wood frame structure with a stone foundation. Teachers were hired after being asked in great detail about their moral life and practices by the school board, who made the final decisions. Female teachers were to be unmarried; if a woman did marry, she was to quit her teaching job to become a wife.

Rose Seally was a graduate of Grandville Union School in 1888 in a class of six that year. To graduate from a high school was uncommon, as most students stopped going to school in the eighth grade. Expected to become wives and mothers, it was especially rare for girls to go to high school unless they planned to teach.

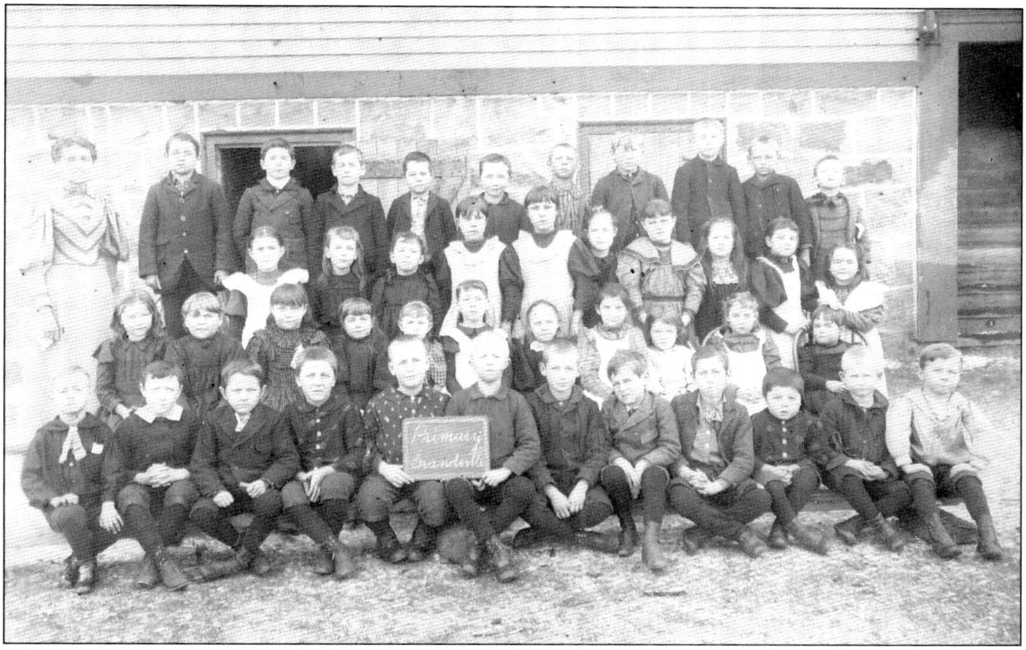

This January 1896 photograph shows the primary class gathered outside Grandville Union School. Parents of children outside the school district paid a small fee; usually there was no choice, as there were no other schools around. Children on the other side of the river, by the current location of Johnson Park, had no way to get across the river except by pole boat. A bridge was not built until 1928, but even with it, a long journey to school each day remained.

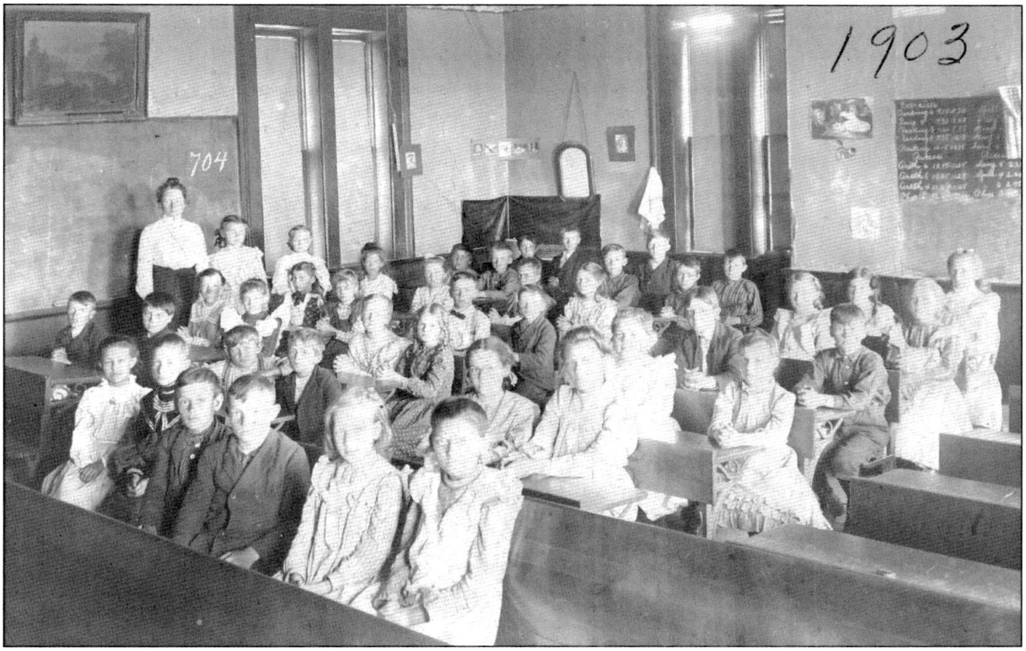

Teacher Nellie Burgess stands with her students inside Union School in 1903. Note how the children have their hands folded and are sitting up straight.

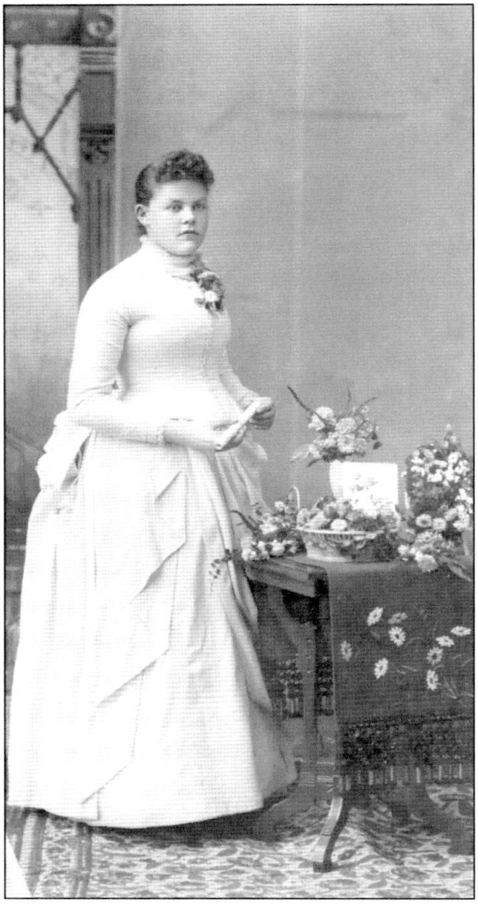

Edith Zimmer also graduated from Grandville Union School in 1888. She was one of six students in the high school class that consisted of four girls and two boys. That year, if a student passed the exam, he or she could teach school after graduation without attending college.

Built in 1869, the Grandville Methodist Church was located on the corner of Washington Drive and Prairie Street. Looking west, the church was once visible from Grandville Union School. In 1880, when in the process of warming stray kittens, some young boys started a fire that spread through the church stables and then to the church itself, burning it to the ground. Money was raised, and a few years later the church was rebuilt.

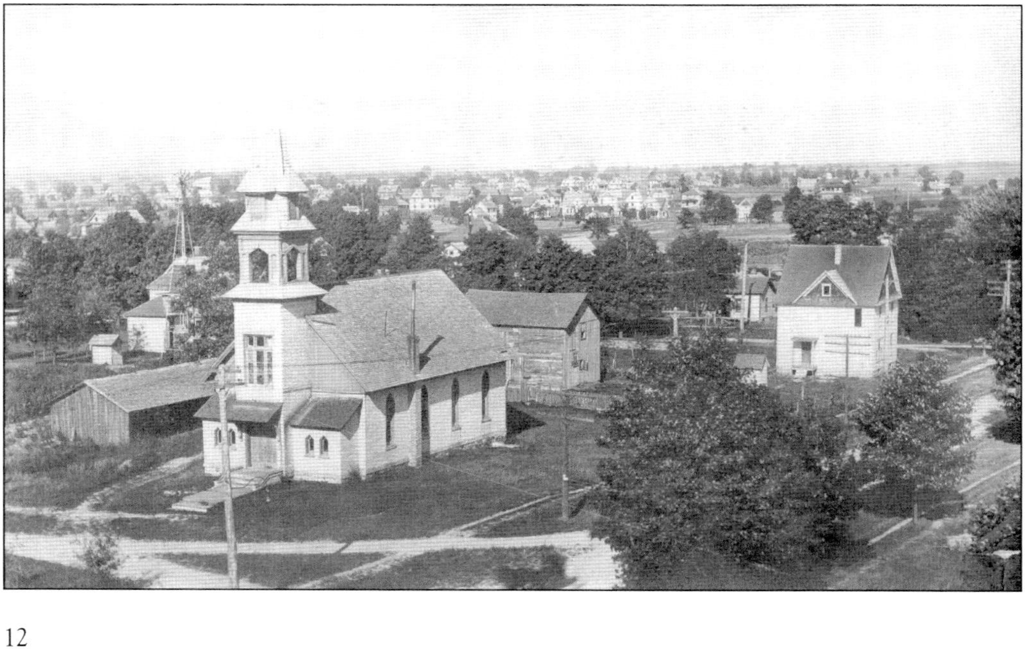

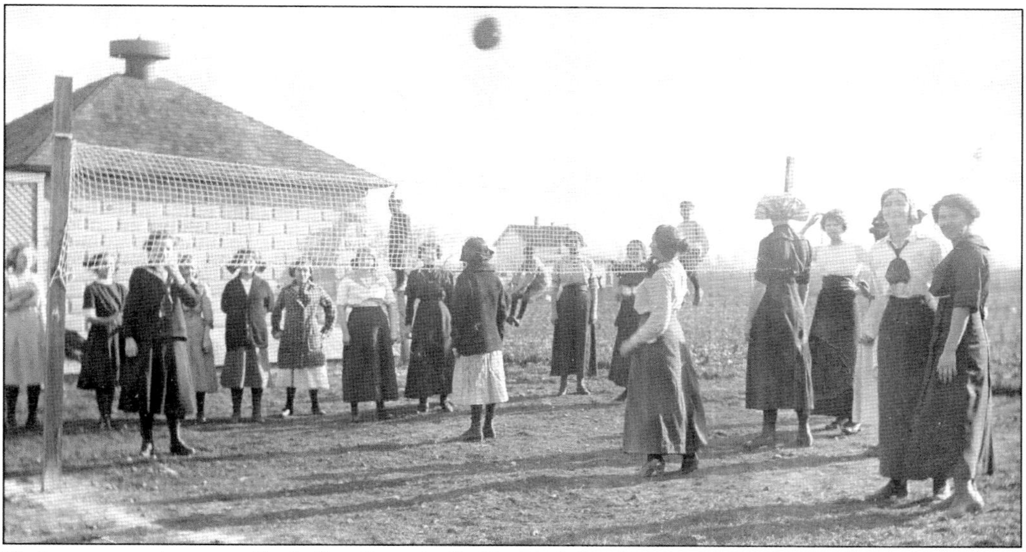

Girls are seen playing volleyball at Grandville Union School in 1900. This is the schoolyard, which later became Wedgwood Field. Equipment was scarce in those days for games like volleyball and baseball, so students had to make their own fun at times. "Kick the Can" and "Eine Inie Over" (throwing a ball over the school) were popular games that required little to no equipment.

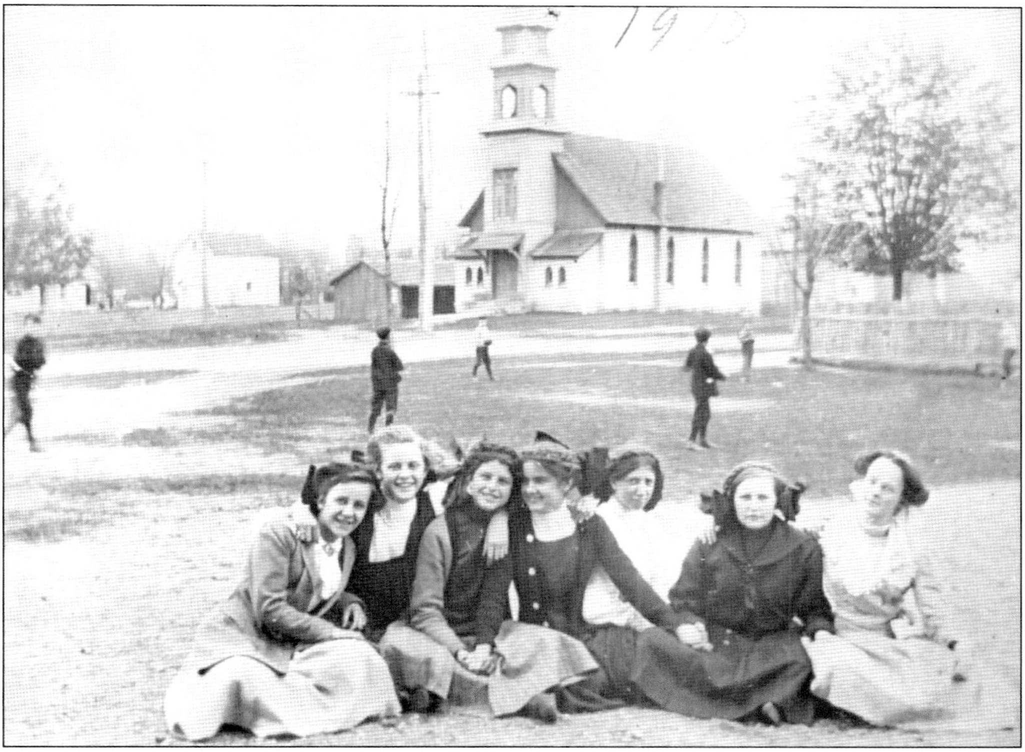

This is the schoolyard of Grandville Union School in 1910. It was located on the corner of Wedgwood Court and Prairie Street. The Methodist church is in the background. The school was torn down the following year, and the foundation was moved to Chicago Drive.

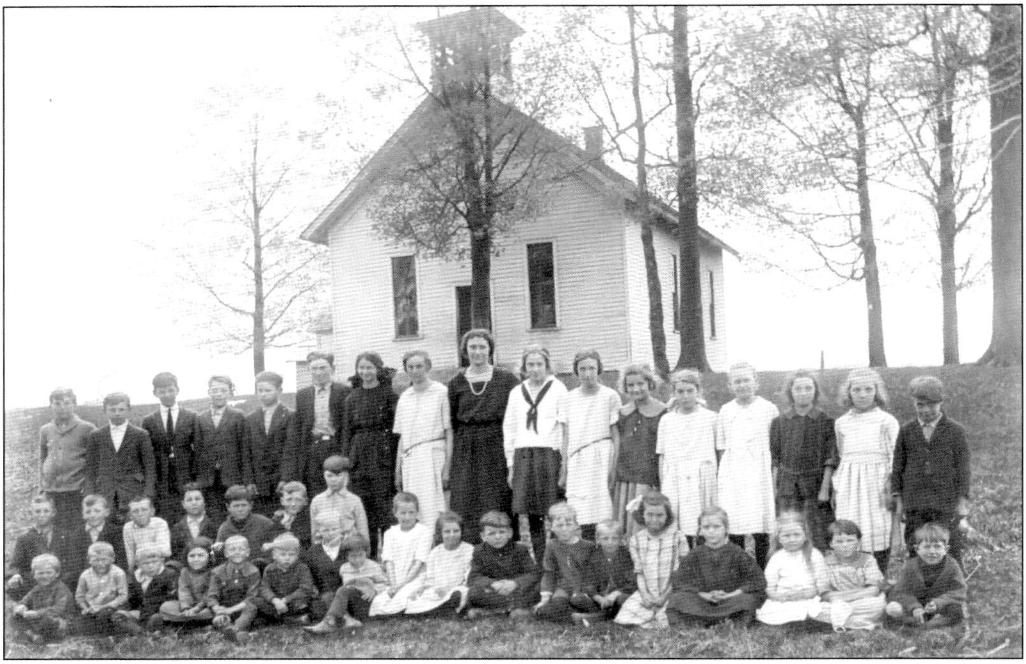

This 1924 photograph shows teacher Florence Nauta with her students at the one-room schoolhouse. The District No. 10 one-room schoolhouse was in use from 1887 to 1958. Built on a hill on Forty-fourth Street, the land cost $50 and the structure $400. The school housed kindergarten through eighth grade. The teacher had to be unmarried, respectful, and able to chop wood and was given a small salary.

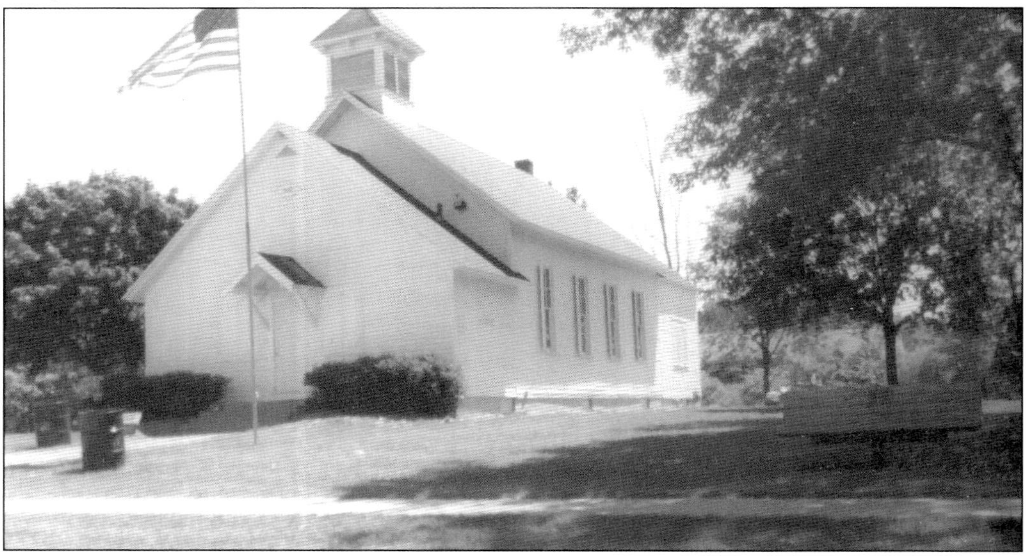

In the 1980s, a movement was spearheaded by the historical commission to save the District No. 10 one-room schoolhouse and move it to its present location in Heritage Park on Canal Avenue, where it is now a working museum free and open to the public. Local elementary students spend a whole day at No. 10 as if it were 1880, dressed in costume with their lunches packed in a tin or a basket.

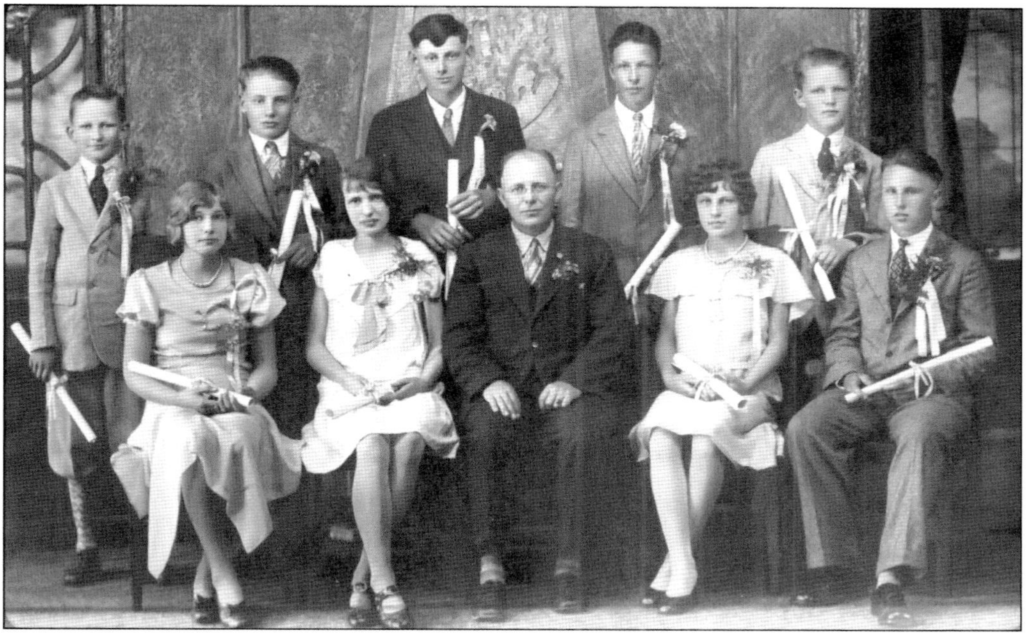

This is the eighth-grade graduating class of 1929 from No. 10. From left to right are (first row) Agatha Schilstra, Gladys Harvey, Howard Walcott (teacher), Charlotte Hazebrook, and Darrell Phillips; (second row) Ken Vredevoogd, Harold Bulliment, Arthur McCuen, Henry Boorsma, and Carlton Vredevoogd.

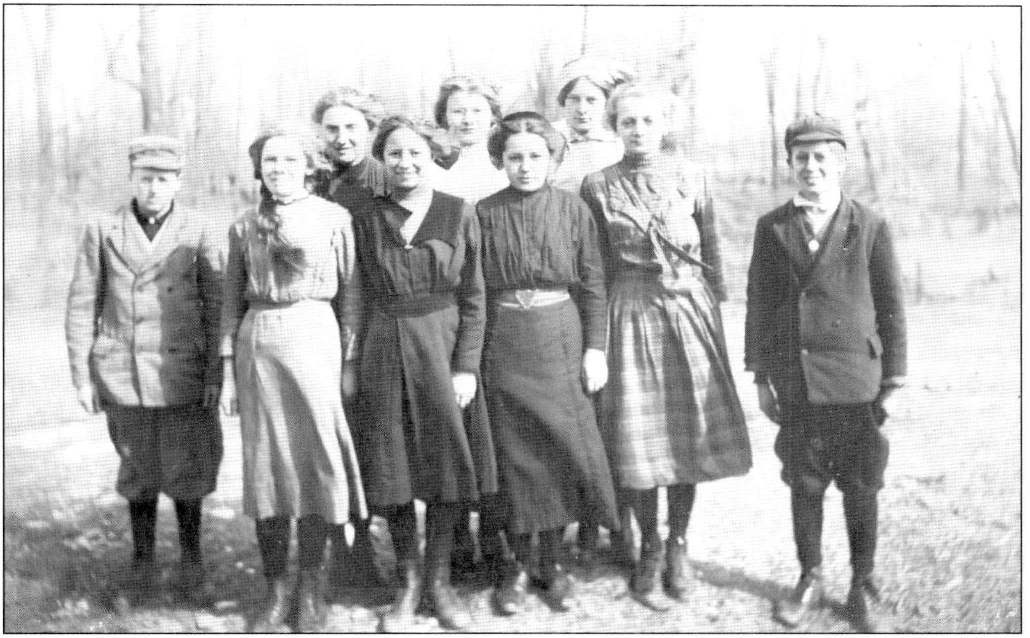

Young people stand in the schoolyard of the No. 10 schoolhouse in 1915. The boy on the far left is Conrad Becker, and the boy on the far right is Wesley Becker; the girl in the center of the second row is Lila Bulliment. Note the knickers on the boys, and the high-top, button shoes the girls are wearing.

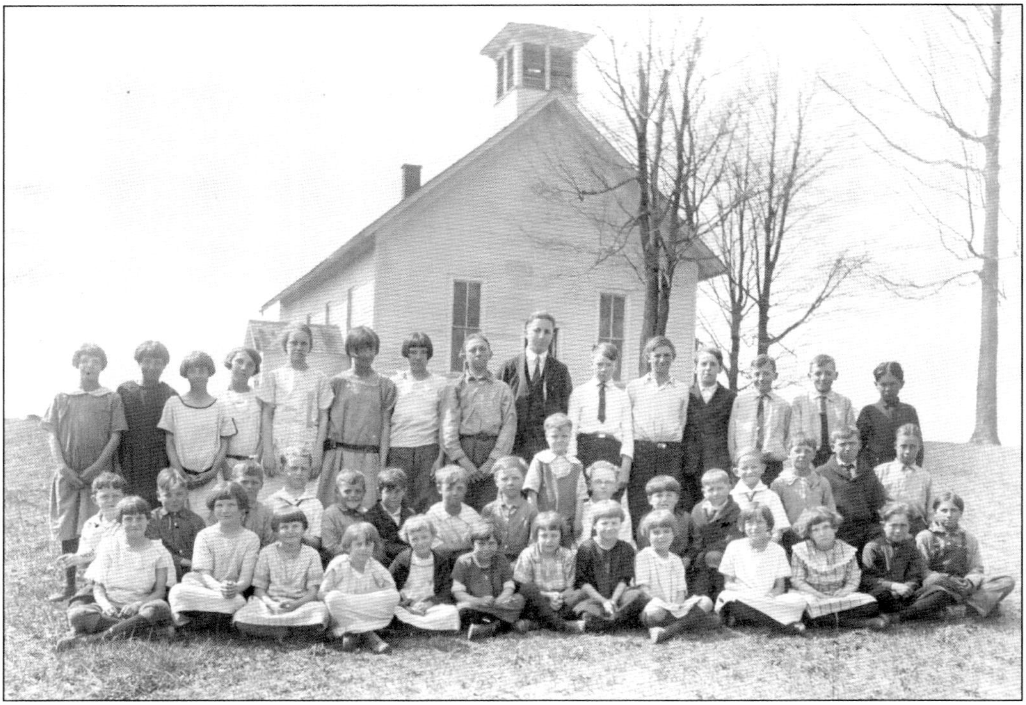

Teacher Mr. Kellogg stands with his students in front of the No. 10 one-room schoolhouse in 1920. Kellogg left the following year to teach elsewhere. He had 43 students in his class that year at different grade levels, and all were taught in one room.

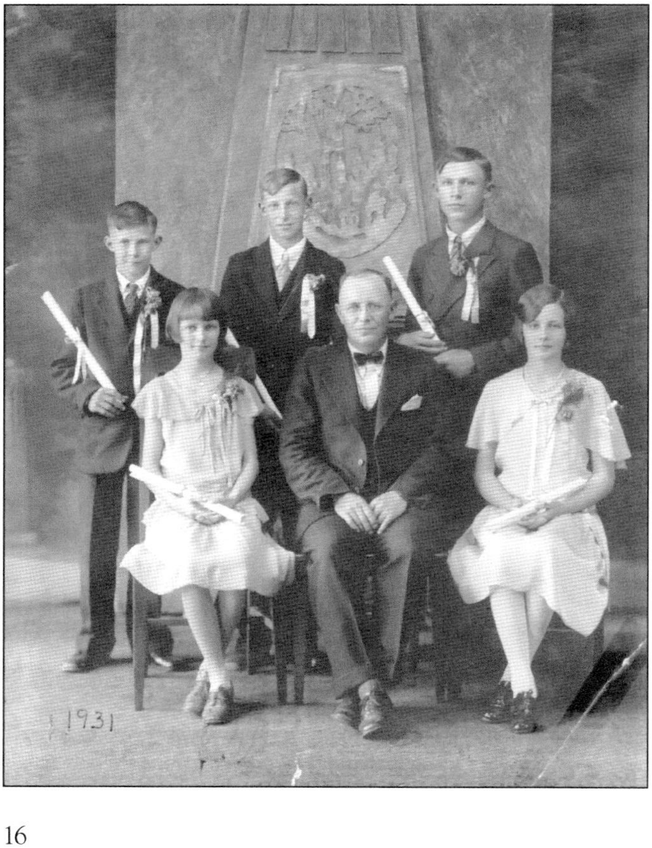

This is the No. 10 schoolhouse graduating class of 1931. From left to right are (first row) Thelma Vredevoogd, Howard Walcott (teacher), and Virginia Bulliment; (second row) Casey Dryer, Ernest "Boots" Boorsma, and Haldane Harvey. Except for a few years at another school, Walcott served No. 10 for his entire teaching career.

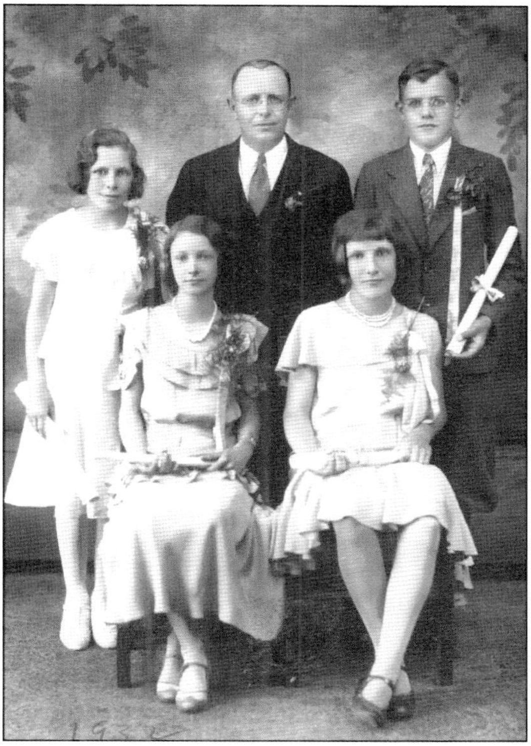

This is the No. 10 eighth-grade graduating class of 1932. From left to right are (first row) Wilma "Babe" Boorsma and Kathryn Mekkes; (second row) Madellan Shoemaker, Howard Walcott (teacher), and Ivan Zwyghuizen.

This is the No. 10 graduating class of 1927. From left to right are (first row) Dena Boorsma, teacher Howard Walcott, and Janet Mekkes; (second row) Nick Dryer, Tressa Katsma, and Paul Hallas. The Grandville Union School, built in 1887 on the corner of Wedgwood Court and Prairie Street, was beginning to show its age and was becoming crowded. So, in the spring of 1910, a brick school was built for $18,000 on the land bordering Prairie, Barrett, Ottawa, and Superior Streets. It housed kindergarten through 12th grade. College entrance exams were then added to the curriculum, along with citizenship classes and home and business management.

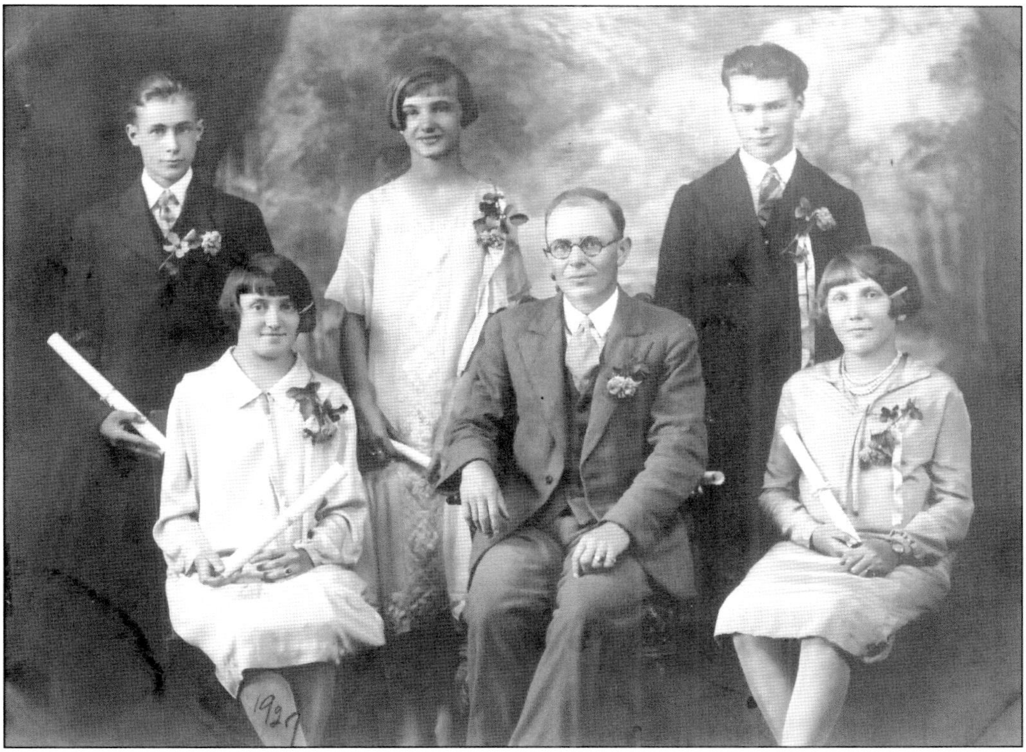

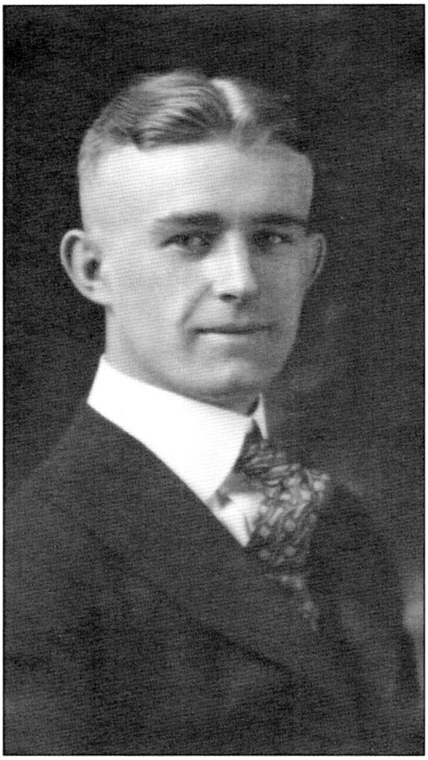

Louis Brunsting was a Calvin College graduate and a teacher at Grandville High School in 1920. Grandville had four high school teachers that year. Brunsting taught science and athletics and was also the boys' basketball coach. There were seven boys on the team, and it accumulated a record of 9-4 playing against such schools as Coopersville, Sparta, Catholic Central, Union, Lowell, Calvin College, and Grand Rapids Junior College. Scores of 6-18, 14-15, and 33-12 were common in that era. Brunsting was also the coach for track and baseball, both of which had a fall and a spring season. No other sports were offered.

Pictured in 1916, teachers posing at Grandville High School on Prairie Street are (first row) Mary Murphy, Lillian Sowersby, Carmaletta Barton, and Ruth Dietz; (second row) Miss Dean, Emma Smith, Albert W. Glas (superintendent of the school from 1910 to 1919), Miss Kelder, Miss La Van, and Francis Maloney.

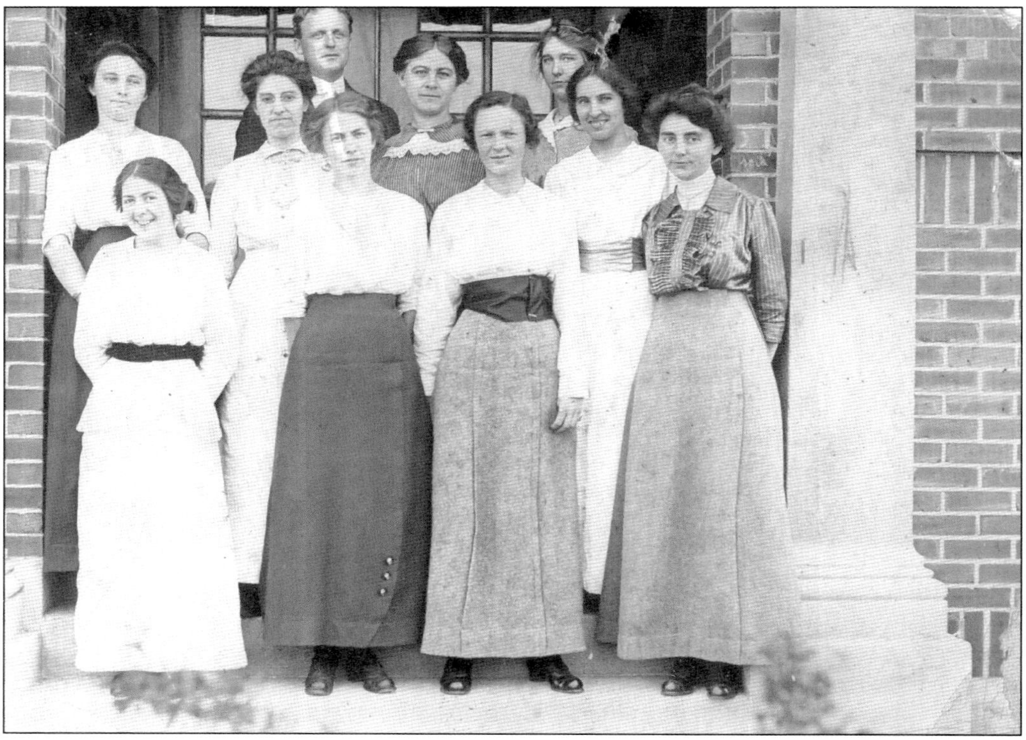

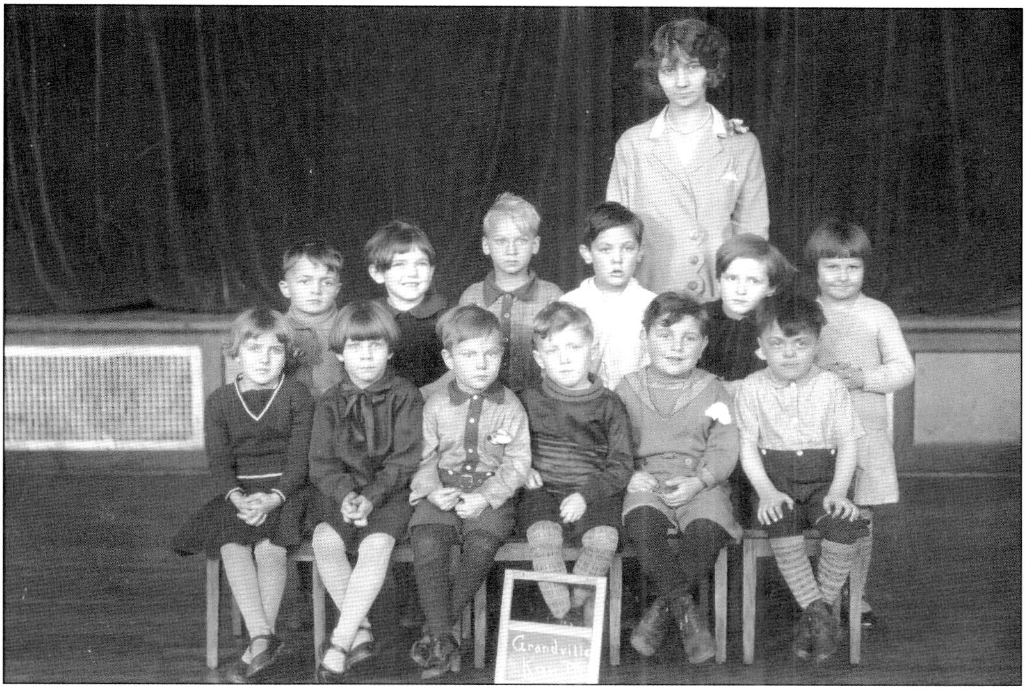

Located on the corner of Prairie and Barrett Streets, this is Grandville School's afternoon kindergarten class in 1928, with teacher Ines Richmond. Note the haircuts and socks of the students.

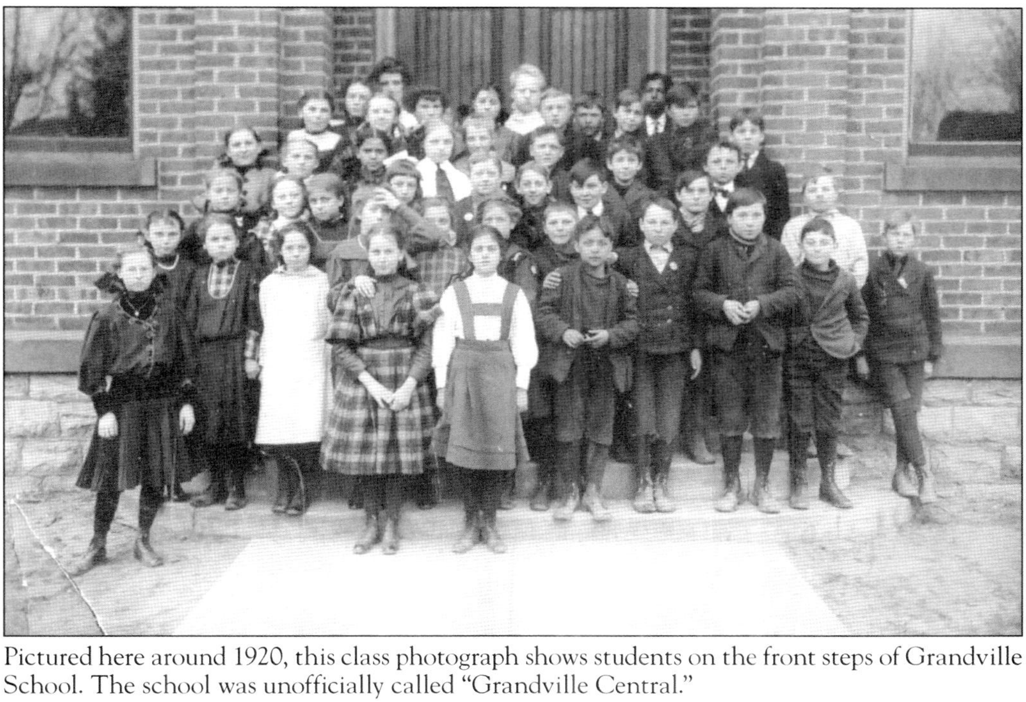

Pictured here around 1920, this class photograph shows students on the front steps of Grandville School. The school was unofficially called "Grandville Central."

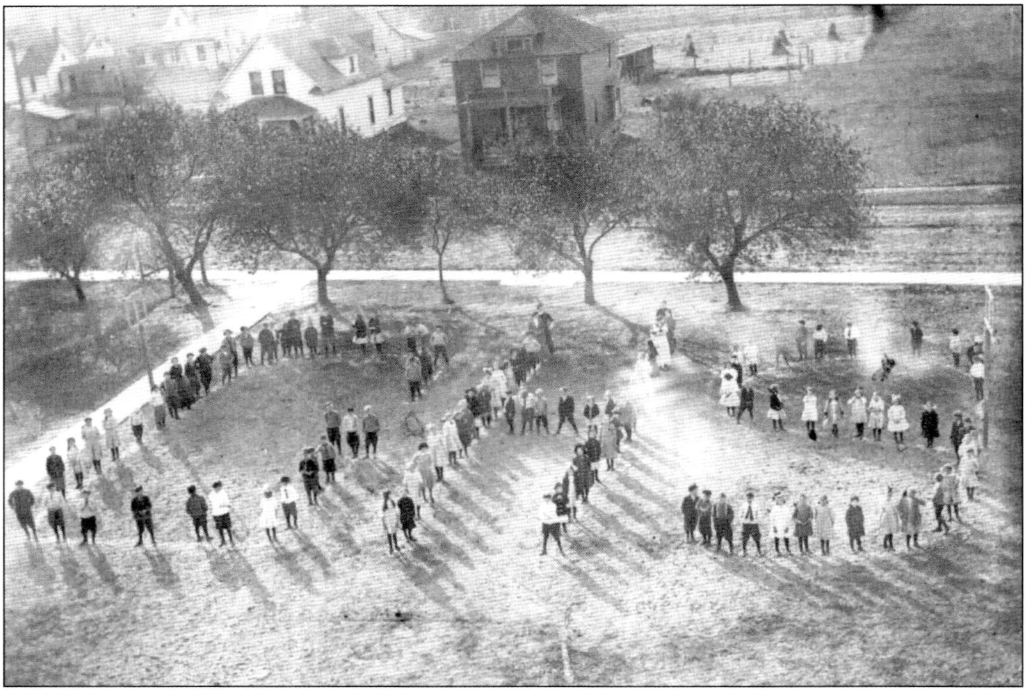

The children form the letters "GHS" on the school playground facing Ottawa Street in 1929.

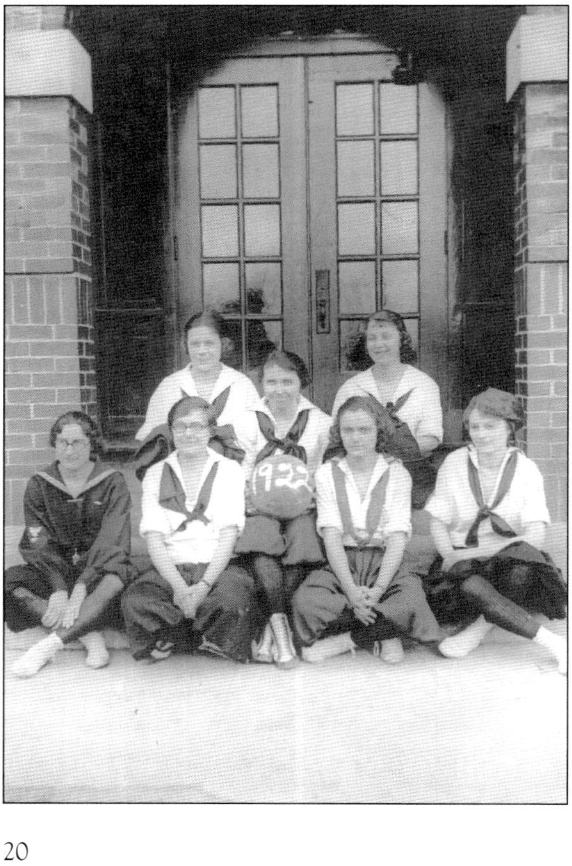

This 1922 photograph shows the Grandville girls' basketball team. The Grandville Bulldog mascot was just beginning to show up in photographs around this time. The school did have girls' athletics at that time, but there was no cheerleading.

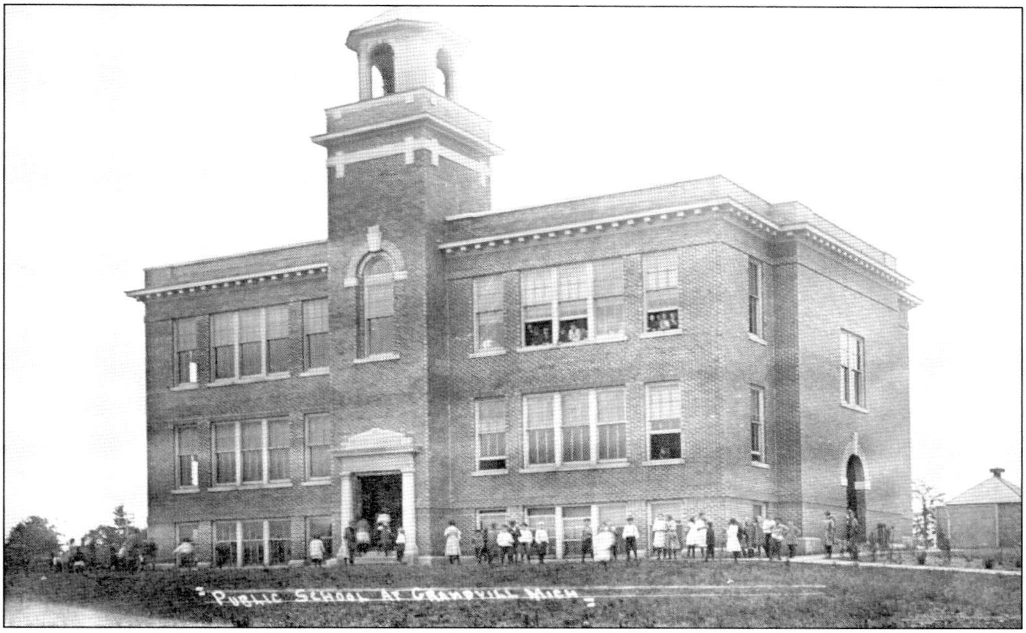

Built in 1910, Grandville High School faced Superior Street. It housed kindergarten through 12th grade. It replaced the Union Grandville High School on Wedgwood Court and Prairie Street.

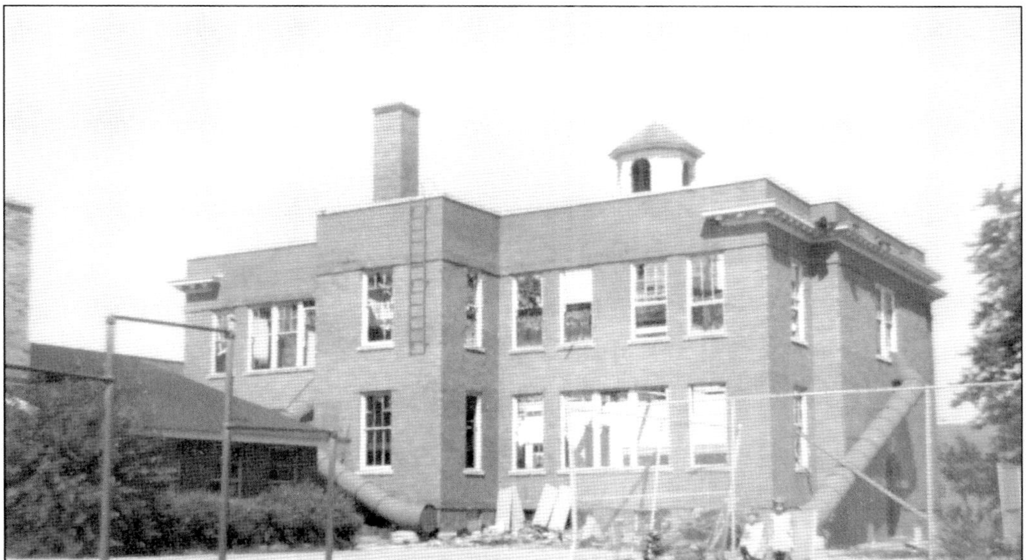

The back part of Grandville High School was torn down in 1964 to make room for a new junior high and cafeteria. The high school was moved to Wilson Avenue that year. Overcrowding made it necessary to build a new school.

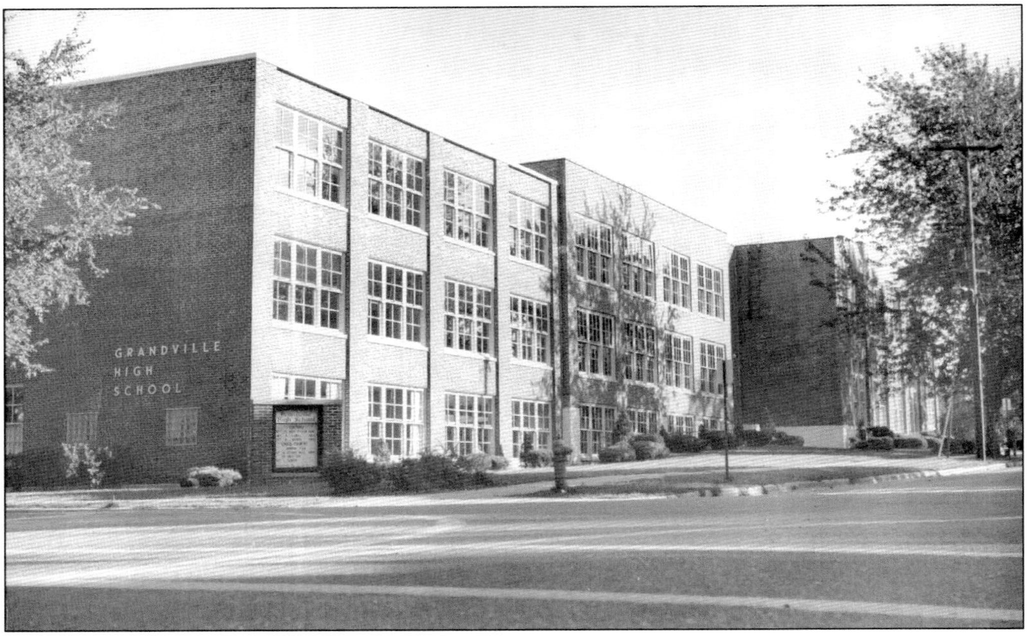

Pictured here around 1960, Grandville High School stood on the corner of Superior and Ottawa Streets. The other side of this building held the junior high. At that time, other elementary school buildings were being built, including East, West, South, and Central Elementary Schools, as well as Christian schools.

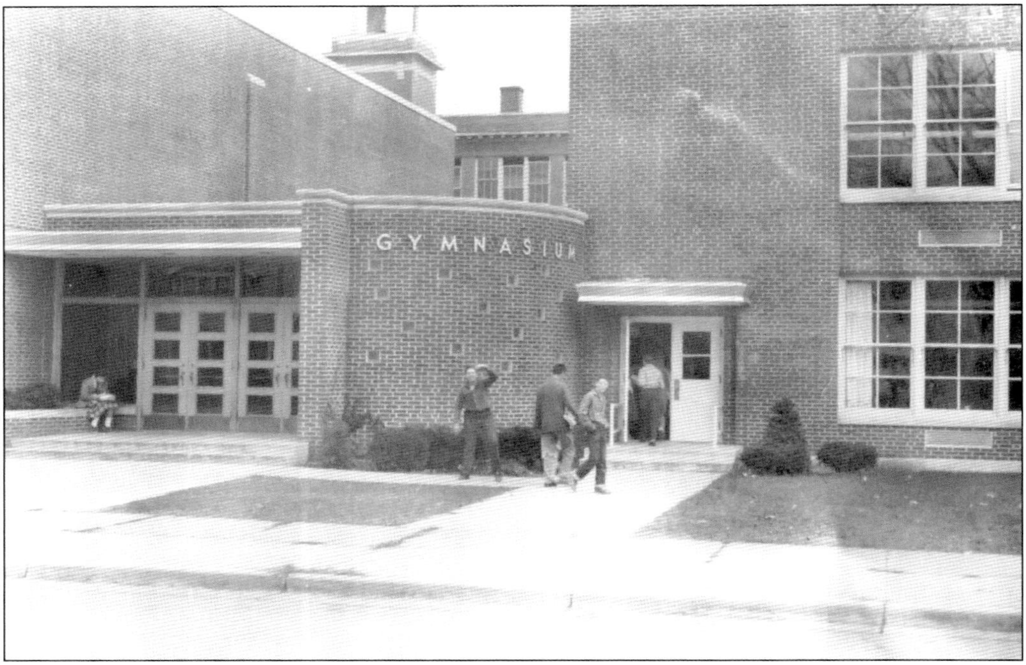

Grandville High School had a very nice gym and stage area, which was well used not only by the school but also by the community. Plays and community events were held there, as well as graduation.

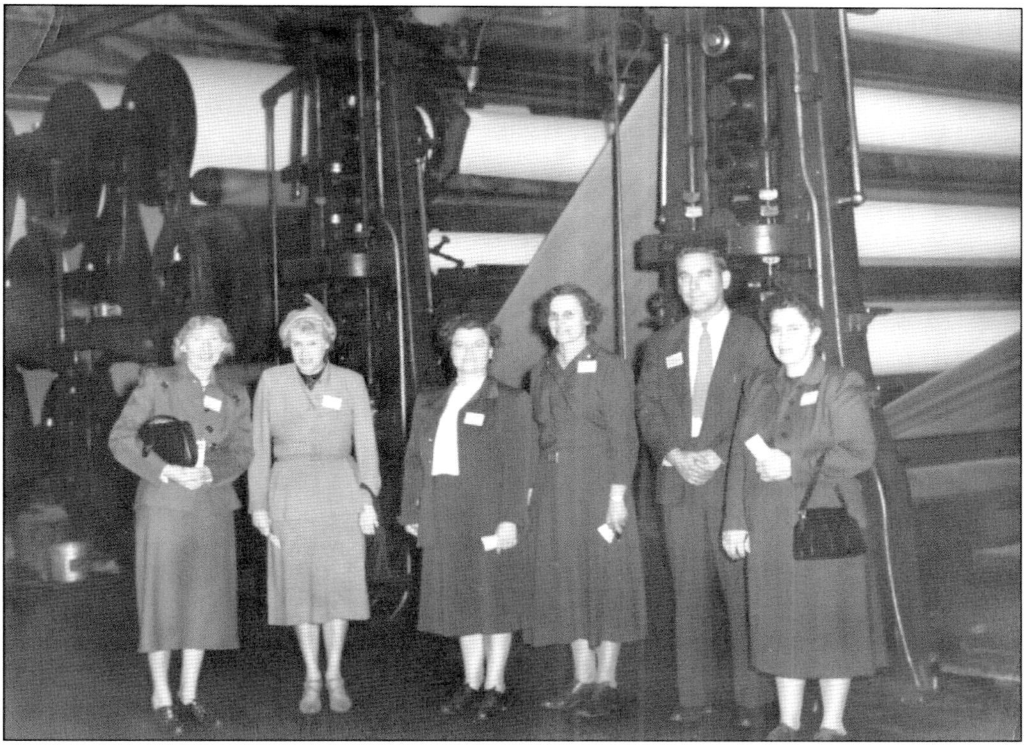

Grandville Elementary teachers visit American Boxboard Company on Market Street in Grand Rapids. Students were treated to a tour and lunch, as well as an introduction to business practices.

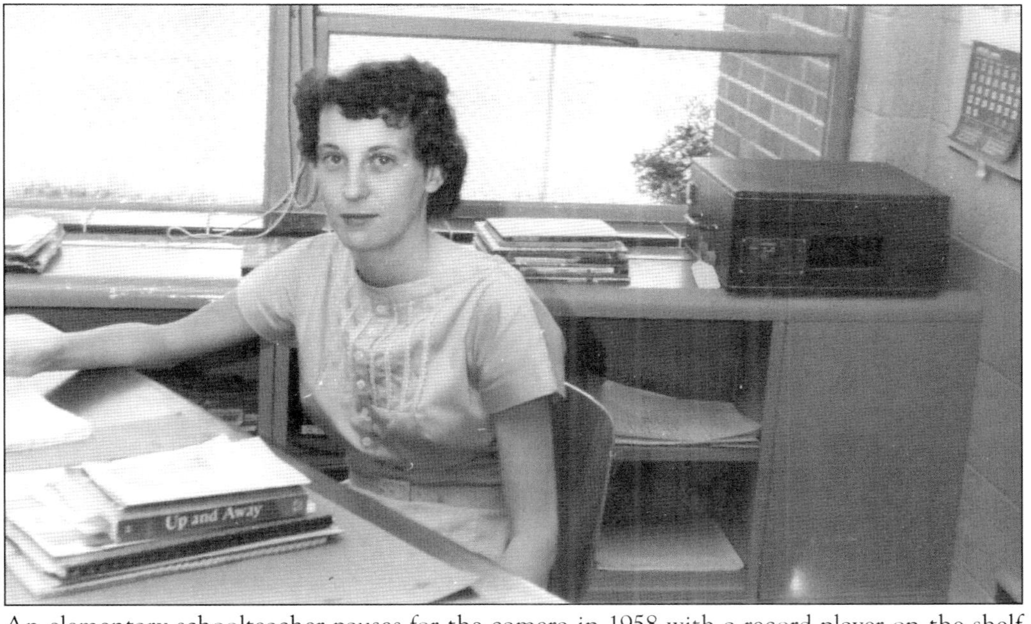

An elementary schoolteacher pauses for the camera in 1958 with a record player on the shelf behind and books in front on the desk. *Dick and Jane* books, beginner readers, were hot items in those days.

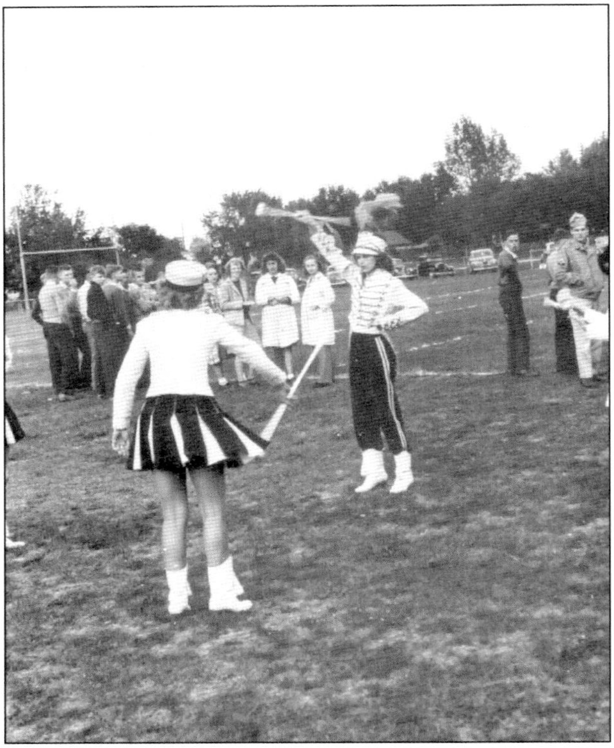

Pictured here are Grandville baton twirlers in 1958, a big part of the high school band. It was important to have a major or majorette to lead the march.

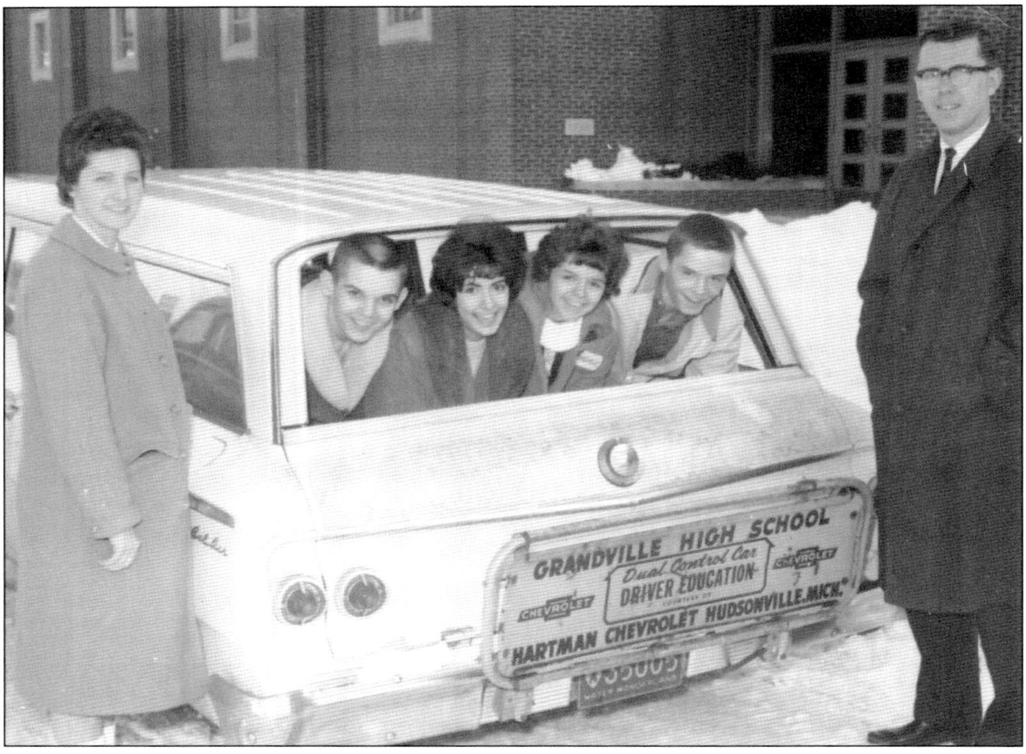

Pictured here in 1962 are Grandville High School students. From left to right are Irene Cooper (teacher), Menno Kraai, Sue Gardner, Laura Roberts, John Moiser, and Donald Reeves. The kids may have been student council members.

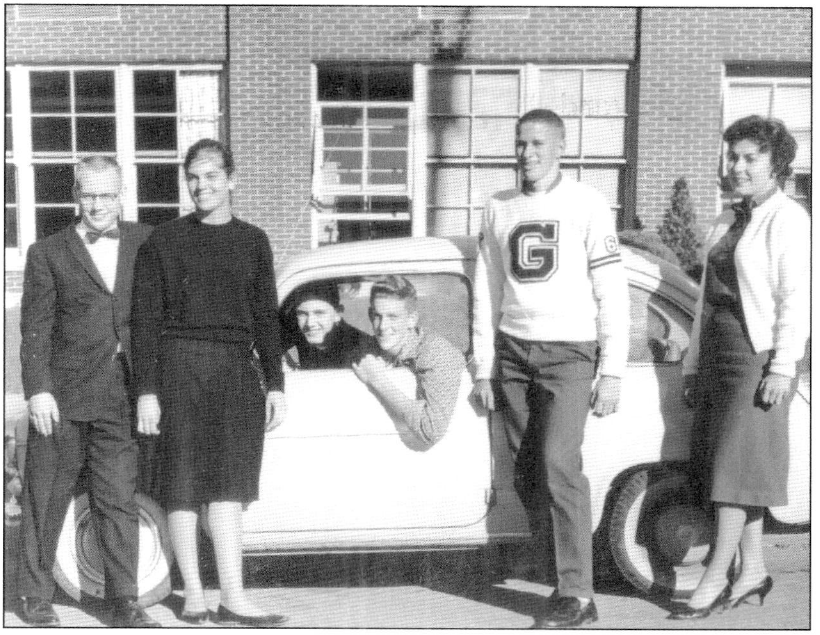

Grandville High School students in 1962 are, from left to right, Mr. Troyer (teacher), Nancy Baar, Jim Ringold, Gordan Dewitt, Larry Nykirk, Lorretta Drewes. The student population at the time was at an all-time high. Even birth rates were up that year.

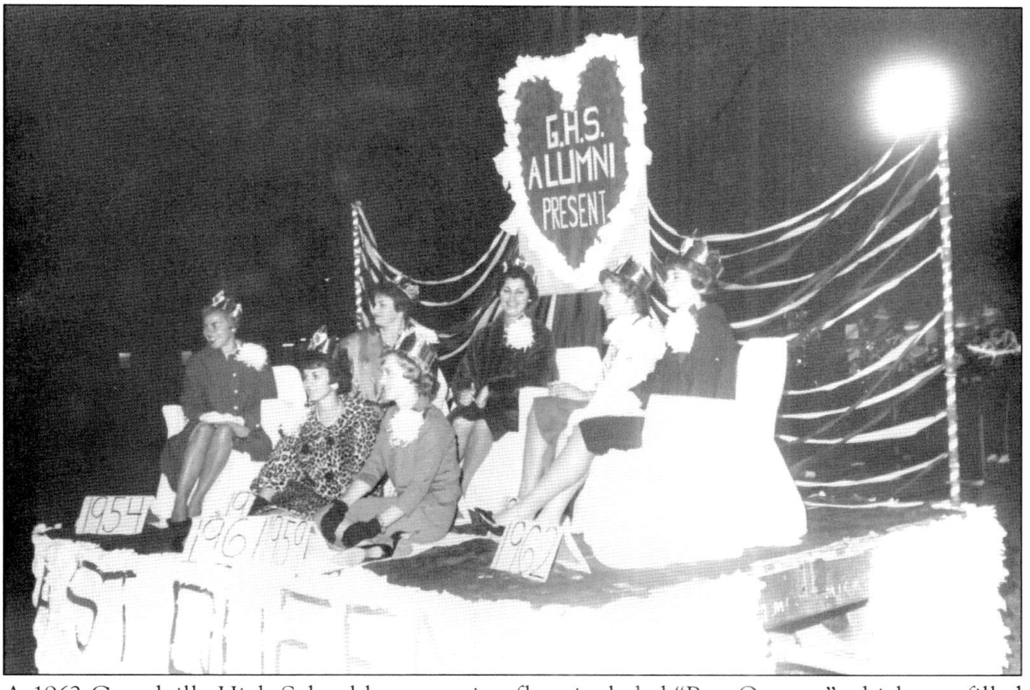

A 1962 Grandville High School homecoming float included "Past Queens," which was filled with returning alumnae queens. There was always a big homecoming parade with floats and of course a football game. That year, the 1936 Grandville city championship football team (some members were sent to the state honors team) and its trophy were brought back to ride on a float in the homecoming parade.

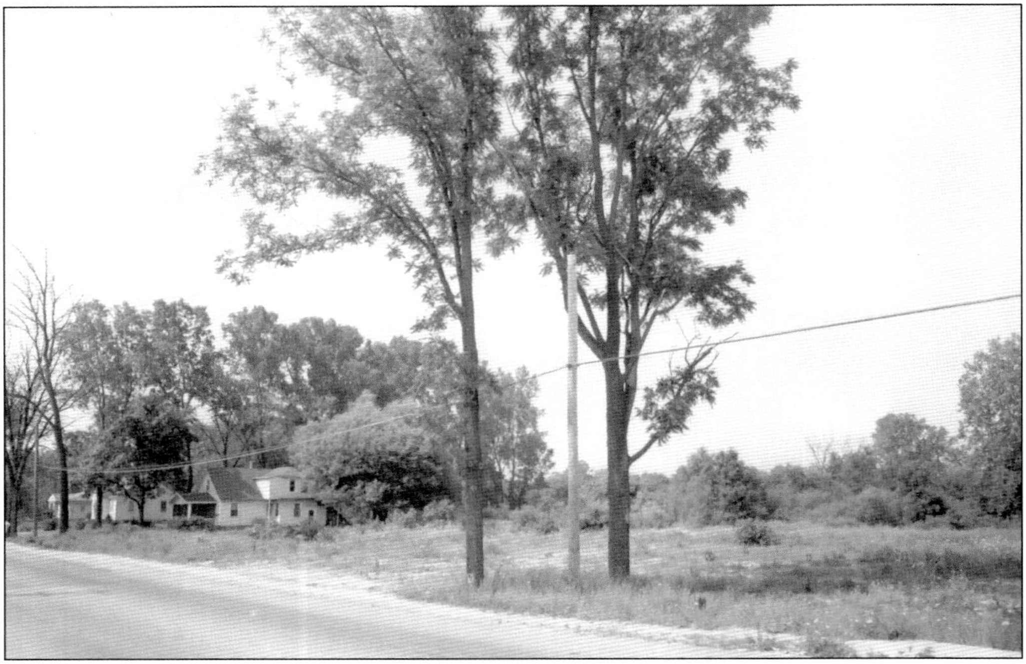

Facing southwest from Buck Creek, land is visible where the new high school would be built in 1964 at 3535 Wilson Avenue. It had been a former gypsum-mining site, with areas of wetlands and marsh.

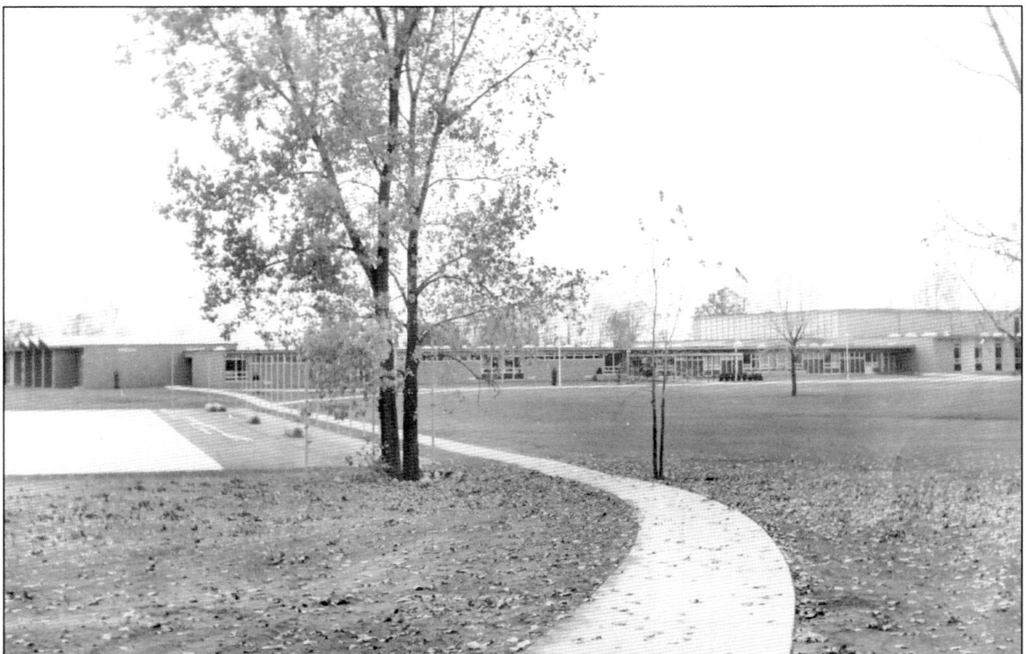

A Class-A school, Grandville High School was built at the cost of $1,607,453 on 29 acres of land. It opened in the fall of 1964.

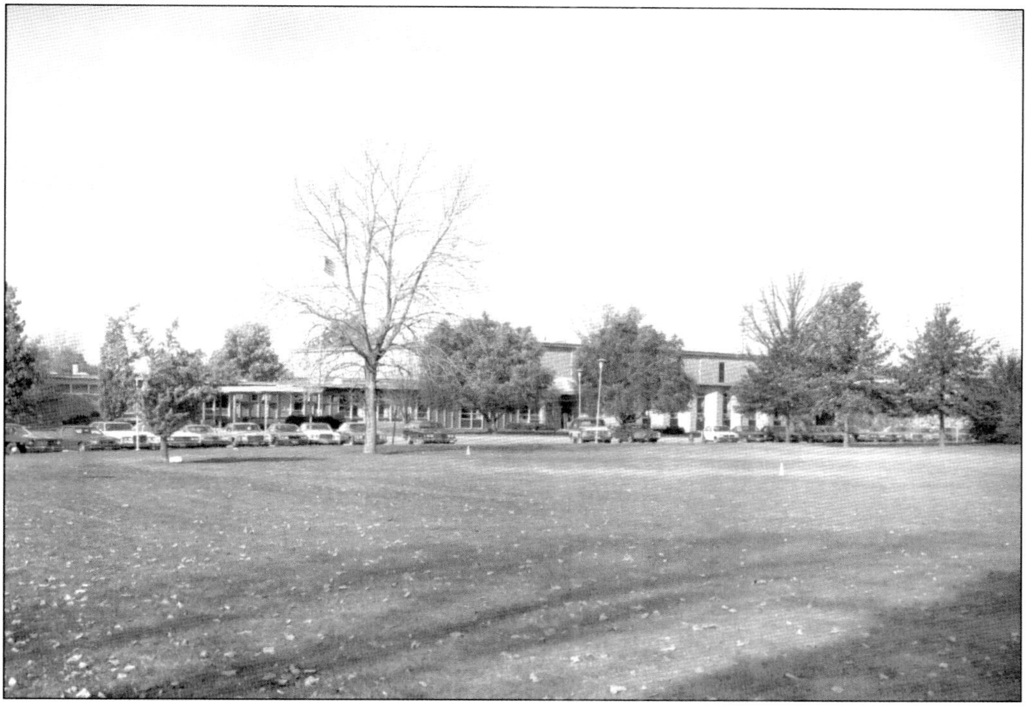

The school boasted an indoor pool, gymnasium, cafeteria, and plenty of classrooms.

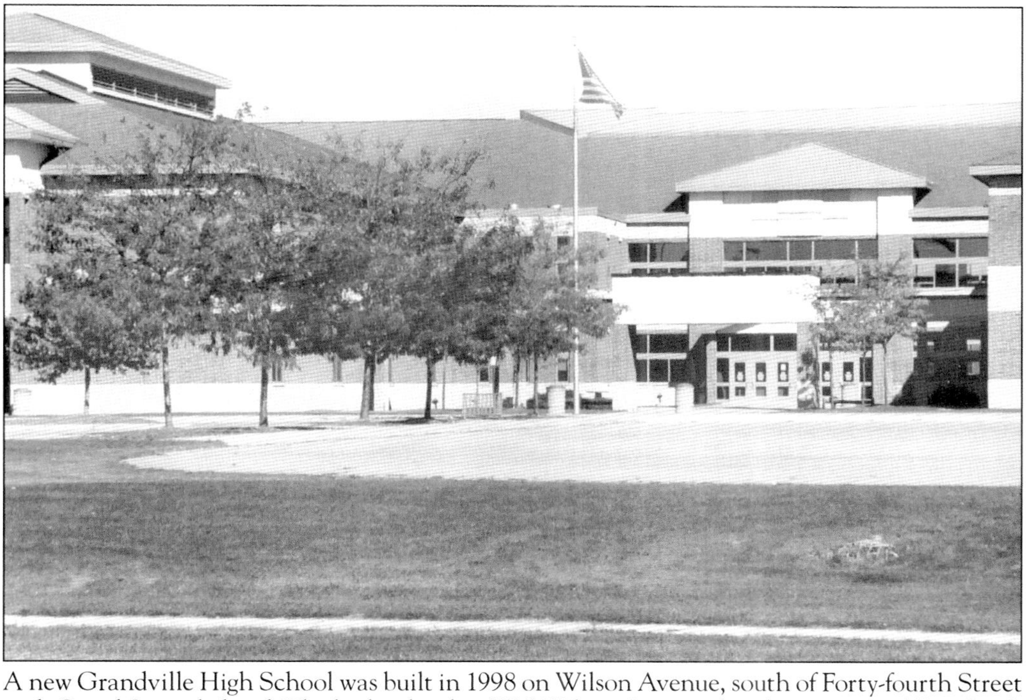

A new Grandville High School was built in 1998 on Wilson Avenue, south of Forty-fourth Street with Canal Street behind. The high school at 3535 Wilson Avenue then became a middle school, while the middle school on Prairie Street became administrative offices.

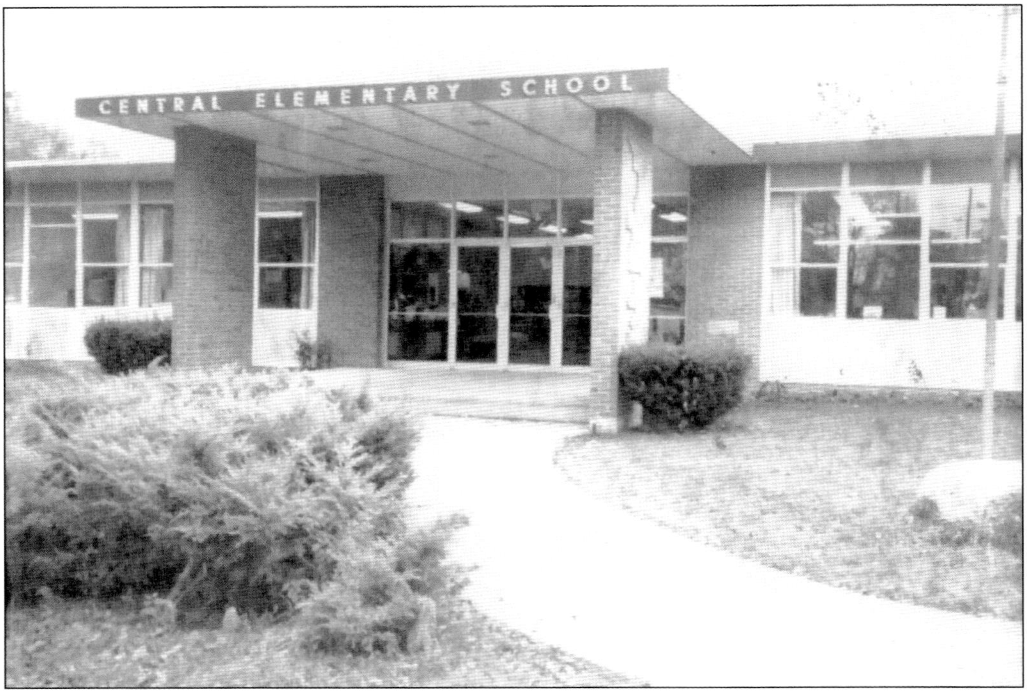

Grandville's population explosion made it necessary to build Central Elementary in 1958 at 4052 Prairie Street at the north end of Wedgwood Field. This was one of the first elementary schools to be built in the area. In the past, all grades (K–12) were housed together.

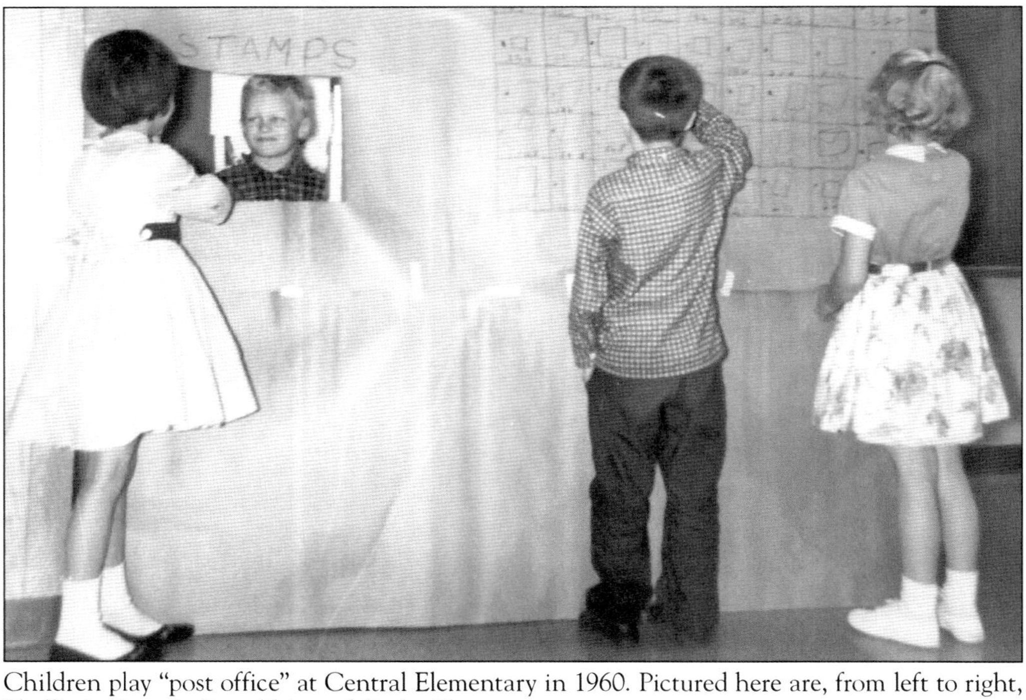

Children play "post office" at Central Elementary in 1960. Pictured here are, from left to right, Phyllis ? , Dave ? , Ronald ? , and Cathy Shaw.

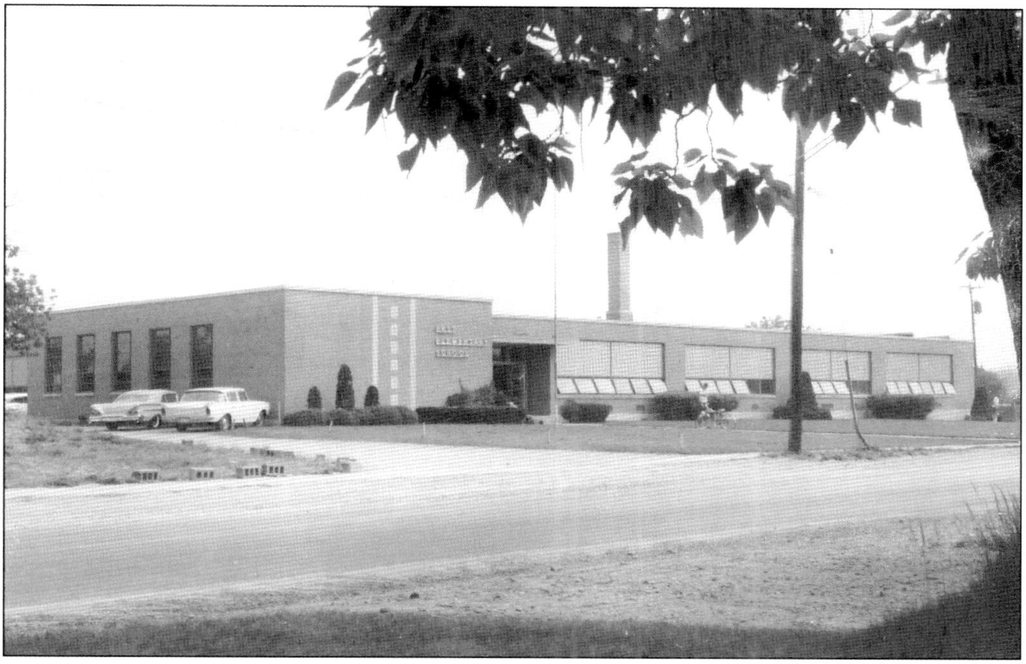

Built in 1951 on Thirtieth Street, East Elementary was located between Locke and Wallace Streets. At the same time, there was also talk of building a park east of the school, but the school was later bought out by a builder. East Elementary had enough land for a baseball field of its own.

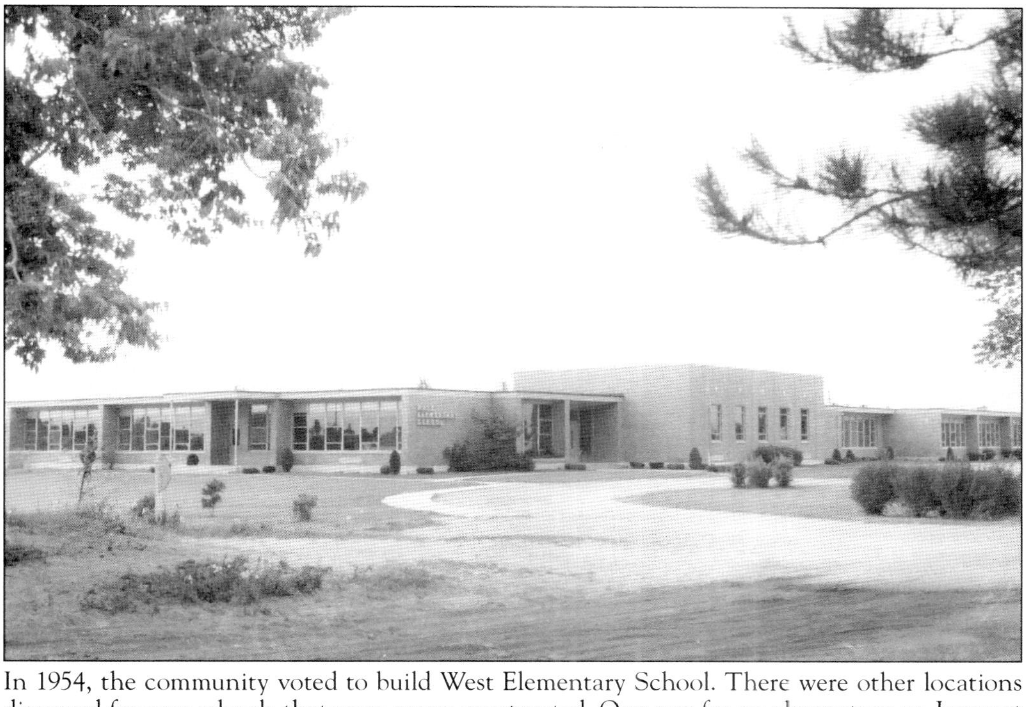

In 1954, the community voted to build West Elementary School. There were other locations discussed for new schools that were never constructed. One was for an elementary on Ivanrest Street, and another was for a school on Forty-fourth Street and Wilson Avenue.

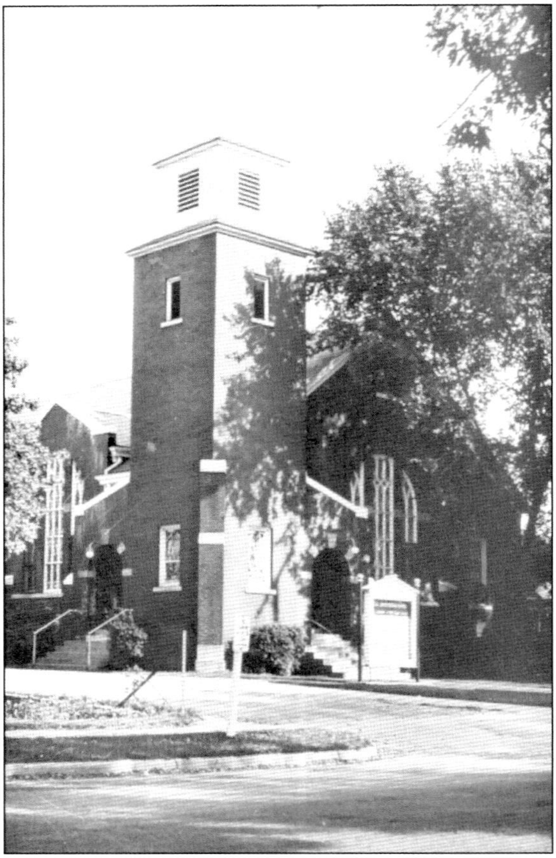

The First Reformed Church of Grandville bought one acre of land on Wilson Avenue and built a church there in 1861. The building was later sold to the city and moved across the street, and a second church was constructed on the site in 1909. Services were held in Dutch in the morning and English in the evening until 1933, when the congregation voted to discontinue Dutch services. In later years, the church grew so much that other churches were established, including Olivet and Zion Reformed.

This 1948 photograph shows Hope Christian Reformed Church. Land was purchased on Barrett Street, and the church opened in the summer of 1941. By 1960, gypsum was found beneath the streets in this area, and some sinkholes were located right across the street from the church.

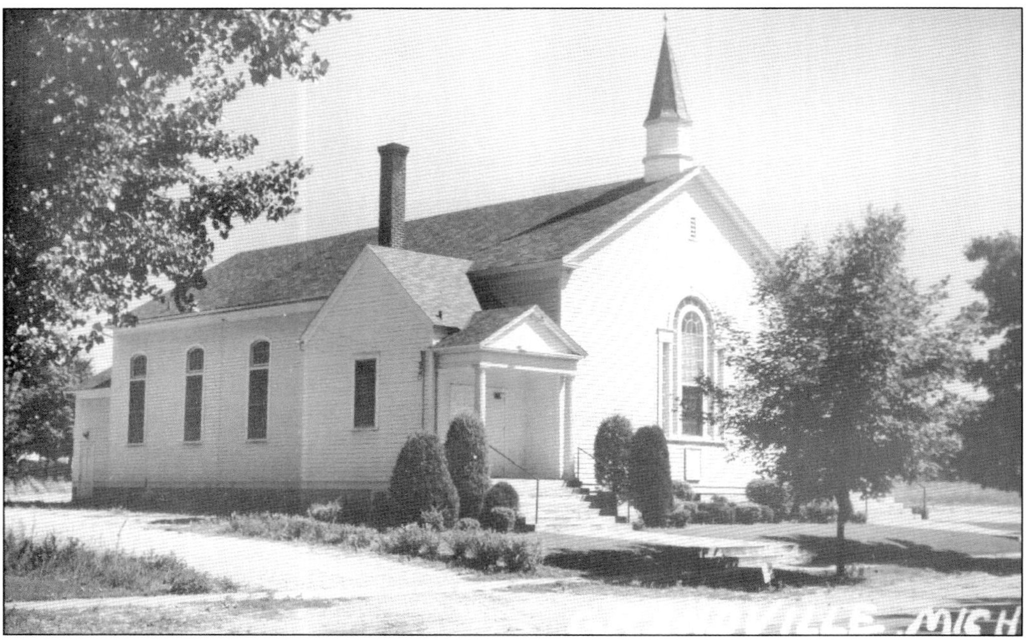

Two

BUSINESS IN GRANDVILLE

Indians, missionaries, fur traders, and farmers came from all over to build a life in Grandville, the little prairie town at the bend in the Grand River.

Grandville was mostly prairie with dense forest to the north. The soil was fertile, so crops were plentiful. The river made it easy to buy and sell by boat: upriver to Grand Rapids and downriver to Grand Haven. Wagon makers and blacksmiths were in demand in town. Trains brought in coal from Chicago and transported out potatoes and celery from Grandville. Plaster and gypsum were also found in the area, so miners came from all over. There was money to be made, and thus the town grew.

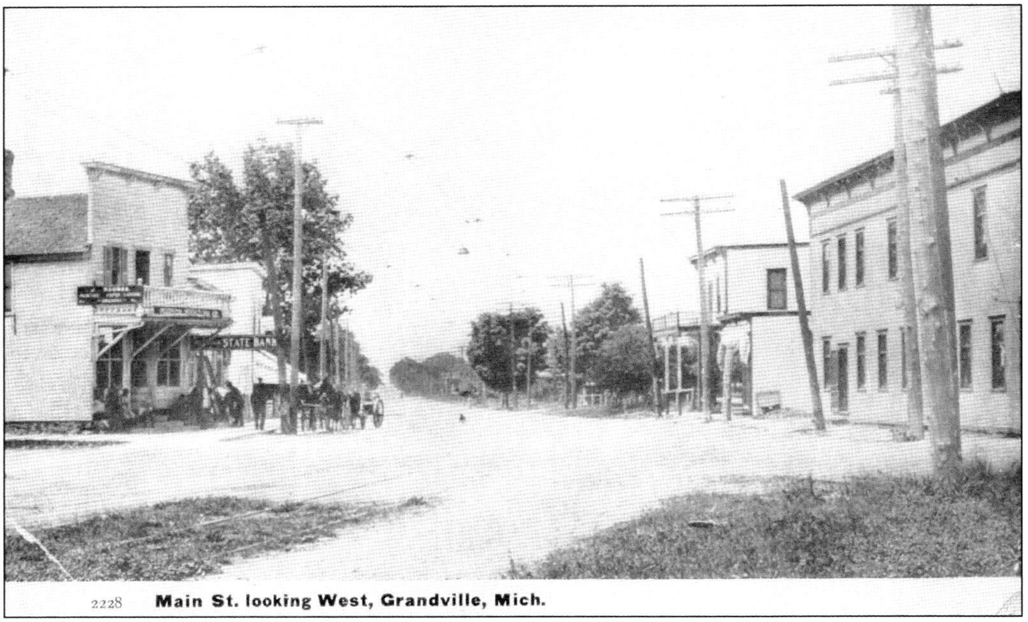

The city business district appears here in the early 1900s at the corner of Wilson Avenue, Thirtieth Street, and Chicago Drive. Not many roads in and out of the city were much good, as most were dirt and a few were plank, having been made with logs. In the spring, mud roads were best navigated on horseback.

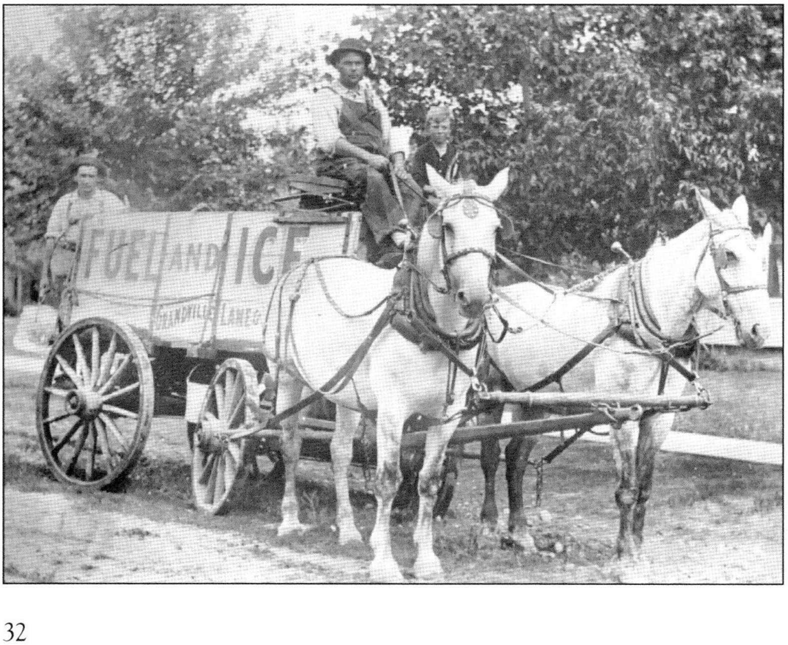

Lane and Company delivered fuel and ice in the early 1900s, providing residents with everyday necessities. Mr. Lane (far left) and Mr. Zandbergen (the driver) stored ice harvested from Buck Creek by bucksaw, which they then sold in the summer. In the winter, they sold coal delivered by train from Chicago.

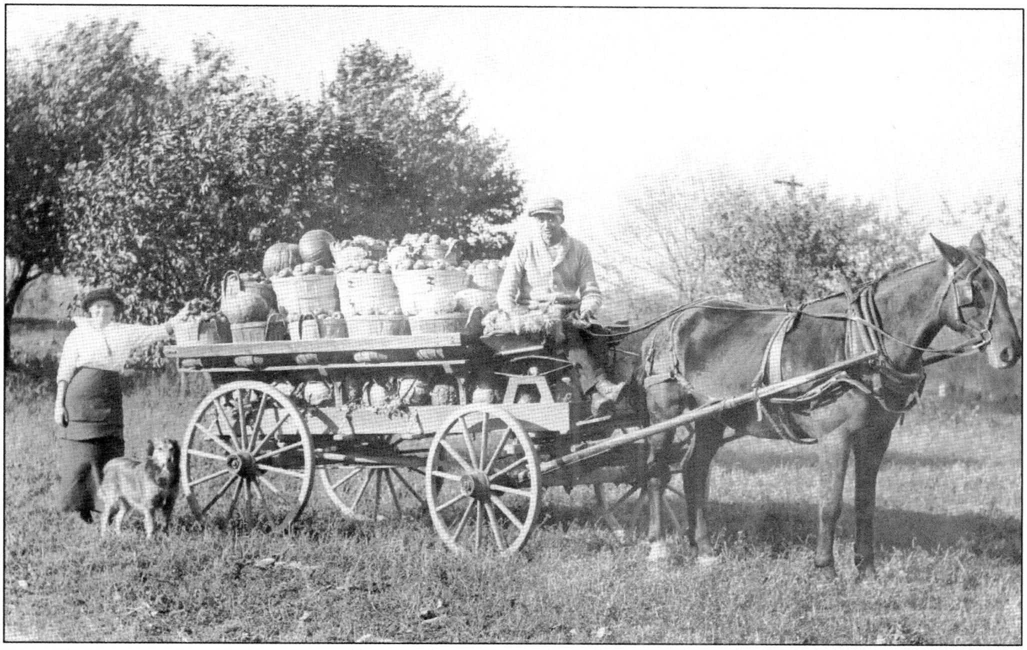

The Bulliment family farm was located on Forty-fourth Street. When the harvest was ready, the produce was brought into town to sell. In this area, October was the big month for the potato harvest.

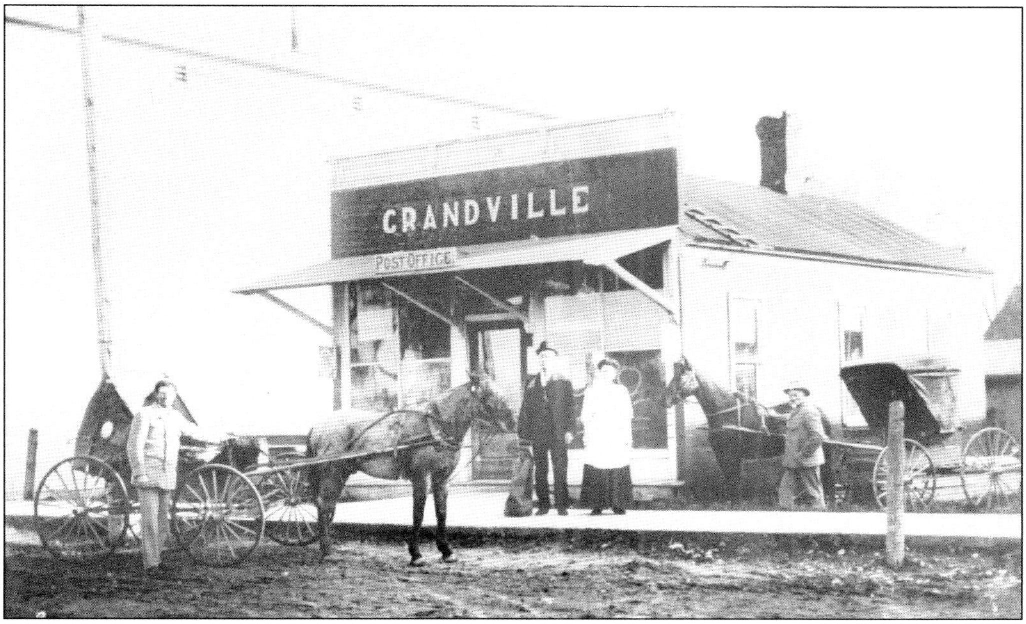

In 1911, the Grandville Post Office was located on the southwest side of Chicago Drive between Wilson Avenue and Franklin Street. From left to right are mail carrier John Degraff, postmaster Milton Velzey, clerk Grace Bullock, and mail carrier Marvin Throop. The main post offices in the region were located in Gull Lake and Battle Creek.

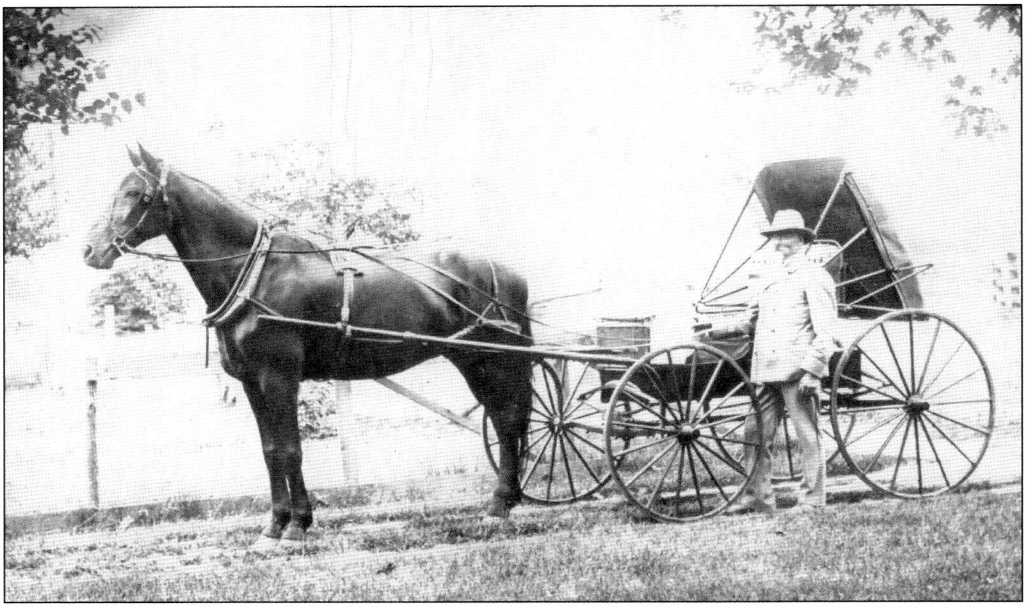

Grandville mail carrier Marvin Throop is shown here with his horse and buggy in 1911. When automobiles became available, a statement to all mail carriers let them know that they could use an automobile, but if any customers complained, they had to go back to using a horse.

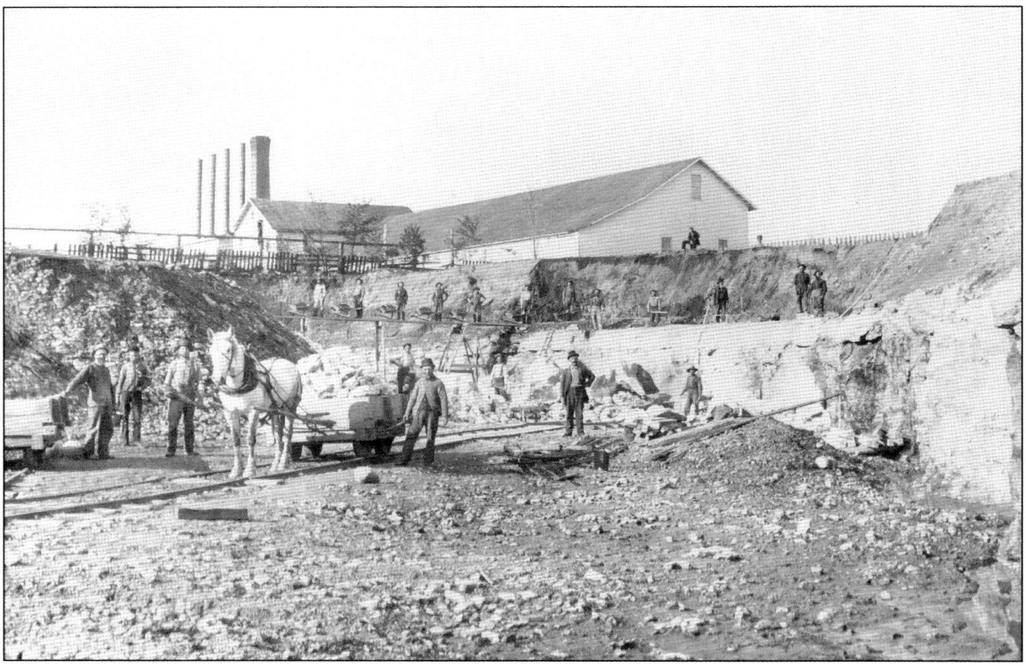

Gypsum and plaster mining was one of the first industries in Grandville. The White Plaster Mill was started in 1842. The work was very dangerous, but it paid well. In the late 1800s, an underground river was discovered while drilling. All of the men escaped the rush of water, but the horses, wagons, and tools were lost. The mill was shut down, and Big Spring Lake took its place, located just off Wilson Avenue.

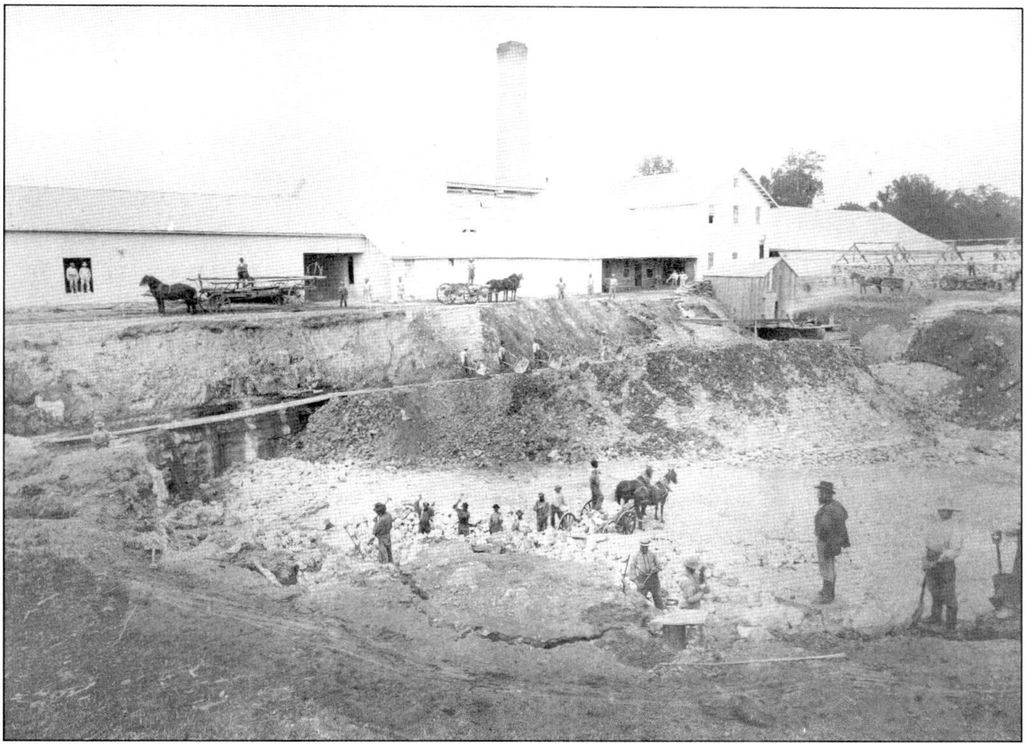

The White Plaster Mill (now the site of Big Spring Lake) was a quarry where topsoil was cleared so that the underlying gypsum could be mined. The rock was carted off across Wilson Avenue to the Red Mill, where the middle school now stands. From there, gypsum was shipped by boat or train to Illinois and Wisconsin.

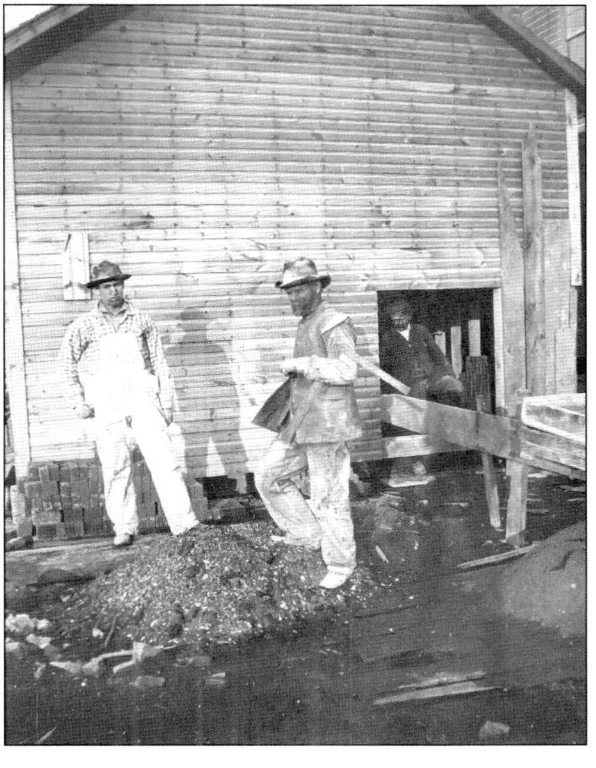

White Plaster Mill workers had hard lives. No safety measures were taken for breathing in any particulates, as seen here with these workers covered in white dust. Dynamite was used and was often a source of injury to workers. Many a worker was hit by a blast, losing a leg or an arm, and a doctor would be called to save the worker's life. If the worker survived, he would be fired, as he was no longer useful to the company. Needless to say, insurance was not part of the equation.

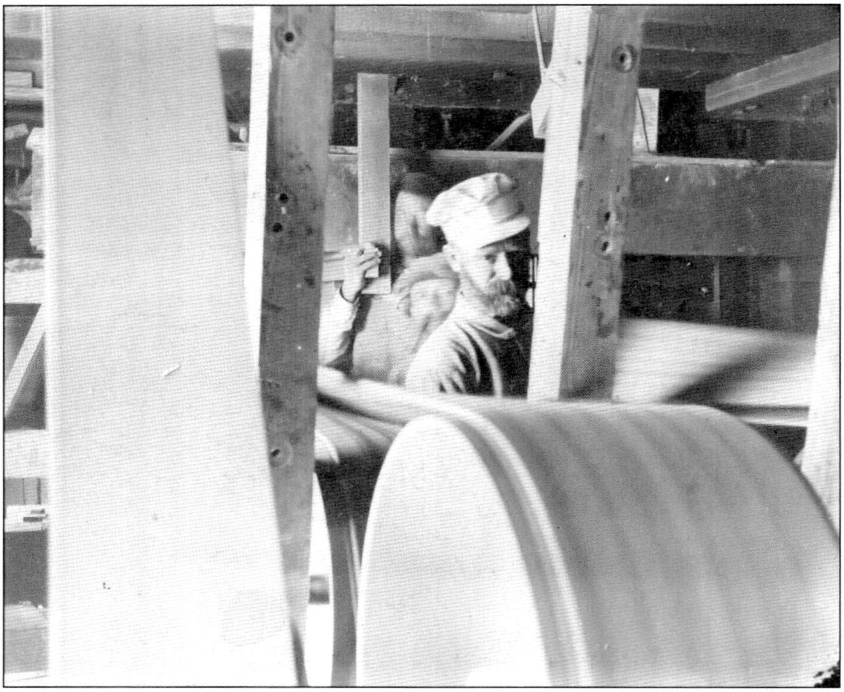

Men are at work inside the White Plaster Mill. This job was easier (and safer) than working in the mine.

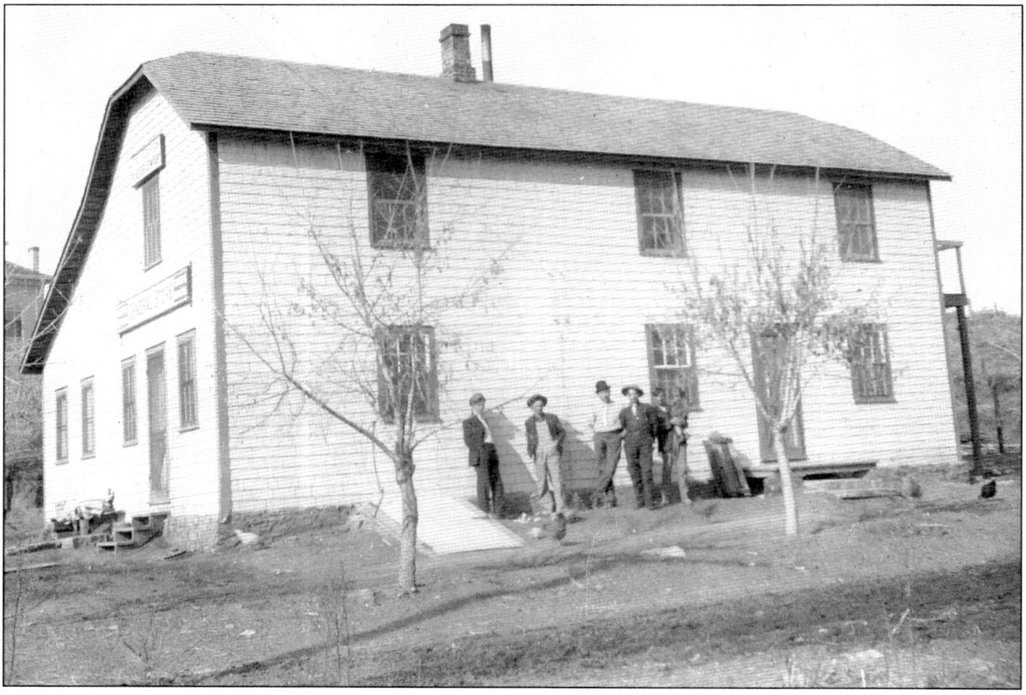

This is the general store and living quarters for the White Plaster Mill. Many men were immigrants, leaving families behind in their respective countries in order to find employment; workers would later send for their families. Single men occupied the living quarters, which provided meals for a slightly higher fee.

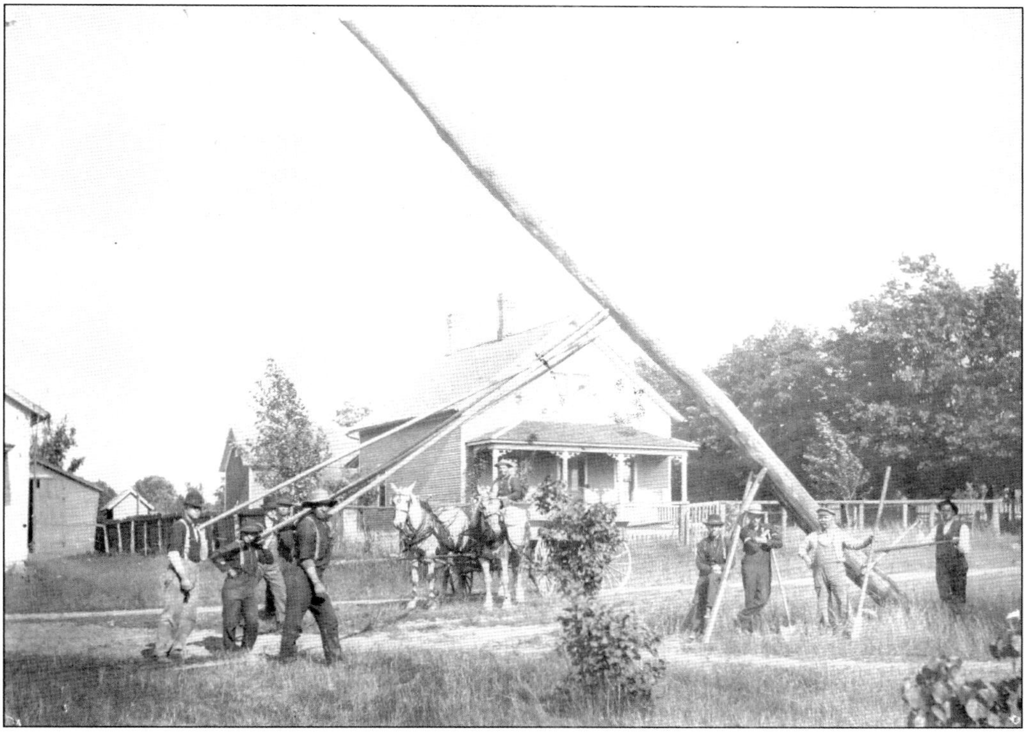

In 1907, utility poles were installed on Fayette Street. Soon, all of Grandville would have electricity. Many of the stores of the day boasted that they had electricity, such as Gustavas Wedgwood, who advertised, "Come see our light bulb." At this time, Elders Electric Company was beginning to have a thriving business.

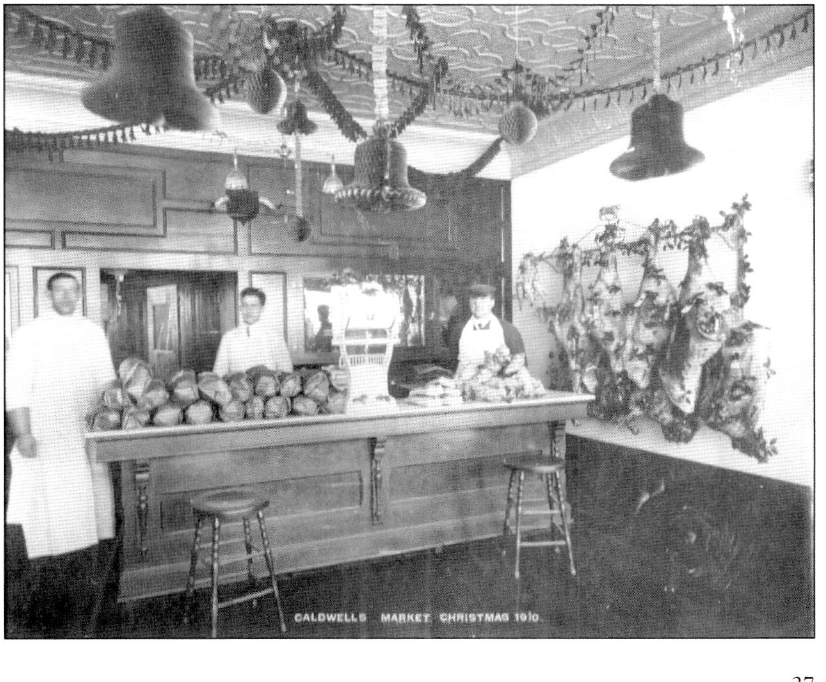

This is Caldwell Meat Market, located on the southwest corner of White Street and Wilson Avenue, around Christmas in 1910. The meat hanging on the wall is decorated for the holidays.

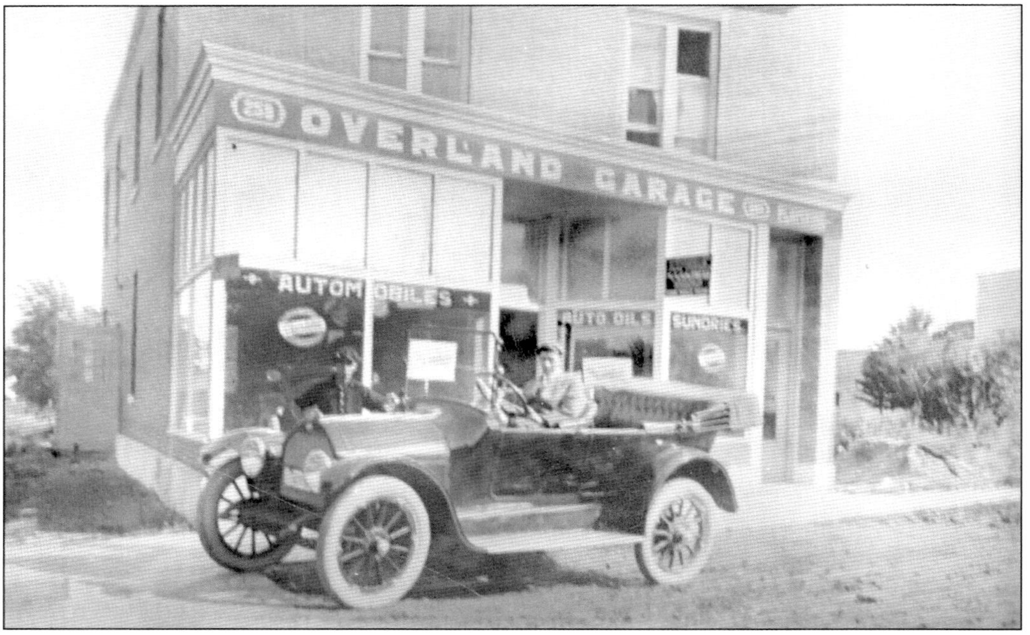

The Overland Car Company was located on the south side of Chicago Drive at Franklin Street. Seen here in 1913, Randall Wedgwood owned and operated the garage with his business partner Dwight Hammond. Overland automobiles were produced up until the 1950s. This garage burned down in 1935. There was no insurance, so it was not rebuilt.

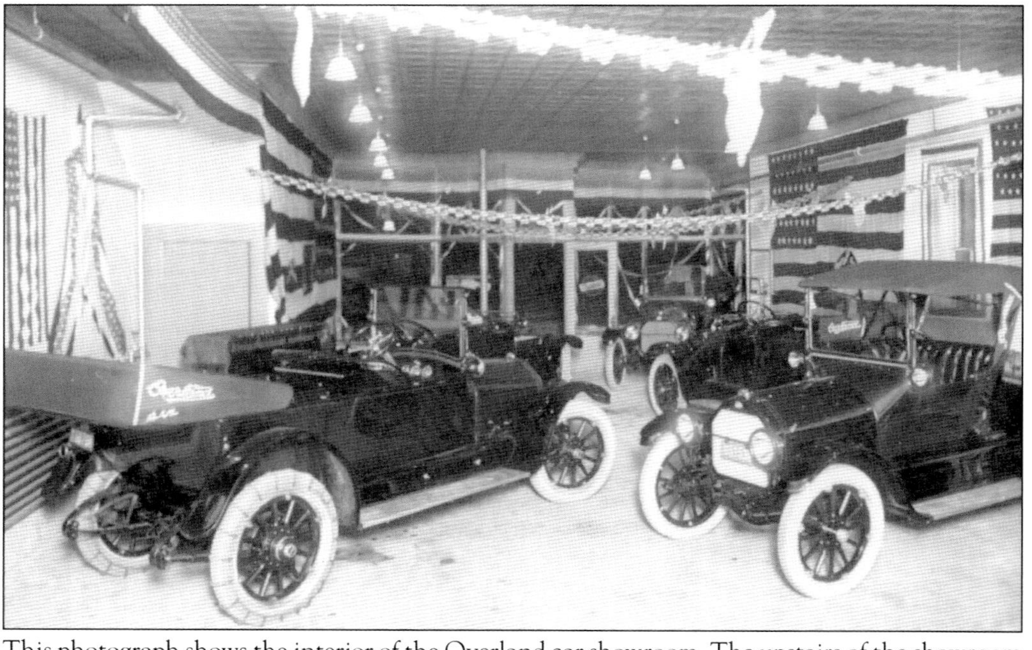

This photograph shows the interior of the Overland car showroom. The upstairs of the showroom was rented out for civic functions. Randall Wedgwood, owner of a sporting goods store and Wedgwood Inn, was one of the first new and used automobile salesmen for Overland cars. There was no such thing as a used automobile at the time, as they were all new in 1913.

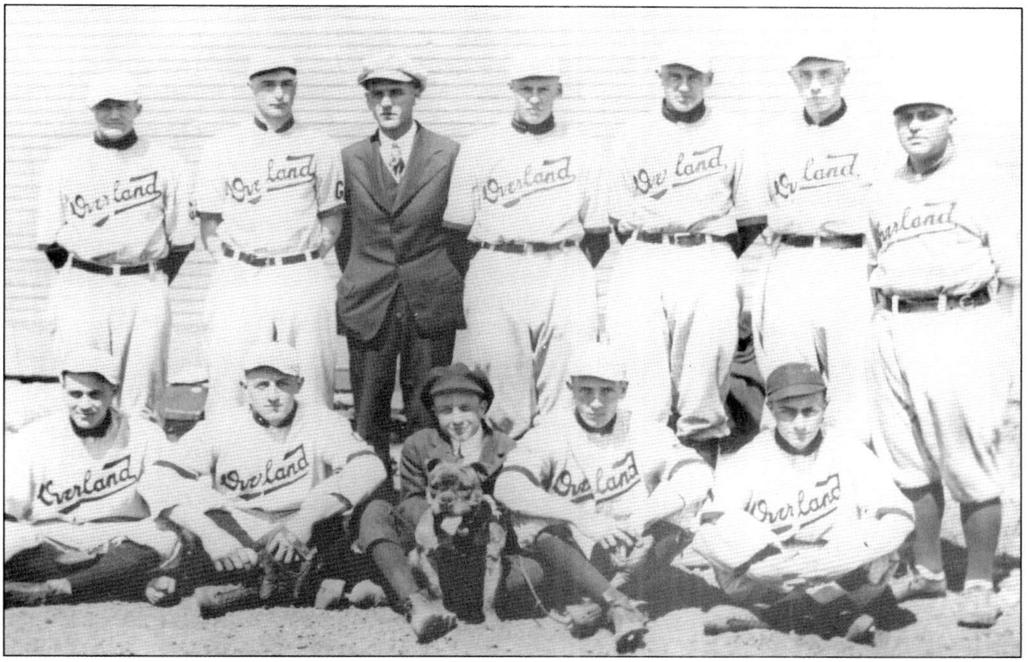

This is the 1926 Grandville Overland baseball team. They played against the Winters and Crampton, Grandville Merchants, and Filmore teams.

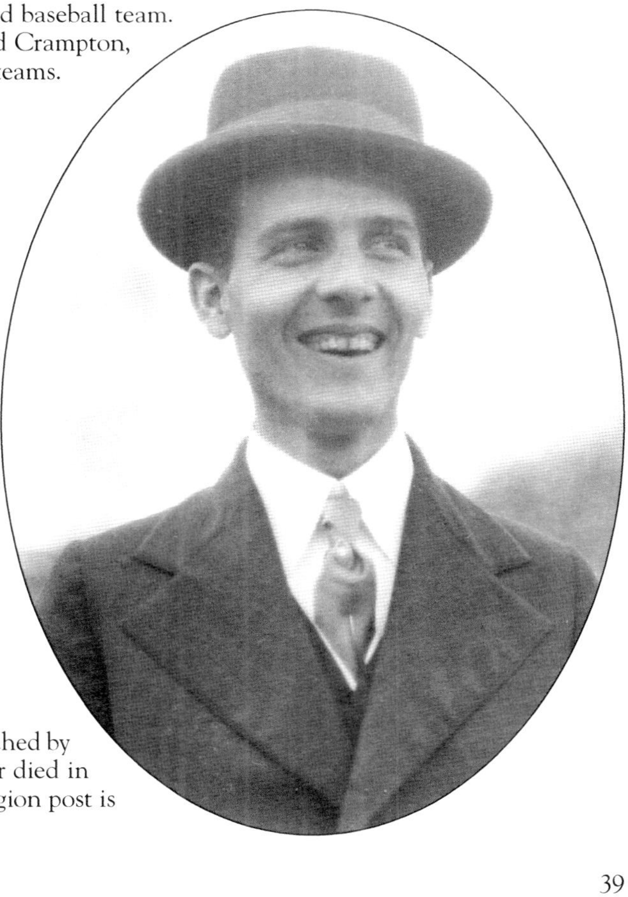

The Overland baseball team was coached by Roy Fonger. His brother Neal Fonger died in World War I; the local American Legion post is named after him.

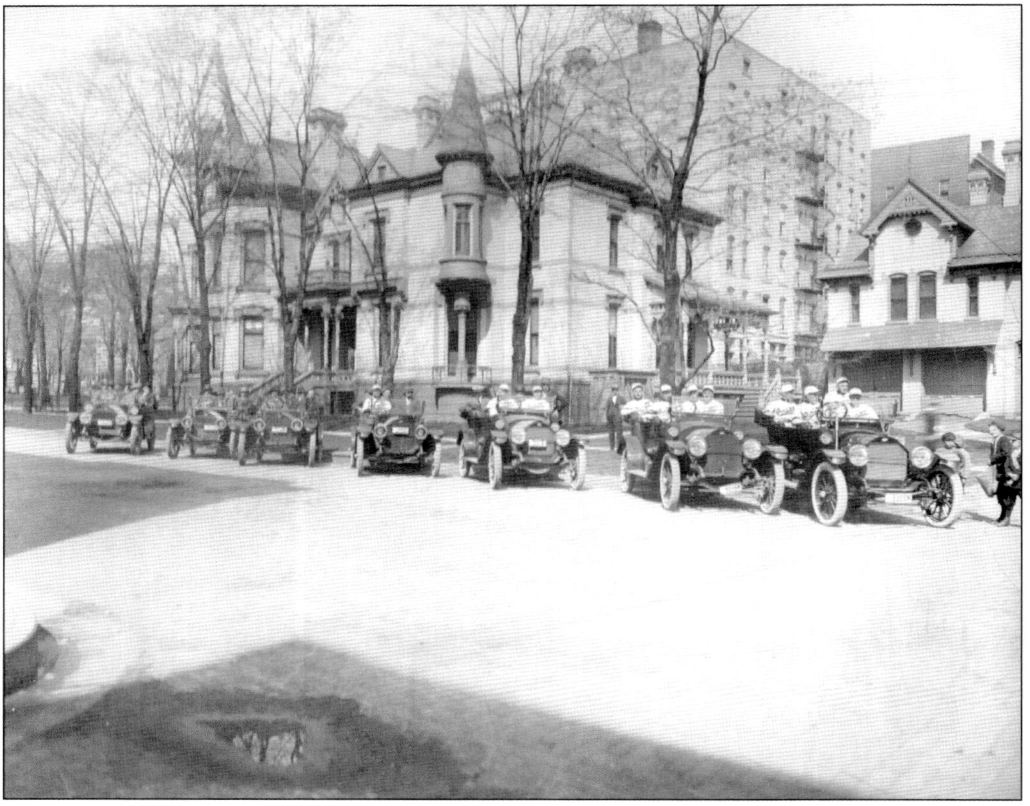

An "Overland Day" was declared, and a parade was set in motion. Randall Wedgwood put the baseball team into his automobiles, and they drove through Grandville and downtown Grand Rapids. They stopped to make speeches and to invite people to the ball games. The *Grand Rapids Press* called "Overland Day" one of Grandville's first "auto shows." It was said to be an overwhelming success.

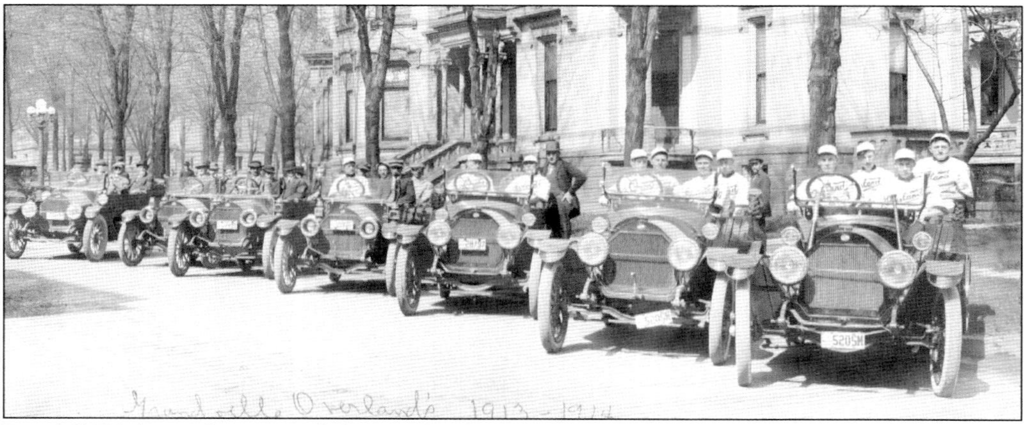

Randall Wedgwood sponsored the Overland minor-league baseball team. Here, the team appears in his cars, advertising and leveraging his business in the community.

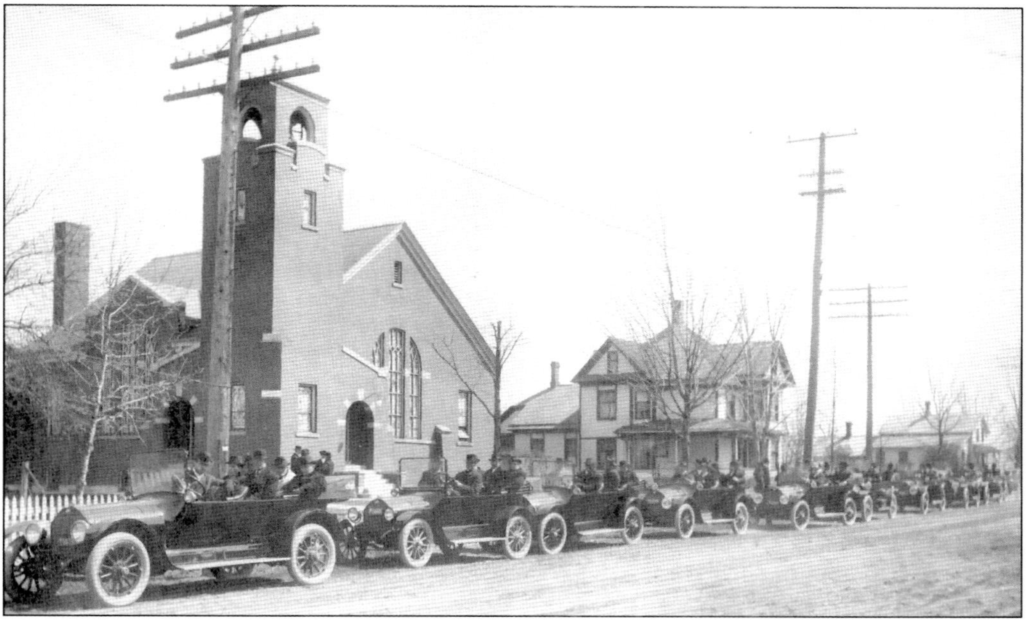

On a separate occasion in 1913, the Overland baseball team drives through Grandville in a convoy of Overland cars, along with many local businessmen and politicians. They are seen celebrating a winning baseball season.

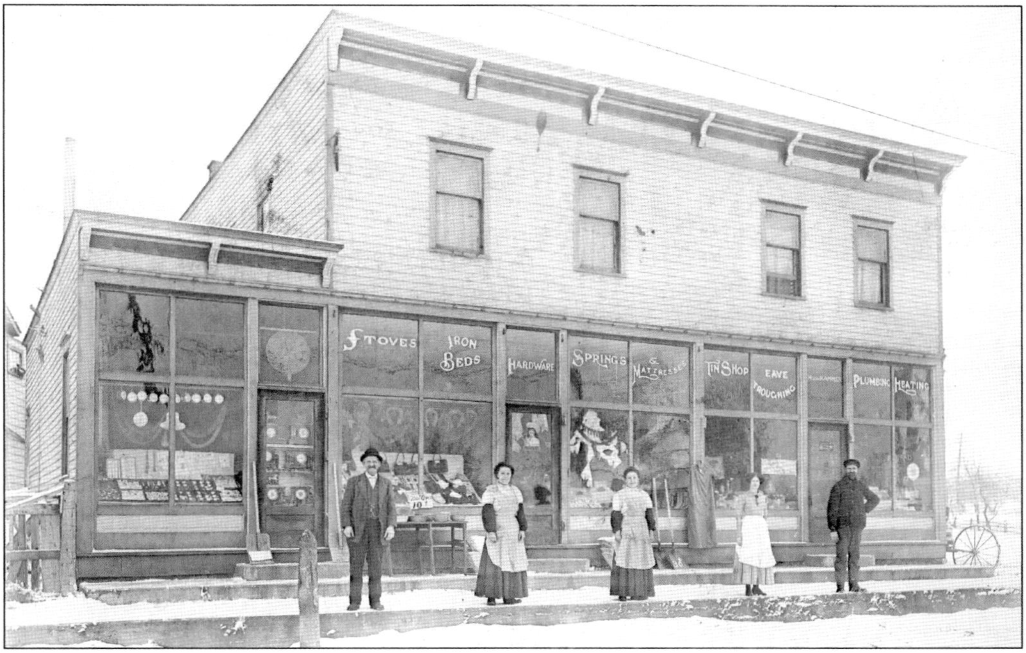

The Van Kammen General Store was located at Chicago Drive and Division Street in the late 1800s. Pictured from left to right are proprietor Jake Van Kammen and his twin daughters Kate and Anne, along with his married daughter Jennie Beukema and her husband, Albert, who helped in the store. In later years, the Beukemas inherited the business. The store carried everything from iron bed frames to shovels, stoves, and groceries.

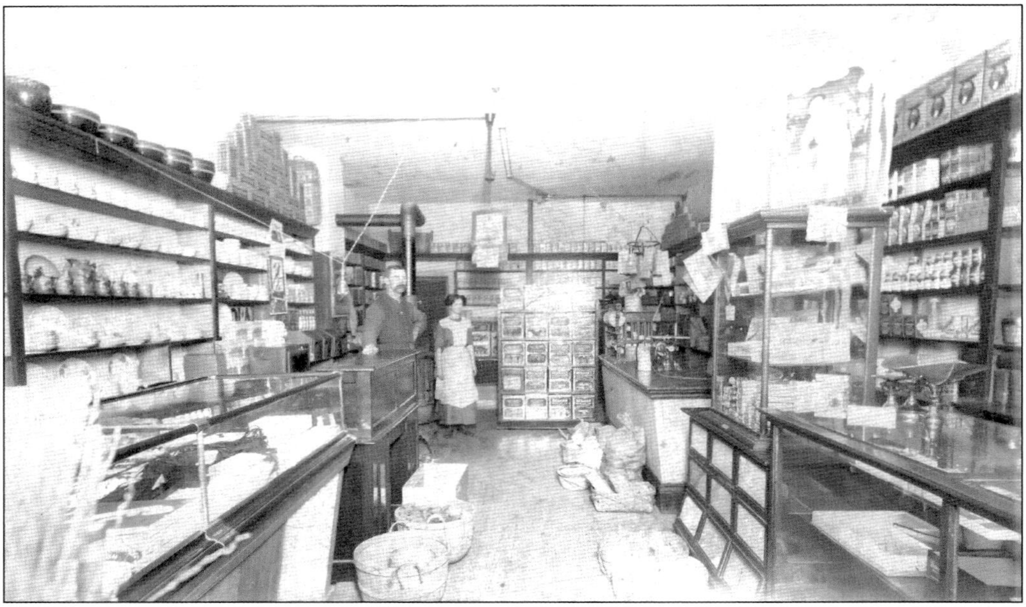

Pictured here are Jennie and Albert Beukema inside Van Kammen General Store. Note the flour and sugar on the right and the fine china on the left. Inventory for the store was purchased from commercial boats traveling on the Grand River.

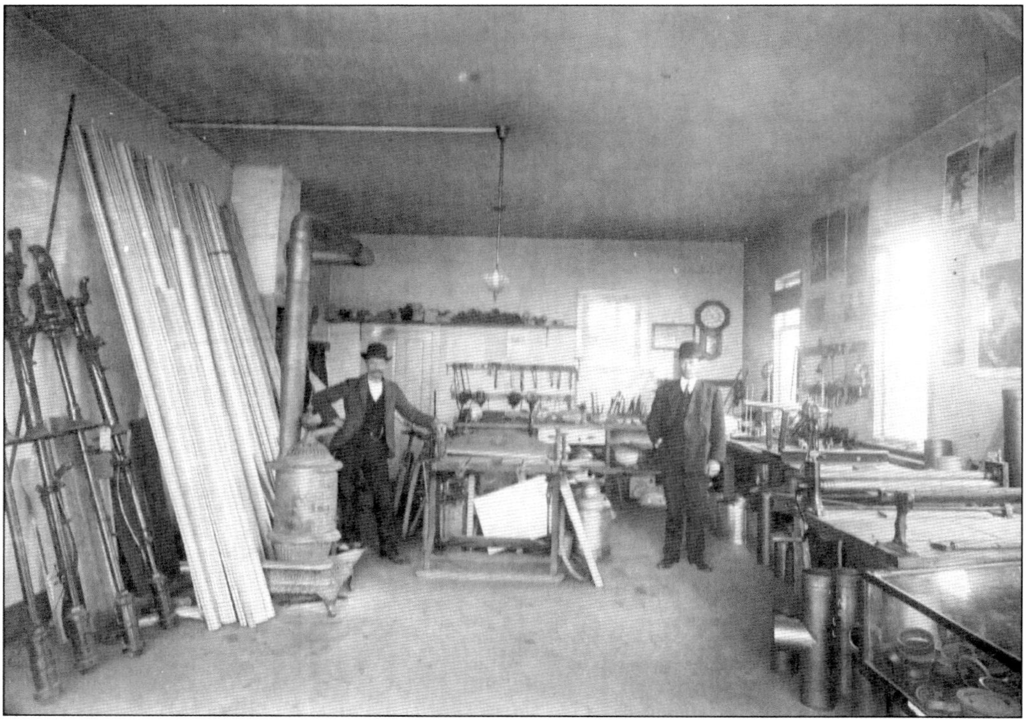

Shown here from left to right are Jake and Herman Van Kammen waiting to help customers in the tin shop. Note the hand pumps for wells on the left and tin fittings for potbelly stoves on the right.

A Sunday afternoon stroll ends at the sawmill by Buck Creek. No one worked on Sundays. Most people had picnics in the cemetery in the summer or strolled along the river. In the winter, they had to be more inventive. Often on Sundays, Bible study was an afternoon pastime.

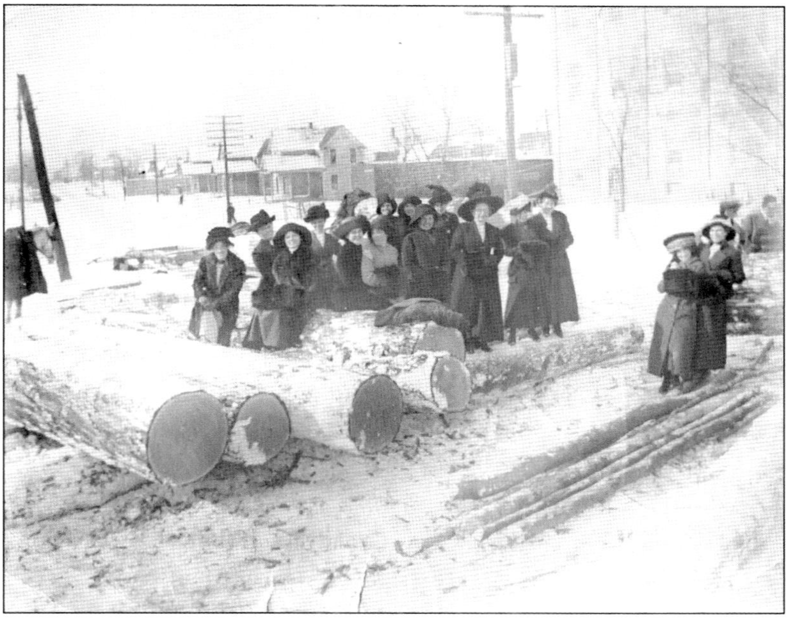

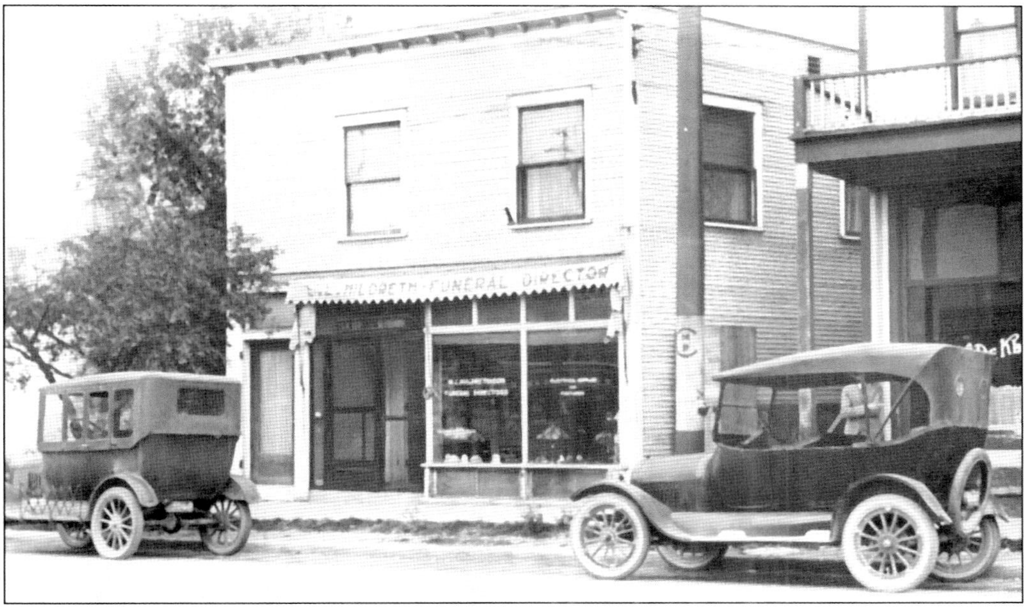

Hildreth Funeral Home and Elders Electric Store are pictured here in 1928. The funeral home was in the front of the store and the electric store was in the back. Elders flourished as electric lights made their way into Grandville homes. The business was also one of the first to sell fans and cooling units. Oddly enough, Elders customers had to walk through the funeral home to get to the store. Lotan Hildreth would be called upon to transport the deceased to his funeral home. After he prepared the body, he would return the deceased to their home, where the funeral would then take place. If the person had died of a contagious disease, the deceased would be placed in the window of the family home, and people would pay their respects from the outside.

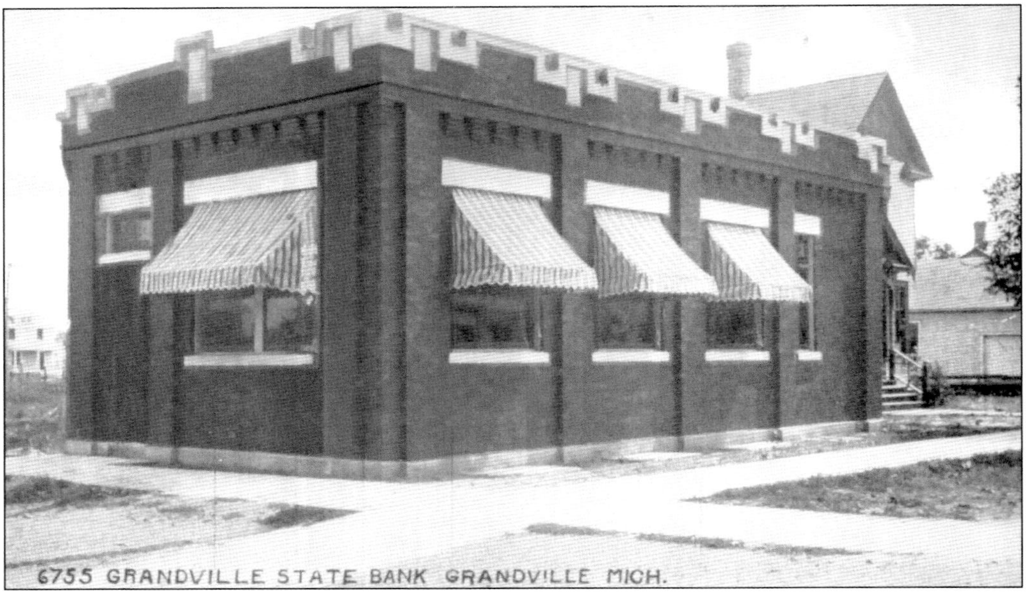

In April 1907, Grandville State Bank constructed a one-story building on the corner of Wilson Avenue and Chicago Drive. The building stood for 20 years. The current two-story structure was built in 1927 over the foundation of the original bank. Terra-cotta bricks were made in Pennsylvania and shipped by rail to Grandville. In 1937, during the Depression, the bank failed and the property was sold. Over the next four decades, the building housed other banks, dentists, insurance agencies, and finally, today, a law firm.

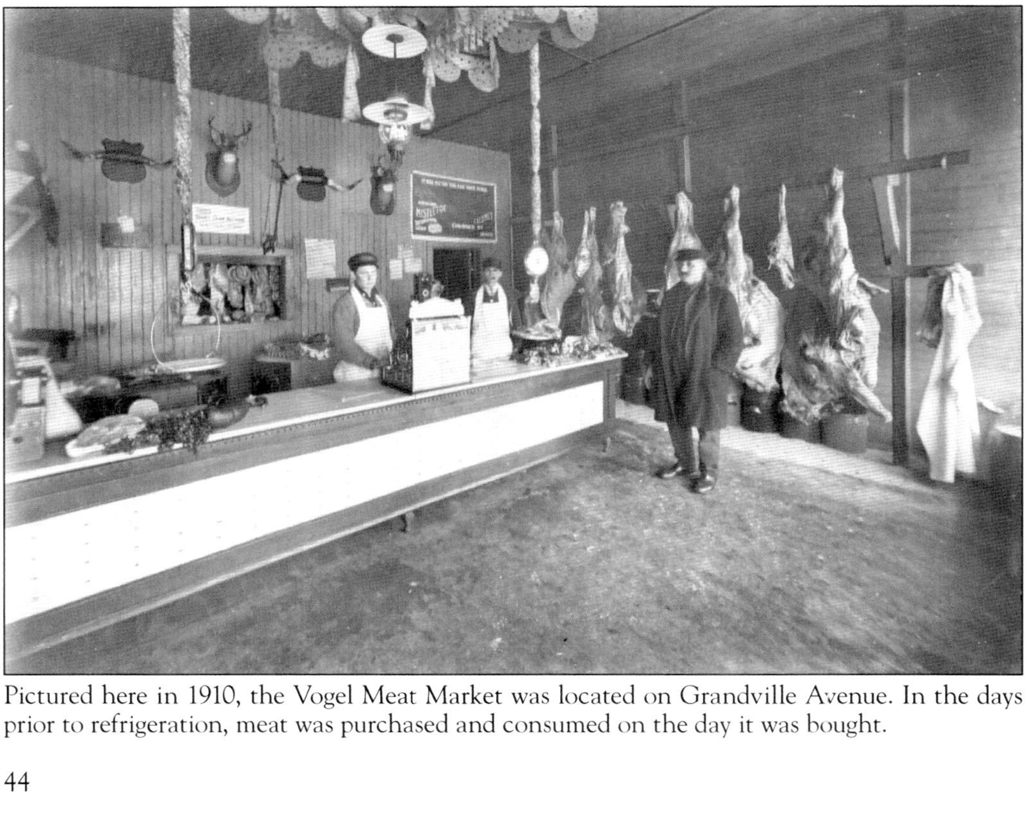

Pictured here in 1910, the Vogel Meat Market was located on Grandville Avenue. In the days prior to refrigeration, meat was purchased and consumed on the day it was bought.

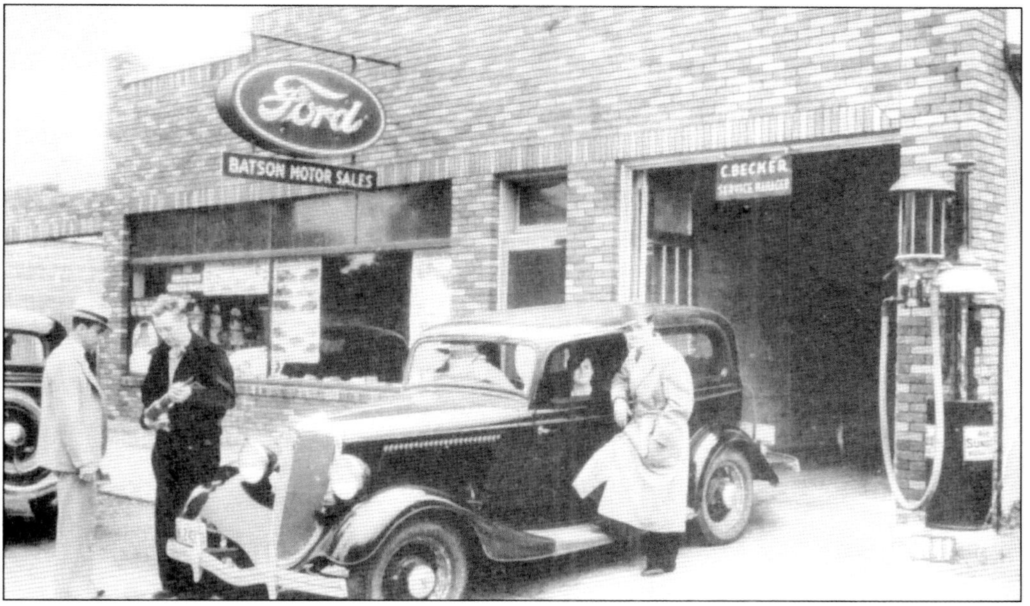

Conrad Becker opened Batson Motors in 1923 on Chicago Drive, where he did a thriving business. The store carried auto supplies and provided mechanic services, including engine repair. Batson Motors was handed down from father to son for generations. No longer specializing in automobiles, the Becker family still operates a business in Hudsonville today.

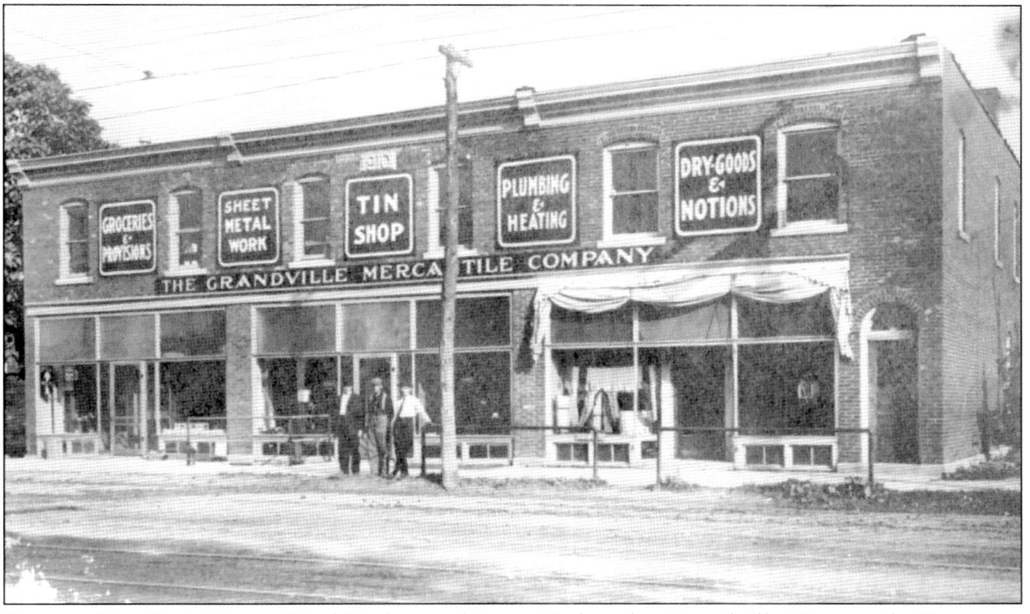

Operated by Kiah Green, Fred Taylor, and Leon Taylor, the Grandville Mercantile Company occupied a brick building, located on the corner of Washington and Chicago Drives, in 1910. It was a general store that also carried a variety of goods, including groceries, plumbing, tinwork, and clothing. Because it was brick, the building was less likely to catch on fire, which was a big concern in those days.

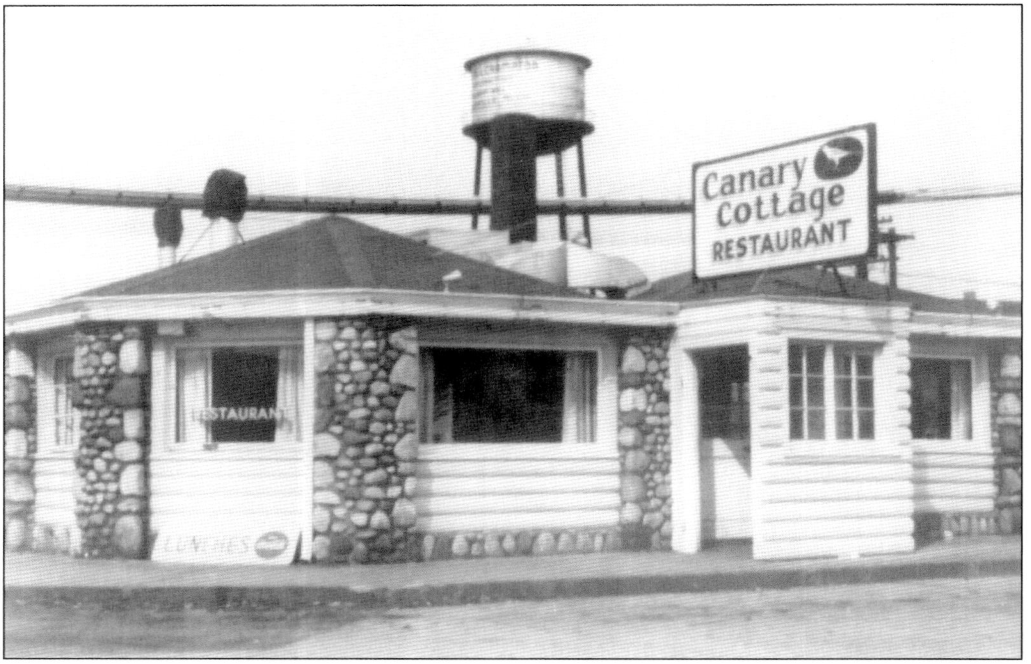

In 1930, the Canary Cottage Restaurant occupied a beautiful stone building on the northeast side of Chicago Drive at Wilson Avenue. It was a family restaurant, serving the best-flavored root beer in town, Vernors ginger ale on draft, and golden fried chicken in a basket.

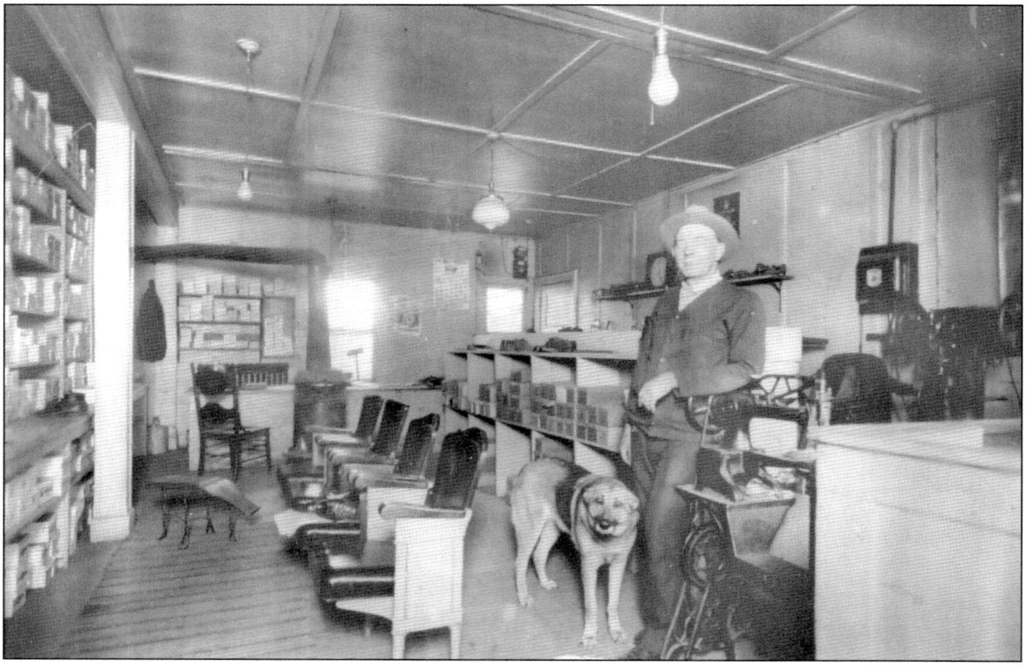

Ysbrandt Groendyk, who emigrated from the Netherlands, owned this shoe store, shown here in 1935. He was a cobbler by trade, and he sold and repaired shoes in his Wilson Avenue store. He was in business into the 1980s.

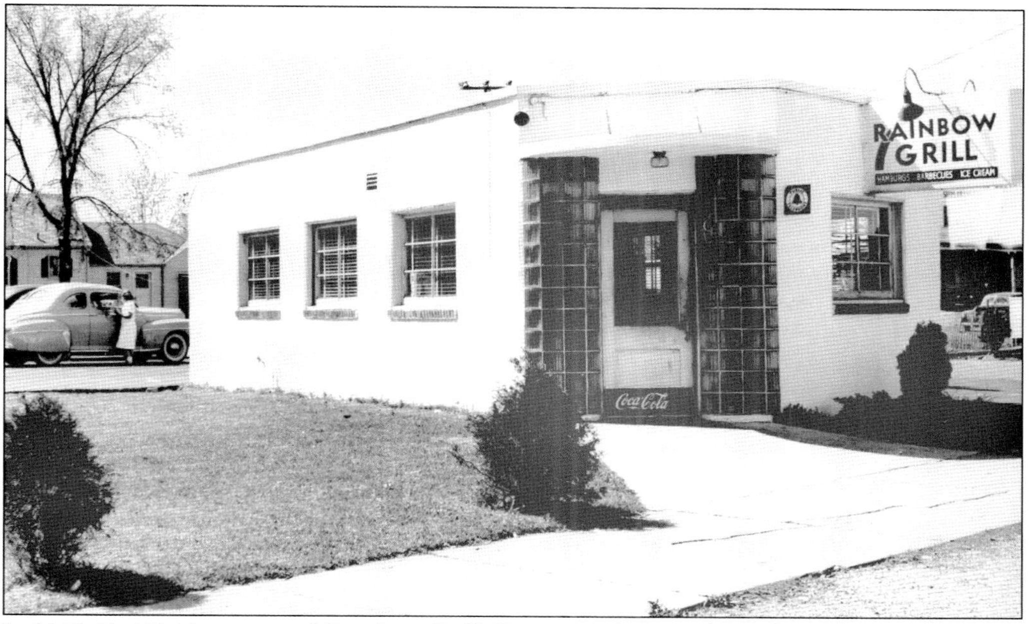

In 1946, Earl Zuidema owned Rainbow Grill. Known at the time for its burgers, malts, and tray service, business continued to grow. In the back left, a tray is being delivered to a parked car.

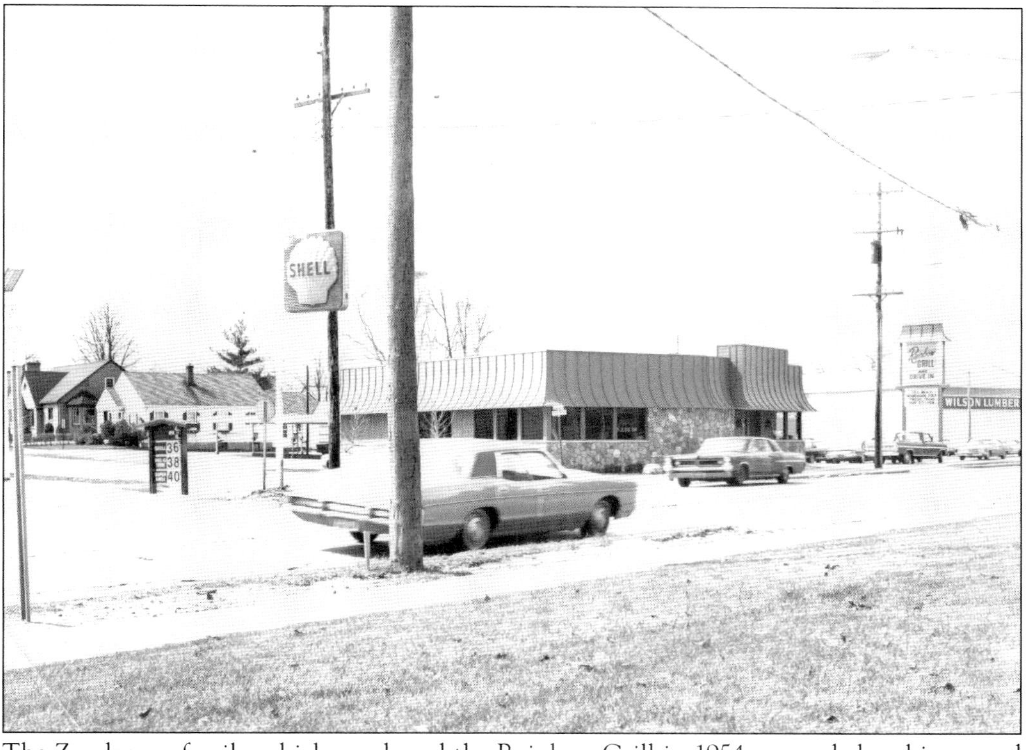

The Zondervan family, which purchased the Rainbow Grill in 1954, expanded and improved the family restaurant. Since then, it has become a community-gathering place. Rainbow Grill is located on Fayette Avenue and Chicago Drive. Note the gas prices on the sign.

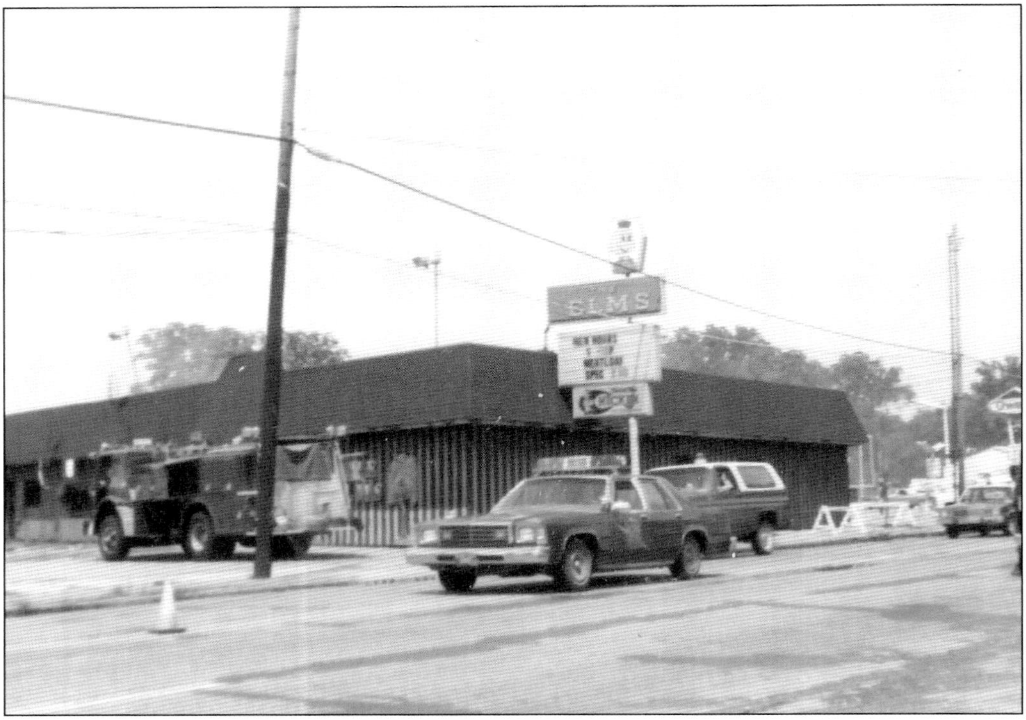

The Elms restaurant was run by Jack Alkema, who purchased it in 1962 from Harold Becker. It was a 25-year landmark in Grandville until it burned down in 1980. Located on Chicago Drive, the family restaurant offered an outdoor tray service. It had just been remodeled with a banquet room and improved family indoor dining when it was struck by lightning during a rainstorm and burned.

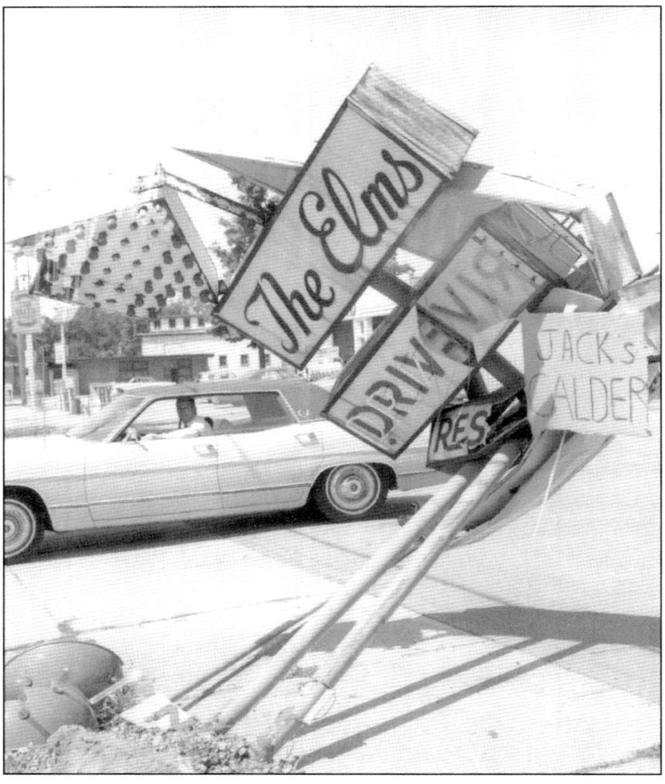

Pictured here in 1969, The Elms drive-thru sign is more than a bit mangled. A drive-thru was a novelty at the time. Food was ordered through a speaker, and when the food was ready, it was placed on a tray that was attached to the window of the car.

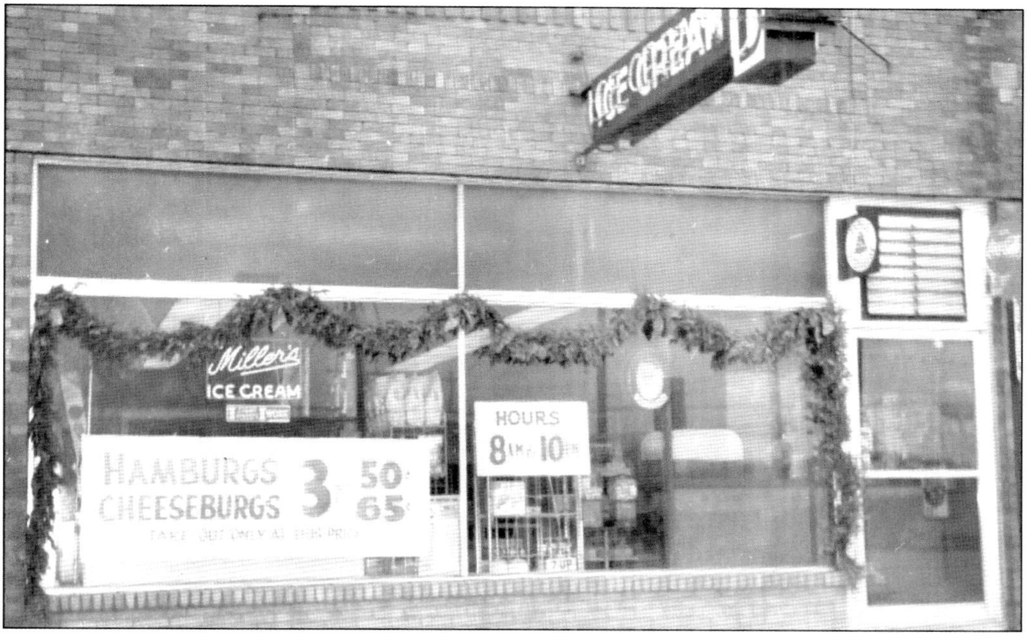

In 1967, Adrianse was located on Thirtieth Street. Note that hamburgers are three for 50¢, and the restaurant was open until 10:00 p.m.; a phone booth was also available.

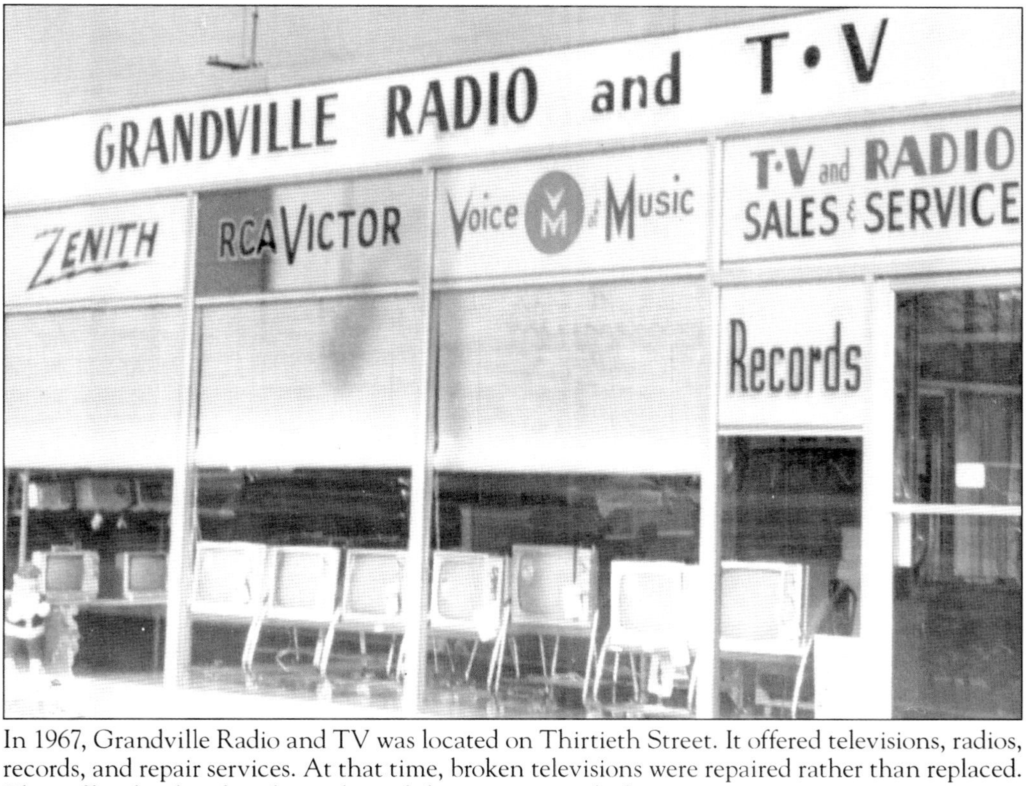

In 1967, Grandville Radio and TV was located on Thirtieth Street. It offered televisions, radios, records, and repair services. At that time, broken televisions were repaired rather than replaced. They offered only a few channels, and there was no such thing as a remote.

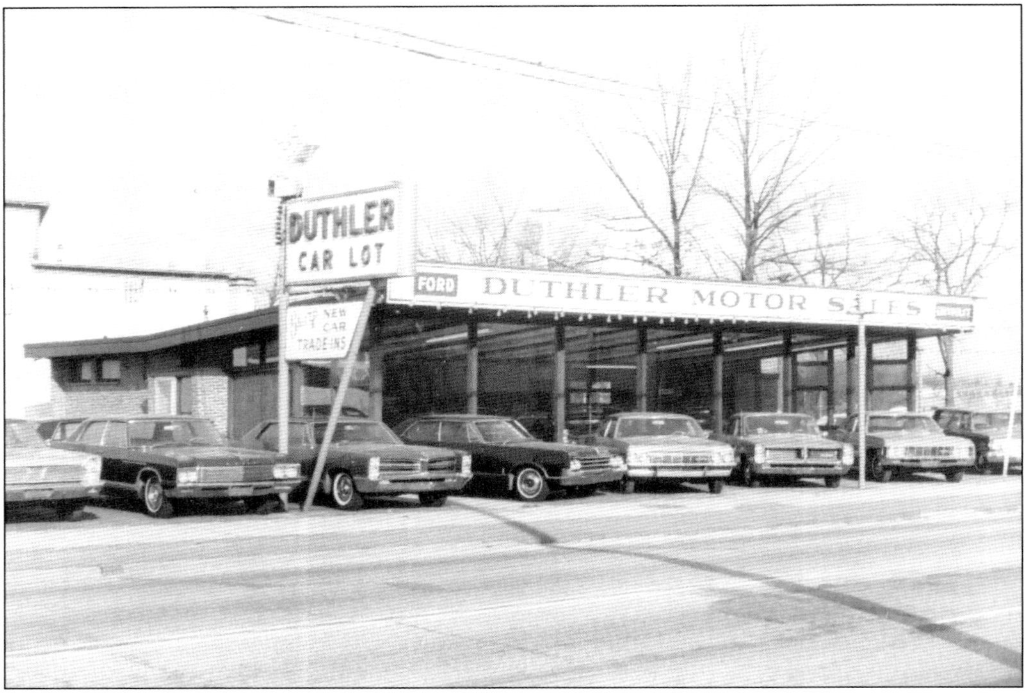

In 1967, many automobile dealers were located in Grandville. The Duthler dealership was built on Chicago Drive at Canal Avenue. It specialized in Chevrolets.

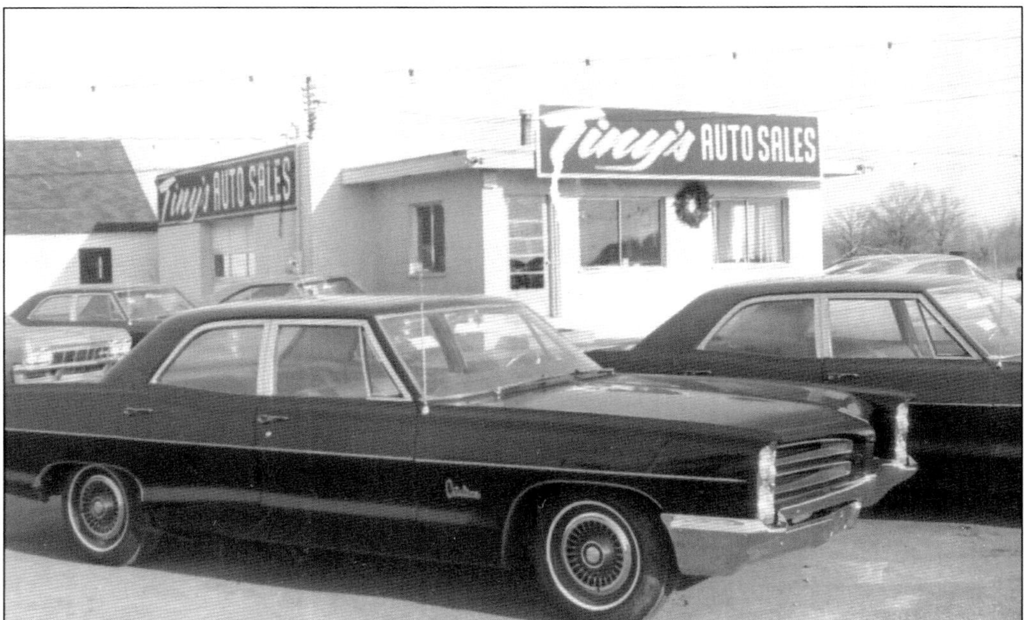

Pictured here in 1967, Tiny's Auto Sales was located on Twenty-eighth Street. It is still in business today, and Tiny himself still owns it. He claims to have been in business for over 50 years, starting out on Chicago Drive, moving to Division and Hall Streets, and then to Twenty-eighth Street, where it has been located for years.

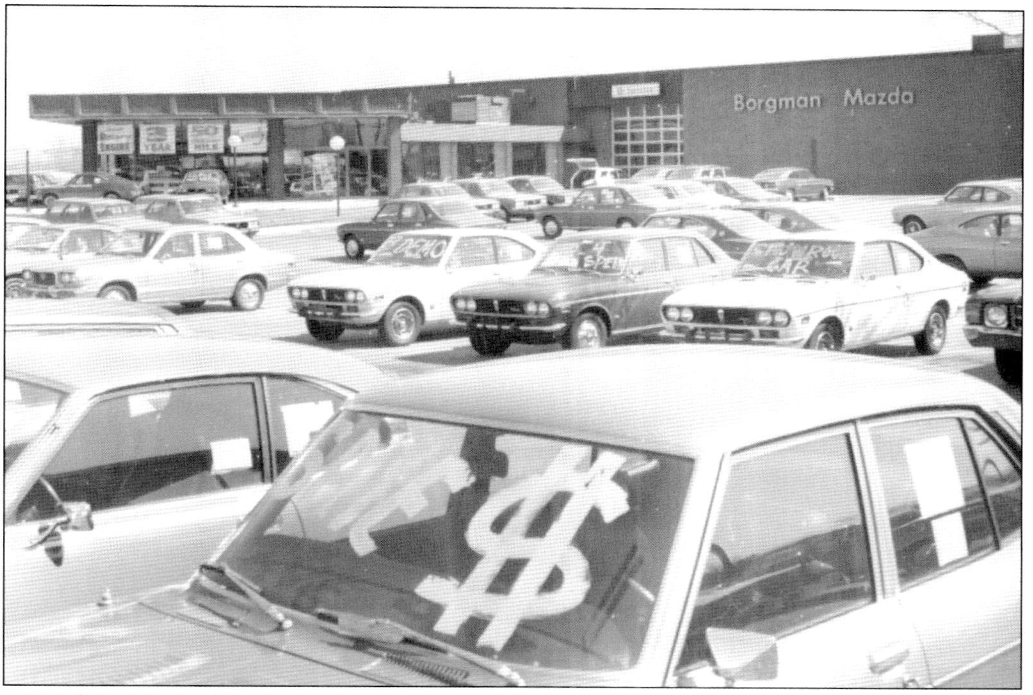

Started in 1960 by Fred Borgman, Borgman Mazda is still located on Ivanrest and Twenty-eighth Streets.

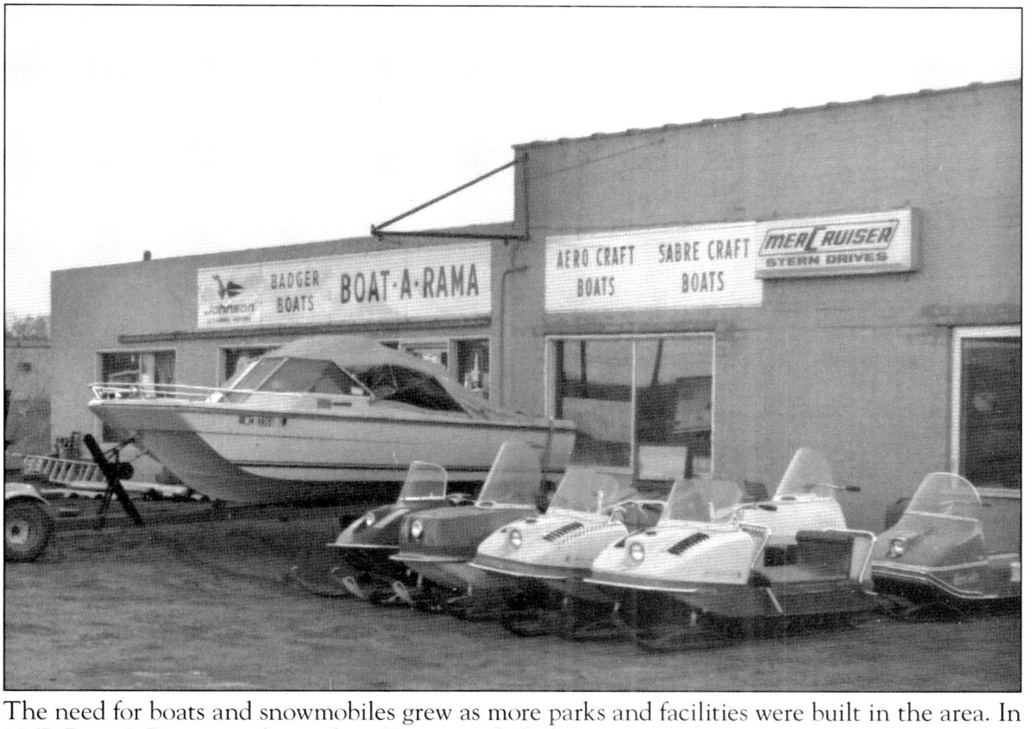

The need for boats and snowmobiles grew as more parks and facilities were built in the area. In 1967, Boat-A-Rama was located on Twenty-eighth Street.

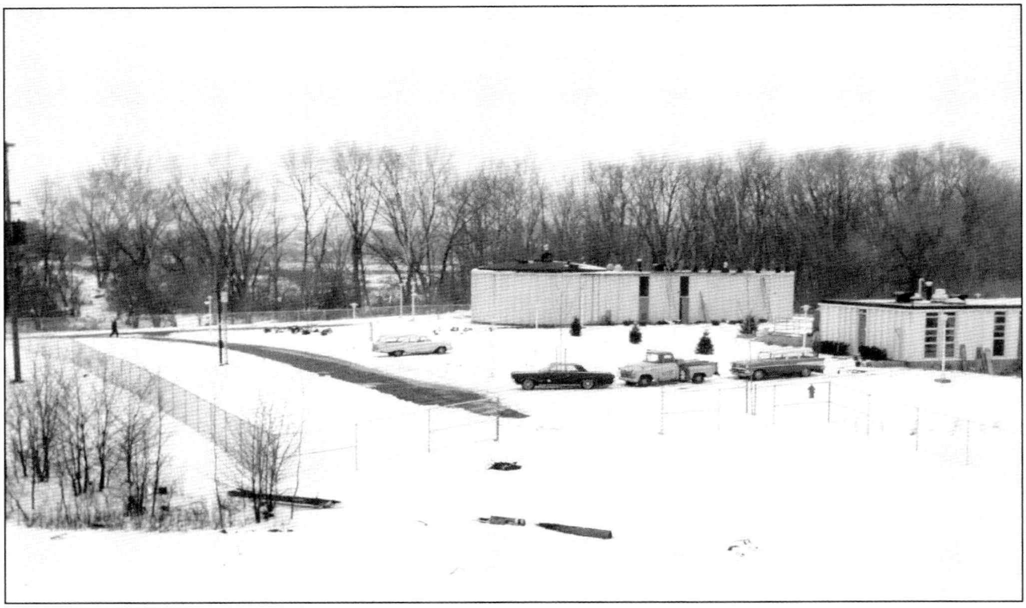

The water and sewage treatment plant was built in 1964, and it was improved in 1968 when the system was converted to a Lake Michigan water supply. Located on Chicago Drive, the city still maintains its own water and sewer system today. The bike trail through Grandville passes by the treatment plant.

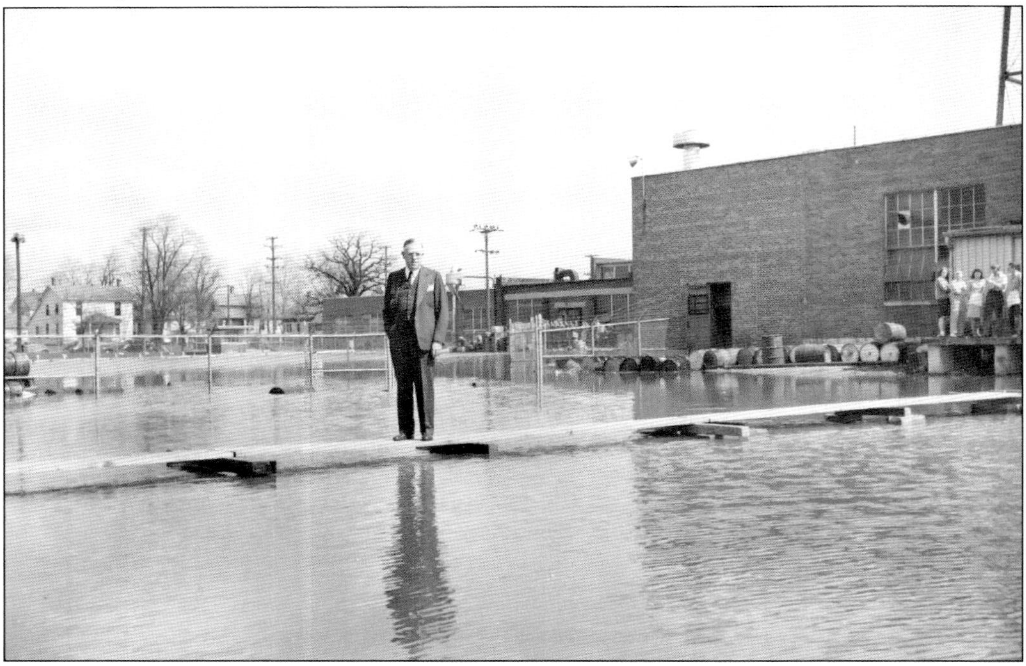

Winters and Crampton, shown here during the 1947 flood, employed hundreds of people in the Grandville area. It was used during World War II for war work, but it also made Kelvinator and Whirlpool hardware and parts. The business began operations in 1929. Later renamed Jervis and Alloy Tech, it was located on the east side of Wilson Avenue next to the railroad tracks.

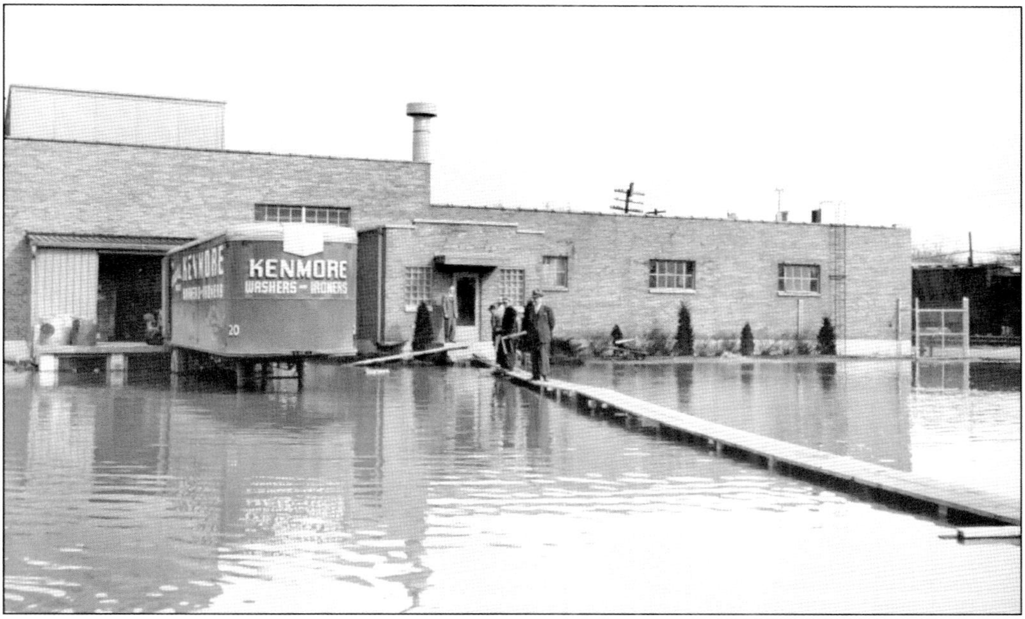

This is a different view of the flood of 1947 at Winters and Crampton. Boardwalks were put in place so employees could walk between the buildings. Cars were made to park farther down the street where the flooding was not as rampant. Business went on as usual despite the weather. Note the Kenmore truck parked at the loading dock.

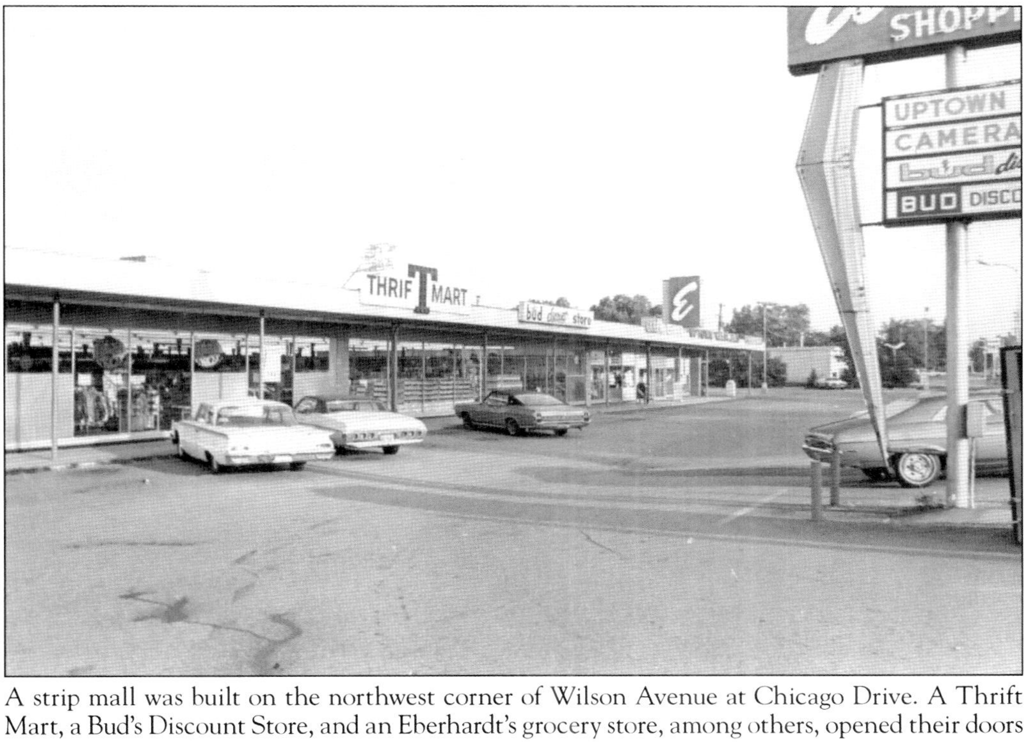

A strip mall was built on the northwest corner of Wilson Avenue at Chicago Drive. A Thrift Mart, a Bud's Discount Store, and an Eberhardt's grocery store, among others, opened their doors to the public in the 1960s.

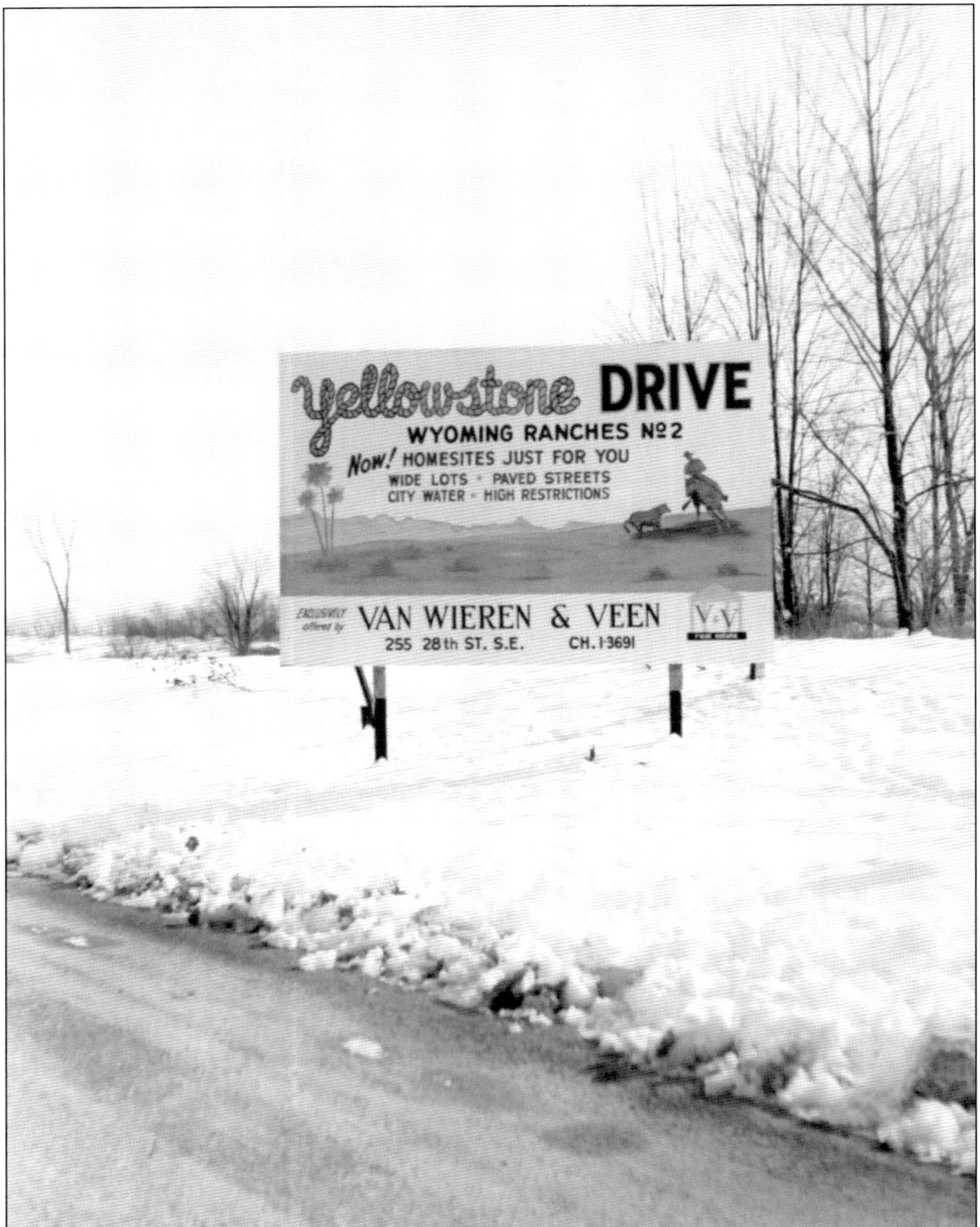

As the city grew, the need for new homes was also growing. Grandville, the sleepy little bedroom community of Grand Rapids was coming into its own. More and more businesses were opening, and the town was becoming a shopping and living destination. Here, a new housing development is advertising lots.

Three

Transportation

Need to get somewhere? That thought is taken for granted nowadays. There was a time when walking was the norm, and the lucky people had horses. Horse stealing then was like stealing an automobile today. In Grandville, the crime was taken seriously; two hangings for stealing horses have been recorded.

The Indian trails, which led down to the rapids, were hard going as they went through dense forest. A boat was a quicker and easier method to head downriver to Grand Haven or up to the rapids in Grand Rapids. However, as the river sometimes ebbed and flowed, it became shallow in the summer, and many a vessel got stuck trying to get upriver. A river dredge crew was sometimes able to help, but manual labor was slow and difficult; more was needed. At one point in time, some hoped to bring big ships up the Grand River, but the river always refused to cooperate.

Trains came, replacing boats as the fastest and easiest mode of transportation. Locomotives also brought goods to market faster. And, with the arrival of the automobile, new roads were installed, and travel in and out of Grandville became much easier.

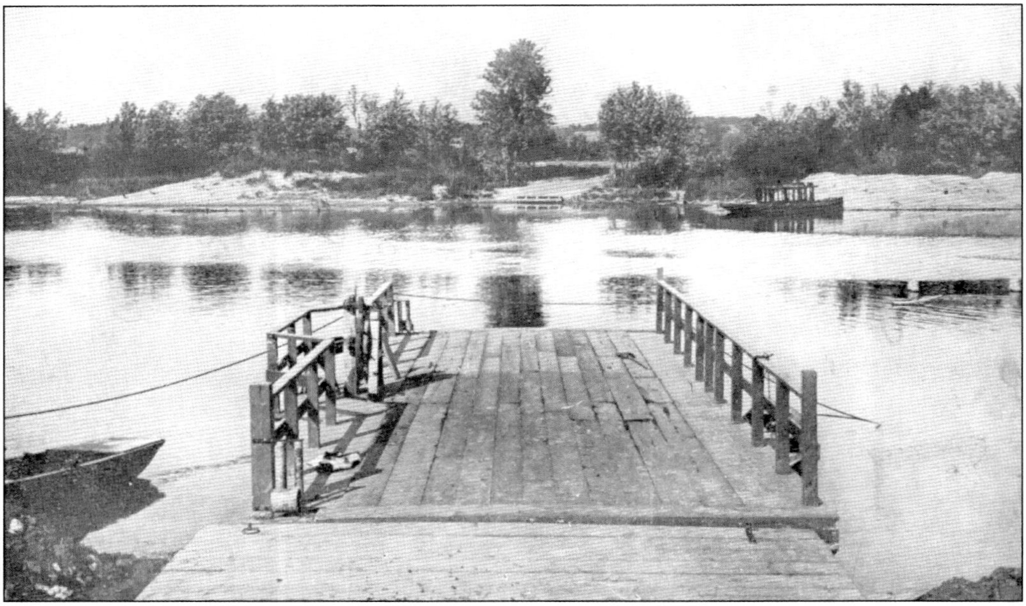

Bike, horse, boat, train, bus, and automobile were just some of the ways to get around Grandville in earlier years. The Grand River, of course, was the reason the city of Grandville was founded at this location. Its natural, sandy shores made it easy for boats to dock, and passengers could get off and on to go to and from Grand Haven or Grand Rapids. The ferry dock pictured here was located at the Jenison–Grandville bend in the Grand River. The ferry was very popular at the time, as bridges in the area had not yet been built so there was no other way to get across the river.

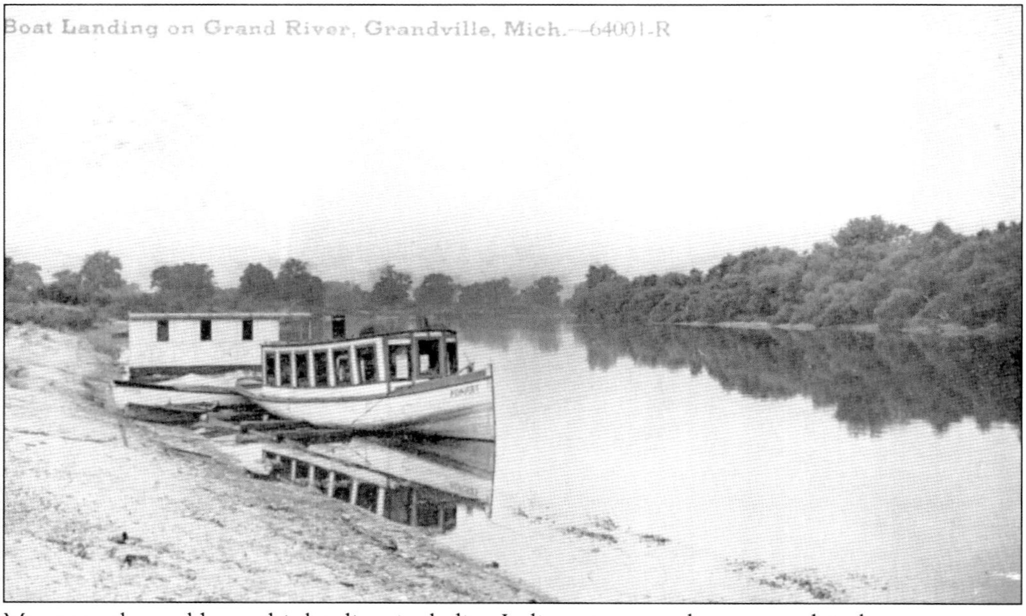

Many people would pass this landing, including Indians, trappers, hunters, and timber prospectors, as there were few passageways other than the river. The water was shallow here, and the shores were sandy—a perfect place for boating or a picnic. Many people chose to dock their boats and spend the day in Grandville.

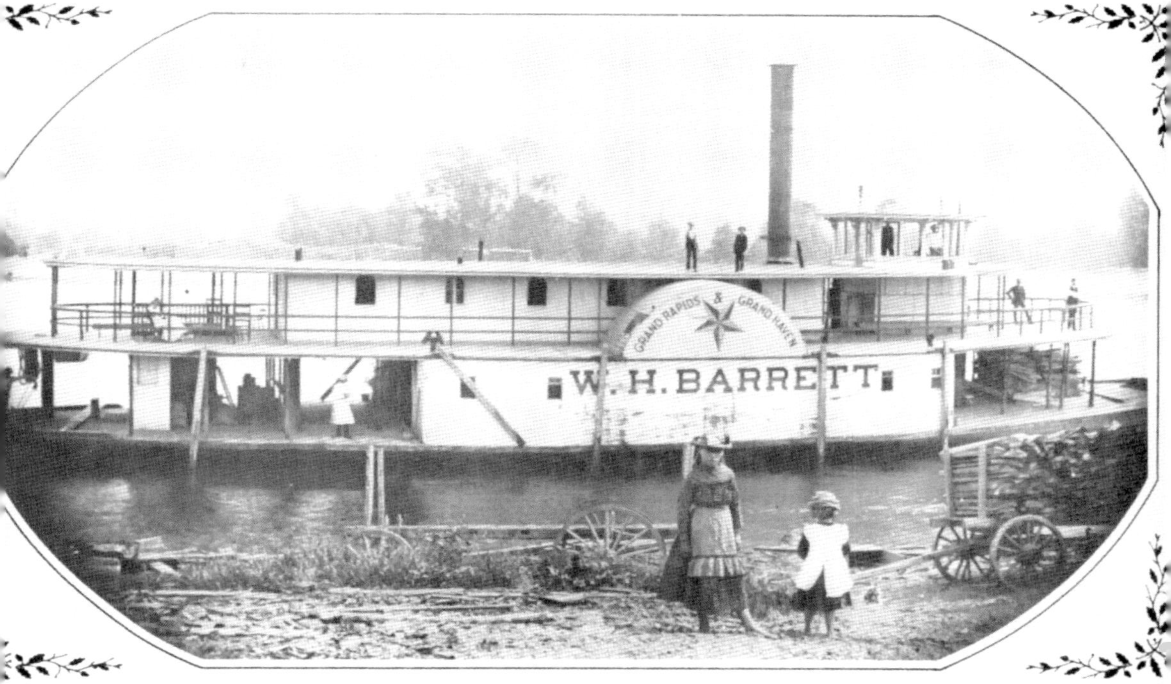

The *W.H. Barrett* was built in 1874 at a time when Ottawa Indian trails led to tall stands of timber and there were no settlements between Grandville and Grand Rapids. Boats were an important link to the outside world, bringing lumber, mail, merchandise, goods to trade and sell, and passengers. People must have come running with excitement hearing the horn of a paddle wheeler. Note the children in the photograph with hats and dresses but no shoes. Lawrence Crowley owned the Grand Rapids Transportation Company and the *W. H. Barrett* among other businesses and ventures. The boat's last days were in 1894.

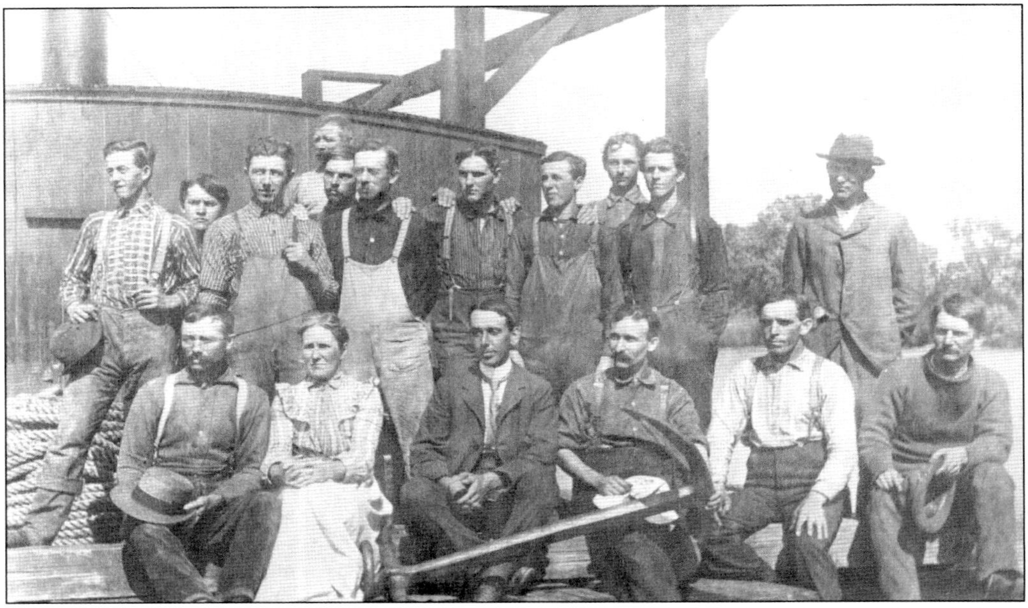

It was tough to be a member of a river-dredge crew in 1900. These men kept the sand from shifting into the river with pickaxes and shovels. The river was constantly being dredged to keep it open for the riverboats. Inspector Amos Evers sits in the middle of the group, wearing a suit and tie.

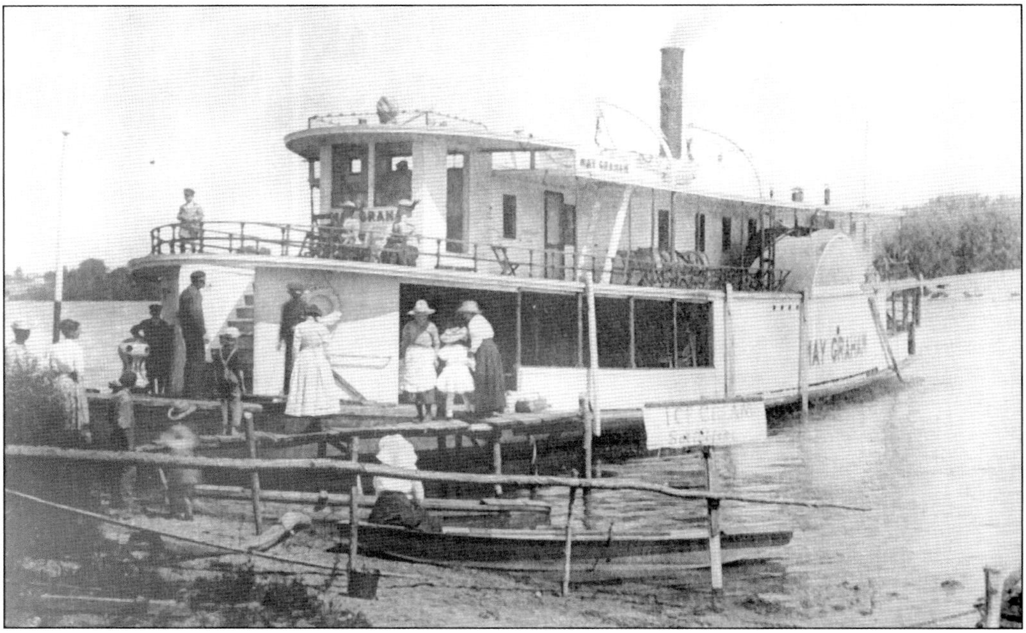

This 1917 photograph shows the *May Graham*. This was one of the last riverboats to ply the waters of the Grand River, as the train became the new mode of transportation. It was a steamer that had been used on the Great Lakes from Benton Harbor to St. Joseph but was really too small for that rugged water. Built in Milwaukee, the *May Graham* became a regular on the Grand River, with a stop in Grandville. It was mainly a pleasure boat.

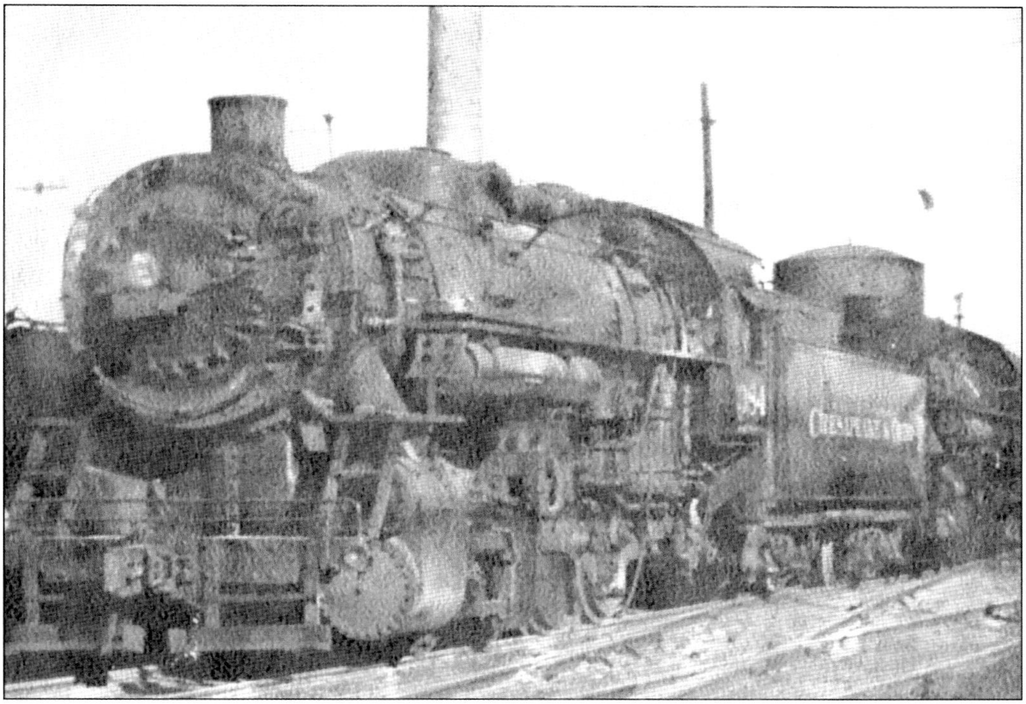

In 1871, the "Iron Horse" came through Grandville. President Andrew Jackson, having never been on a train, rode this one in 1833 and deemed it safe for travel. This steam locomotive was a fixture in Grandville for a while.

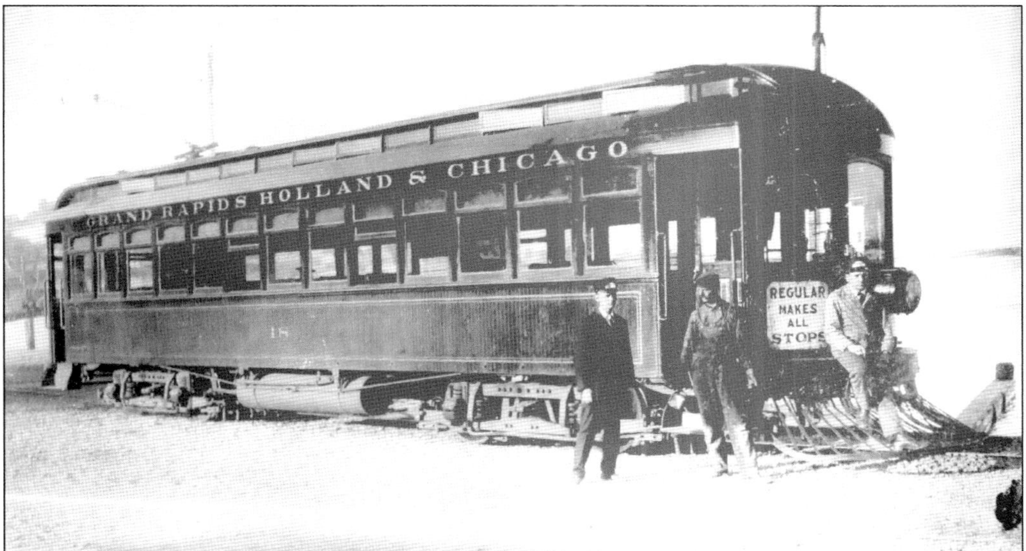

The Grand Rapids and Holland Railway Company was founded in 1870. It built a railway from Holland to Grand Rapids, and in 1871 the project was completed. Immediately, farm products were put on the trains for market. Early into the 1900s, the interurban expanded into Grand Rapids, primarily carrying light freight and passengers. This c. 1926 photograph was taken on a stop between Jamestown and Jenison.

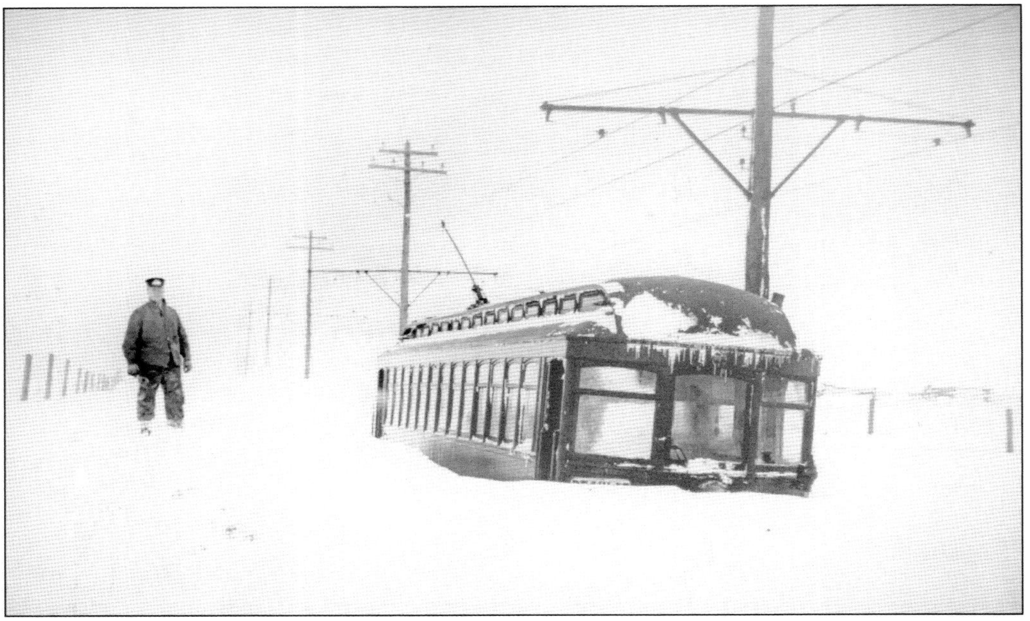

In November of 1908, a snowstorm shut down the city of Grandville and the surrounding area. This interurban train was snowbound for quite some time before it could all be dug out. The whole of Grandville had to be shoveled out by hand.

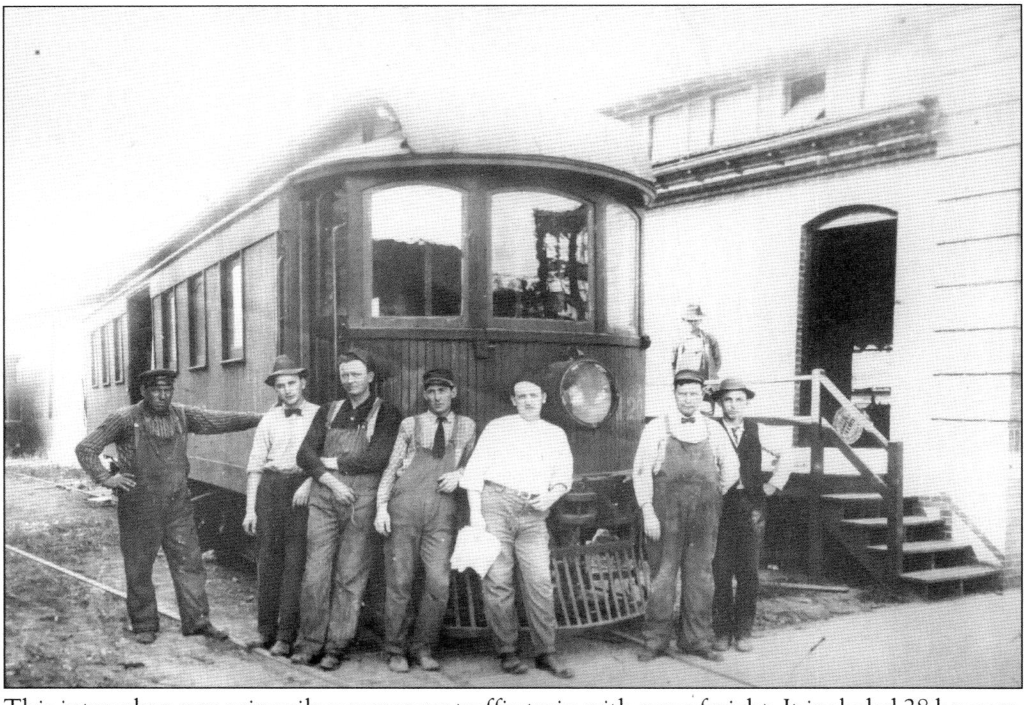

This interurban was primarily a passenger traffic train with some freight. It included 28 boxcars, two motorcars, and five passenger/baggage cars. It operated from 1871 until November 15, 1926, when service ended due to a merger that ended in bankruptcy.

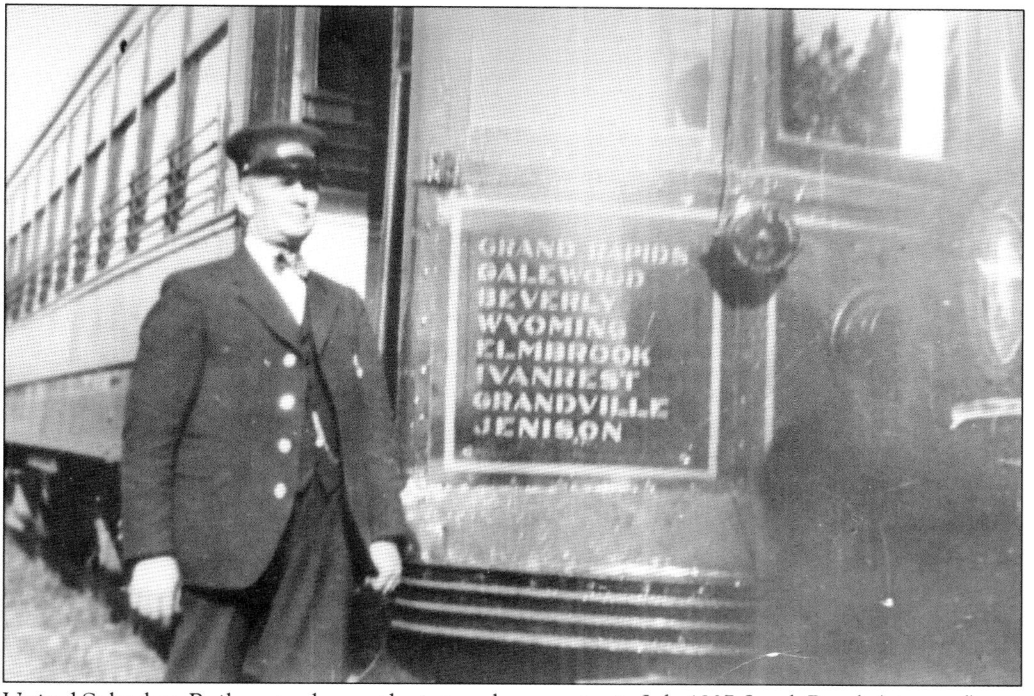

United Suburban Railway took over the interurban service in July 1927; Jacob Brock (pictured) was the engineer. It claimed to be the shortest railway, running only from Grand Rapids to Jenison, with the longest list of stockholders. The sign on the front of the train shows the stops along its route. It went out of business in 1932 because of the automobile.

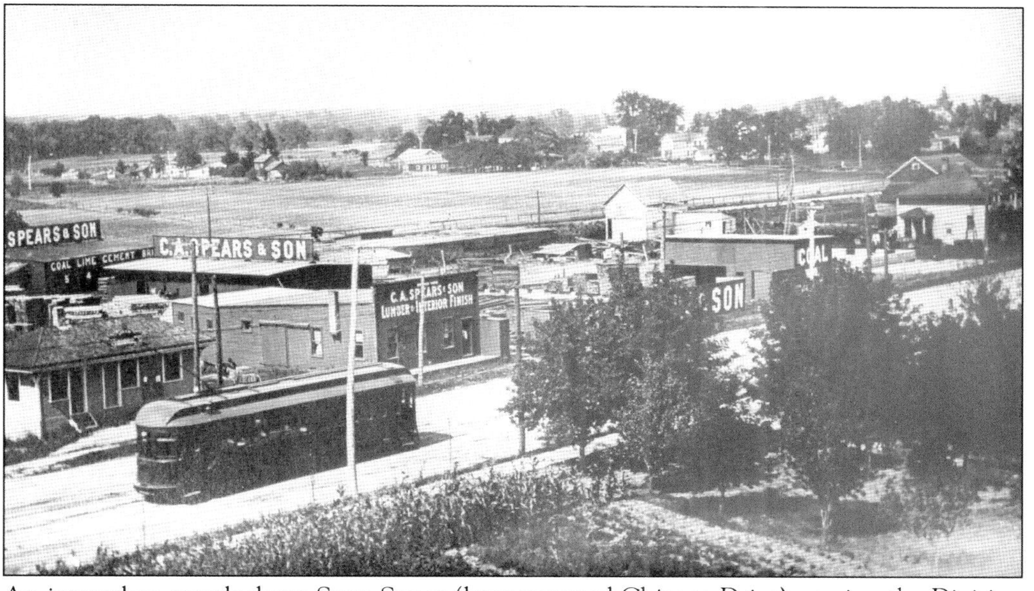

An interurban travels down State Street (later renamed Chicago Drive) nearing the Division Street crossing in Grandville. At that time, passengers not only waited at designated stops, but they also could wave down a train. At night, a light could be carried and used to signal the train to stop.

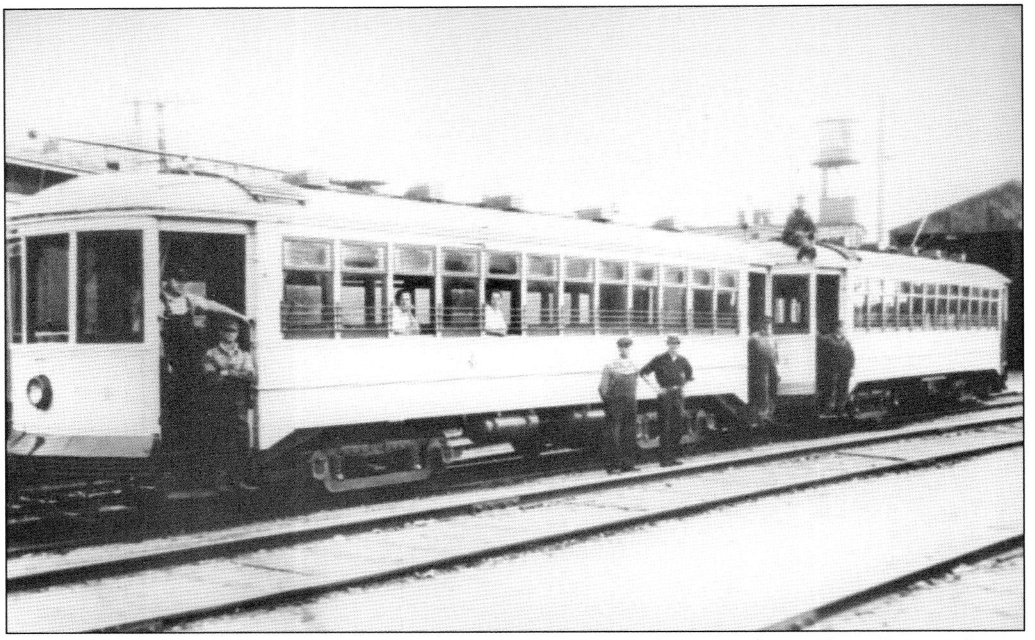

Here are two of the early-1900s interurban passenger trains. The cost of a trip from Barrett Street in Grandville to Grand Rapids was 5¢. Note the man sitting on the roof.

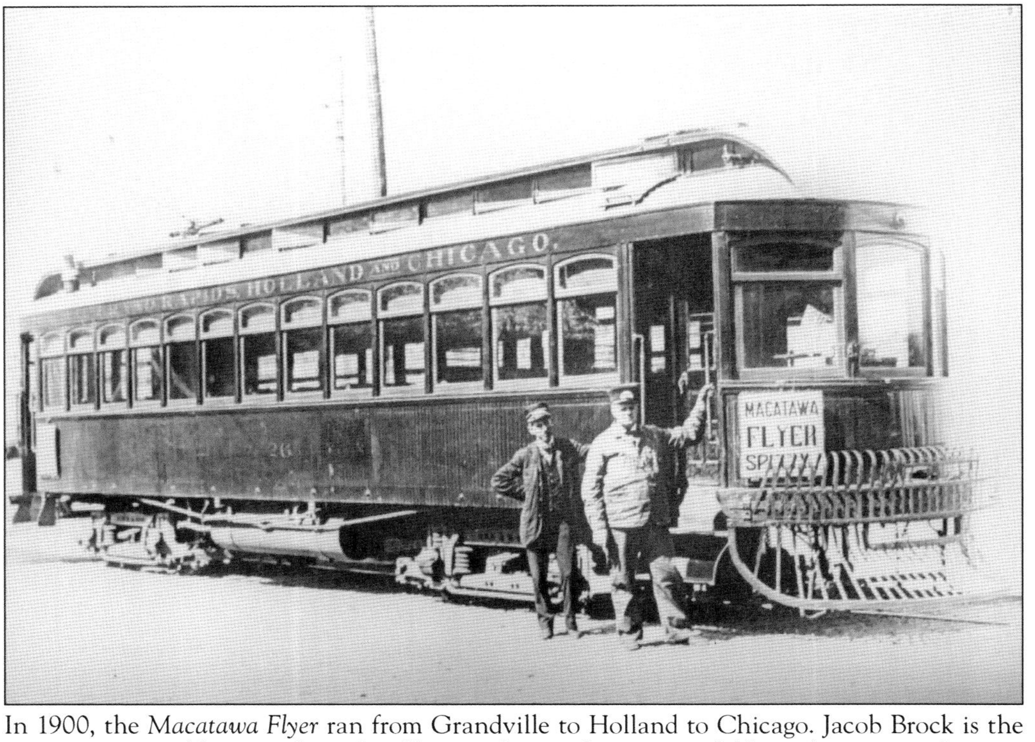

In 1900, the *Macatawa Flyer* ran from Grandville to Holland to Chicago. Jacob Brock is the engineer pictured here on the right. Chartered trains became available at the time, and groups and parties began to use them. Vacations or day trips to Lake Michigan became popular.

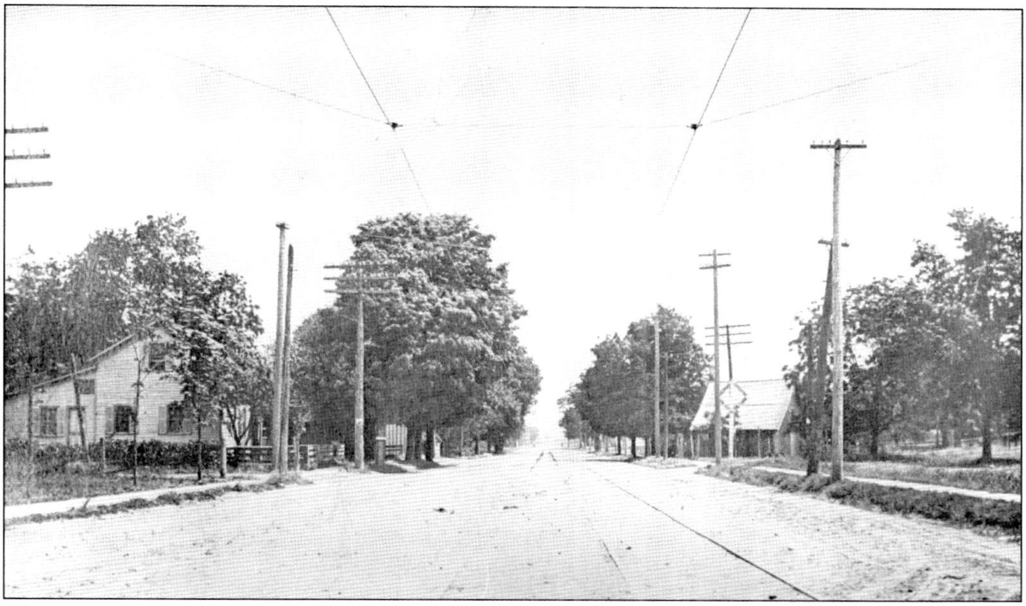

These are the Interurban tracks on Chicago Drive heading out of Grandville.

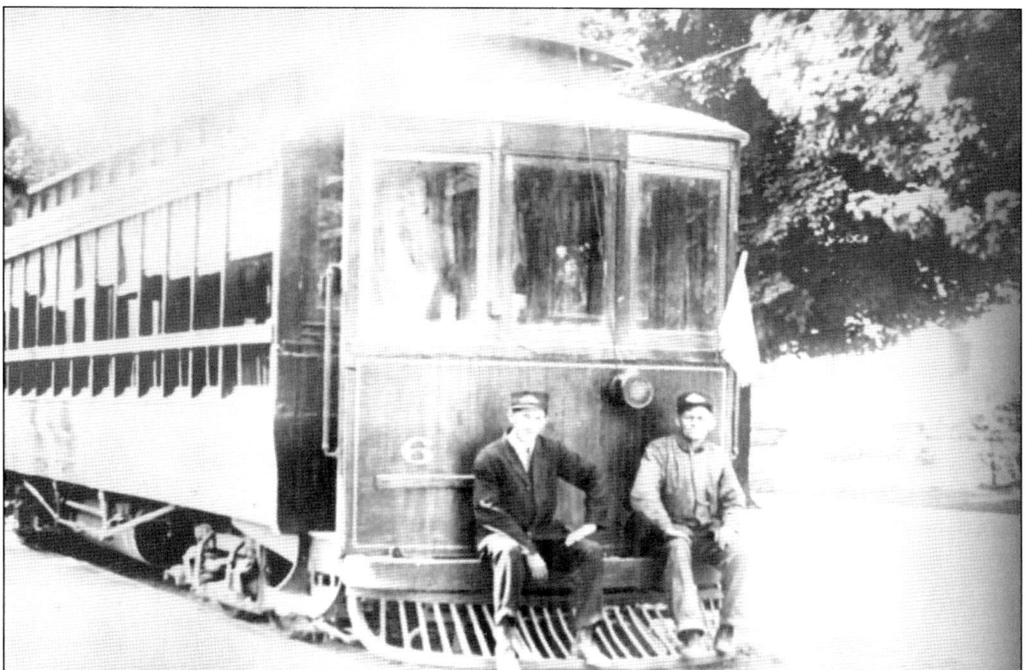

In 1900, Jacob Brock was the interurban engineer. In 1904, the train was given a set speed limit of 8 miles an hour while going through Grandville; automobiles were capped at 6 miles an hour (later upped to 12), and 15 miles an hour was the limit for steam locomotives.

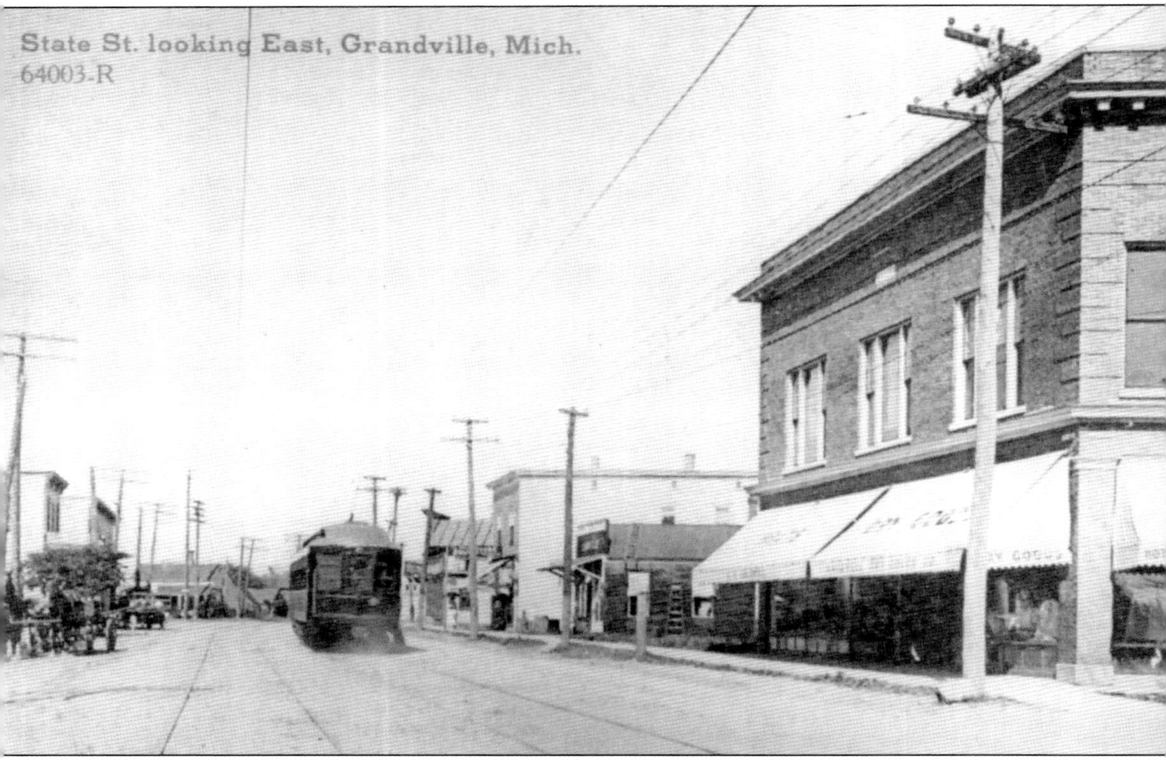

Pictured here in 1910, Chicago Drive near Franklin Street is visible to the east. The city had plank roads and dirt roads at the time.

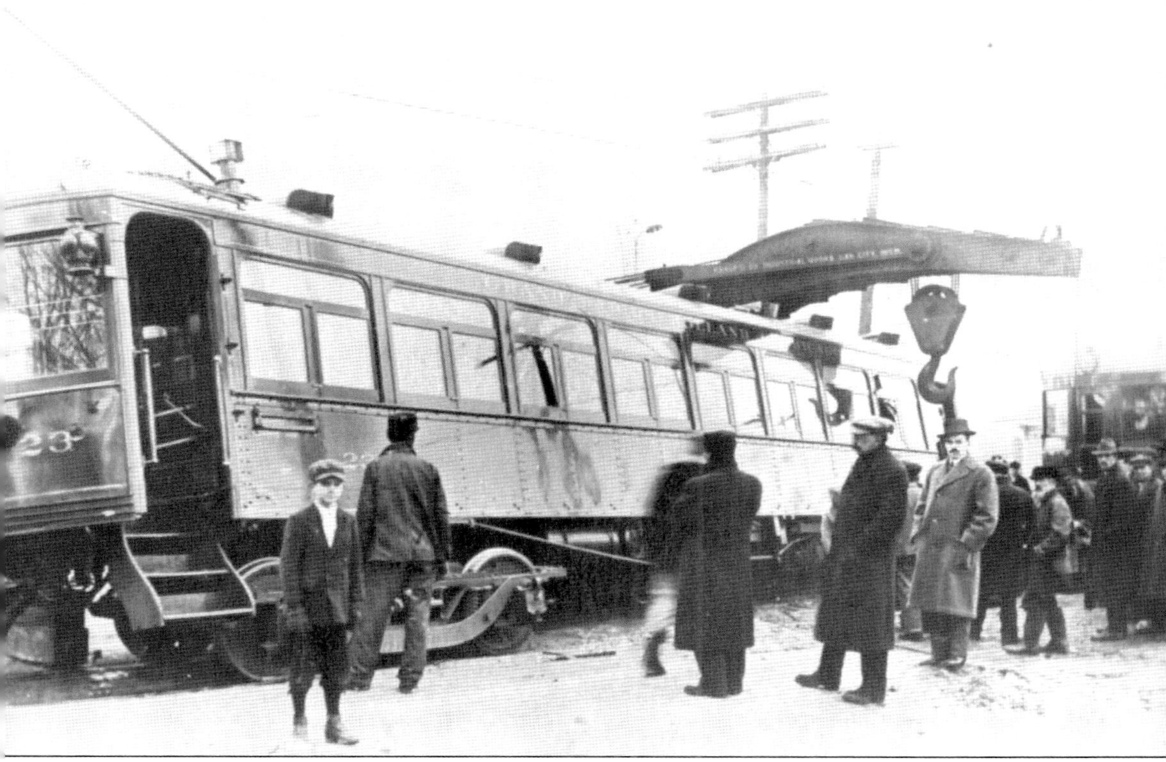

In 1916, this interurban was hit by a Pere Marquette engine just beyond the Wilson Avenue Crossing, injuring 10 people. The young boy in the photograph is George Grutter. There were many accidents between automobiles and trains. There is a story of Dr. Llewellyn Wedgwood's automobile being hit by the interurban at Chicago Drive and Godfrey Crossing; he broke his arm and some of his ribs. Two months later, his brother Randall Wedgwood was also hit by the interurban at Godfrey Crossing; he was seriously hurt and taken to the hospital and lost his dog in the accident. At the time, it is likely that the city had not put up lights. There was another crossing at Jenison, where accidental deaths were a common occurrence.

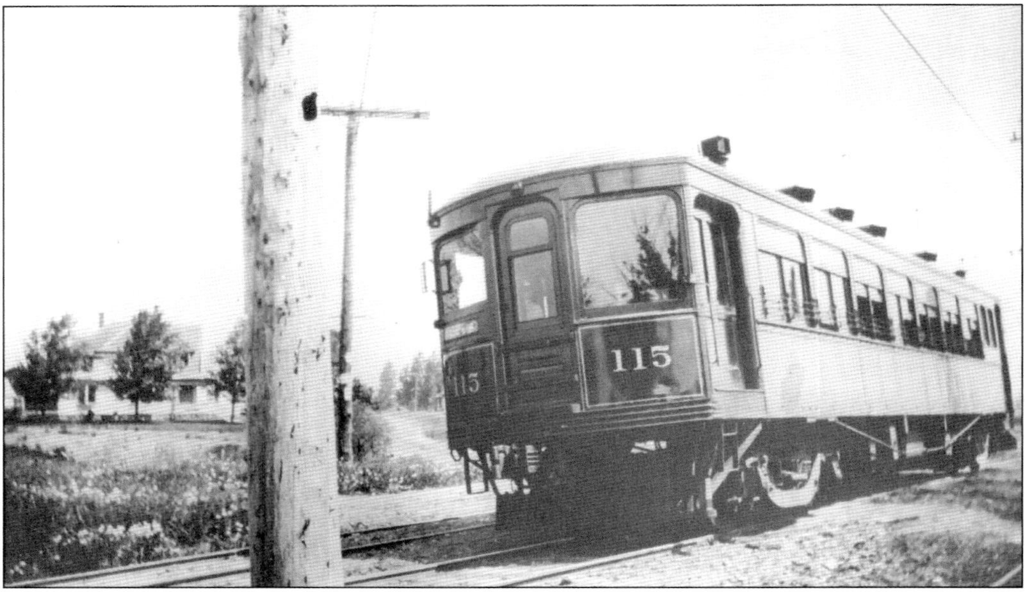

The train line was mostly lined with double tracks, allowing the interurban and steam engines to pass each other on occasion. The rails had been shipped from Detroit to Spring Lake. They started laying tracks there, continuing east until joining in Grand Rapids.

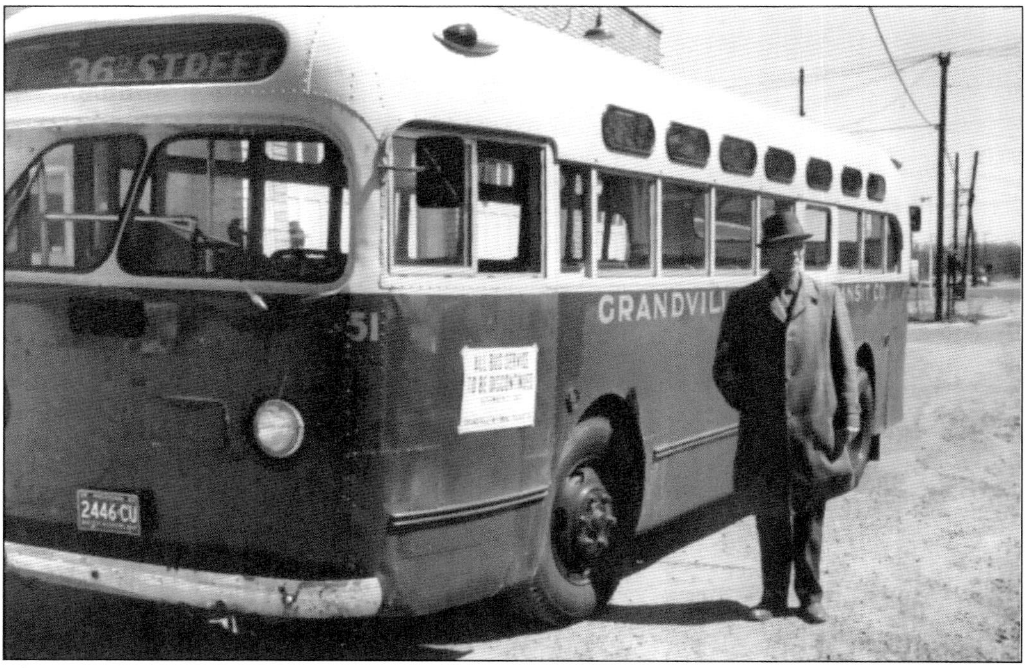

The Grandville-Wyoming Bus Transit Company ran for a little while between the two cities. Lee Johnson is pictured here on the occasion of the last bus trip in December 1962. Bus businesses were never really successful in Grandville.

Four

People and Organizations

Finding a social group or wanting to be a part of something charitable has been a common thread in the history of Grandville. There has always been a group to join in town. Many of these organizations called for formality; they had rules and regulations, or biblical principals, that one had to follow. Some groups were social in nature, with picnics and parties, while others were educational groups, such as the Ladies' Literary Group, which read the latest and greatest by authors and scholars. Schools and churches created vital interaction in the community, as farm life could be hard and lonely at times. There were also groups that raised money for different needs in the area.

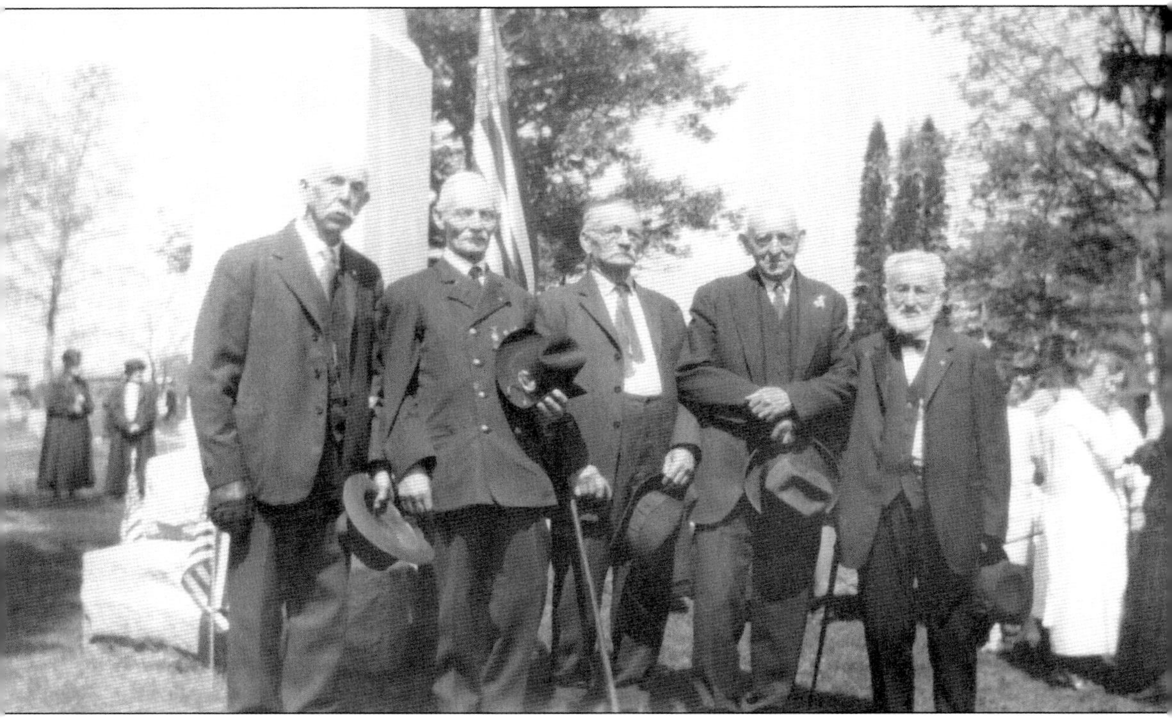

In 1916, money was raised by the women's group Daughters of Union Veterans of the Civil War to erect a Civil War monument on Prairie Street in what is now Grandville Cemetery, replacing a wooden structure. Members asked everyone in the community to donate money, and then they published the contributors' names in the *Grandville Star* newspaper. Kiah Green, Fred Taylor, Leon Taylor, and L.D. Moody laid the foundation, and A. Adrianse donated the gravel. On Memorial Day in 1916, the living Civil War veterans were honored at the dedication of the monument, which can be found today at the front of the cemetery. These veterans are, from left to right, Joseph Whipple, James Beadle, Mr. Burke, Henry Preston (who had the honor of being General Grant's bodyguard), and Henry Swan.

Filled with patriotism, men from Grandville joined up with surrounding communities for the 13-mile walk to the Grand Rapids Fairgrounds located at Hall and Madison Streets. At the fairgrounds, men from the Grandville Civil War Company H met up with the companies from Grand Rapids, becoming a Michigan regiment. Over half of the Grandville men did not return from the war. Every year, Grandville's Memorial Day parade ends at Grandville Cemetery with speeches and a wreath placed at the base of the Civil War statue located in front of the cemetery.

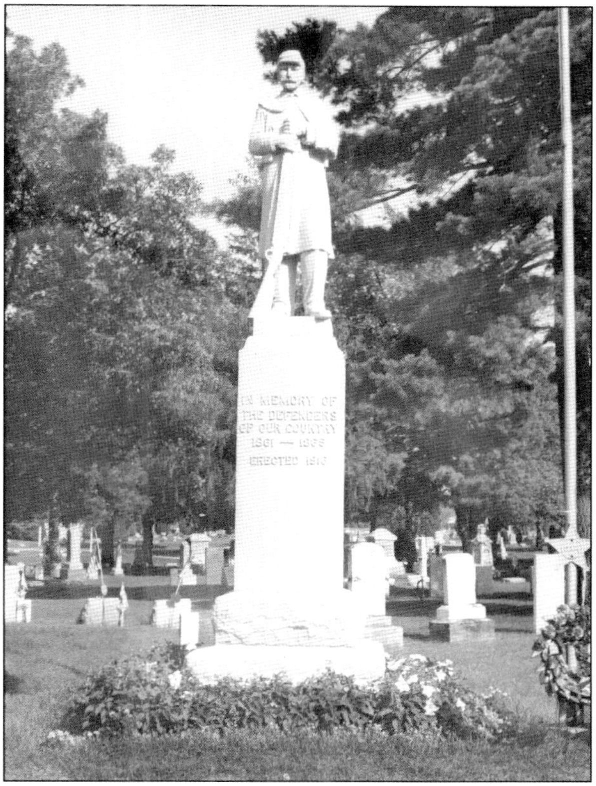

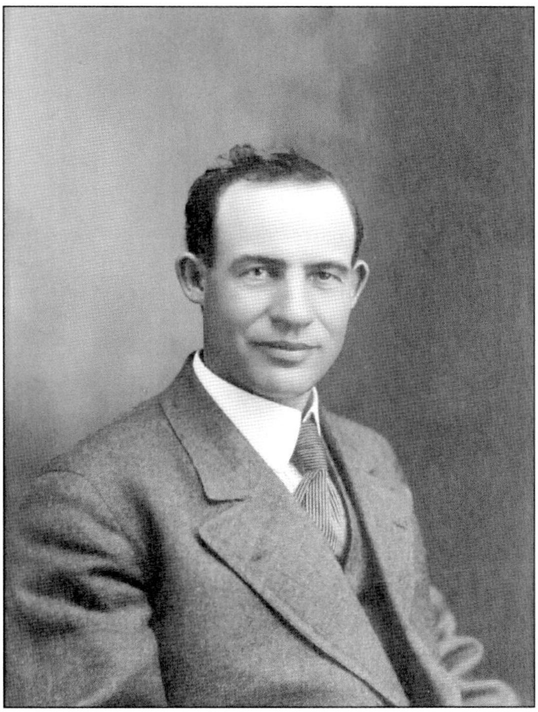

Dr. Llewellyn Wedgwood graduated from Grandville Union High School in 1895 and Wayne State Medical School in Detroit in 1899. After graduation, he started work in Jenison. Two years later, he opened an office in Grandville. Residents without financial means would often pay him in eggs or with a farm animal. He paid house calls by horse and buggy.

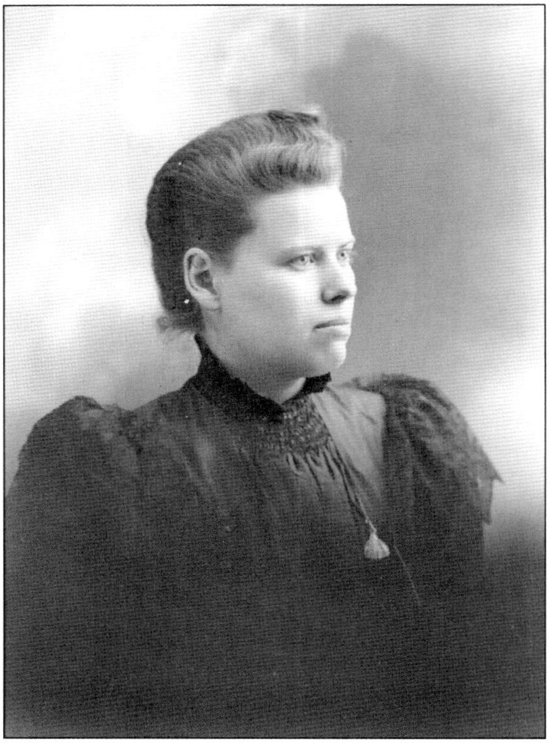

Dr. Llewellyn Wedgwood's longtime receptionist and nurse Lottie Barnaby Cross was said to be the kindest woman around. The doctor's office was located above the drugstore on Wilson Avenue and Chicago Drive.

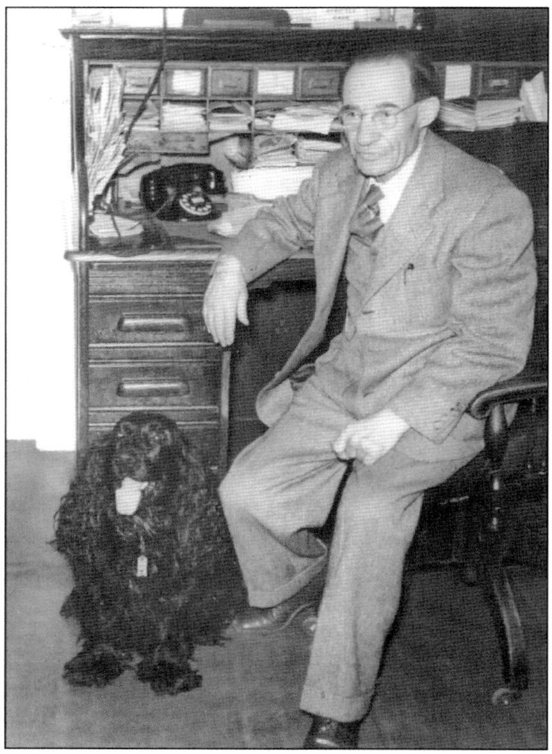

Dr. Wedgwood was given a gold watch by the Grandville Rotary Club at his retirement in 1949. This photograph shows him around the time of his retirement, one week before he died. He was a doctor in Grandville for over 40 years.

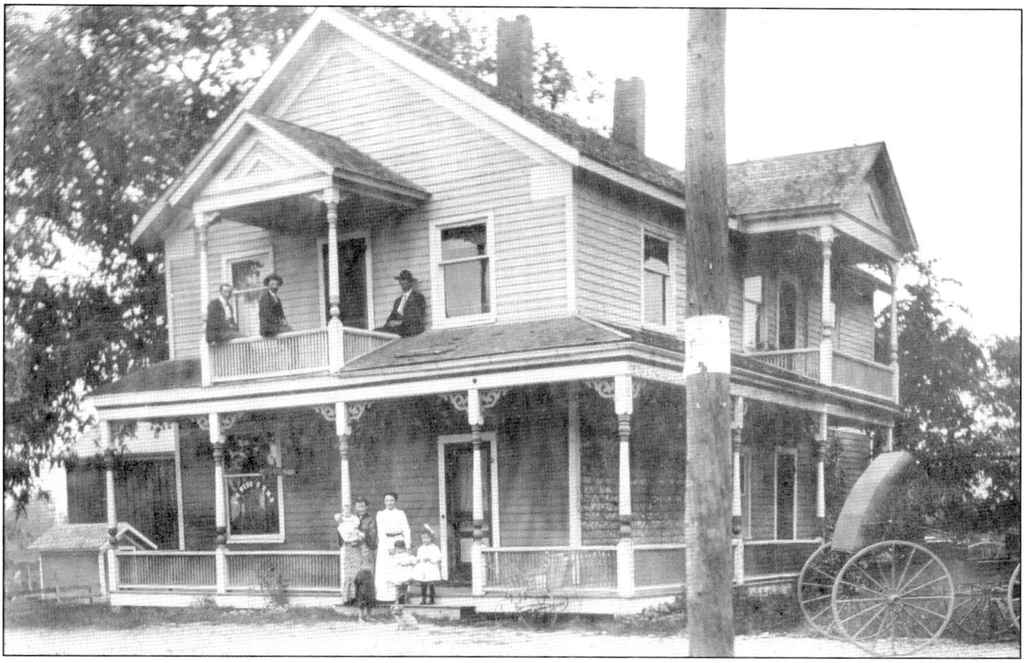

Dr. Llewellyn Wedgwood's house was located on Chicago Drive at Canal Street. Pictured are, from left to right, (upstairs railing) Dr. Wedgwood, his brother Randall, and their father, Gustavas Wedgwood; (first floor, adults) mother, Elizabeth, and Llewellyn's wife, Edith; (children) baby Kenneth (Randall's son), Gladys, and Mildred.

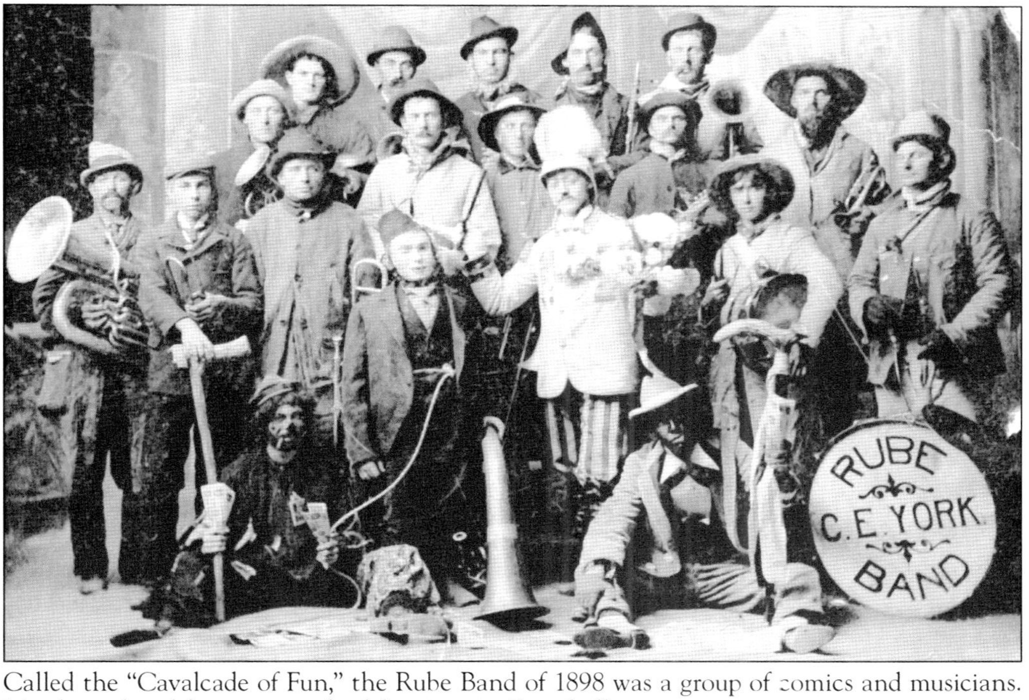

Called the "Cavalcade of Fun," the Rube Band of 1898 was a group of comics and musicians. Members played for events and celebrations in Grandville.

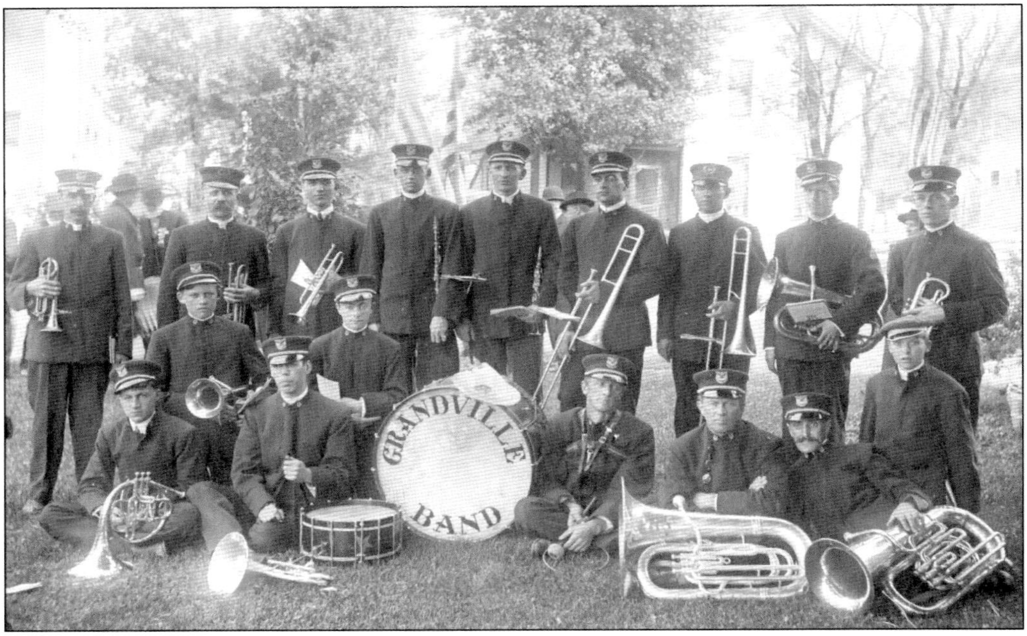

The Grandville Band was formed in 1925 and made its first appearance in March that year. Members were fitted with professional-looking blue and white suits. The *Grandville Star* reported that the band sounded good. The band performed for many years and never had trouble filling a spot if someone left.

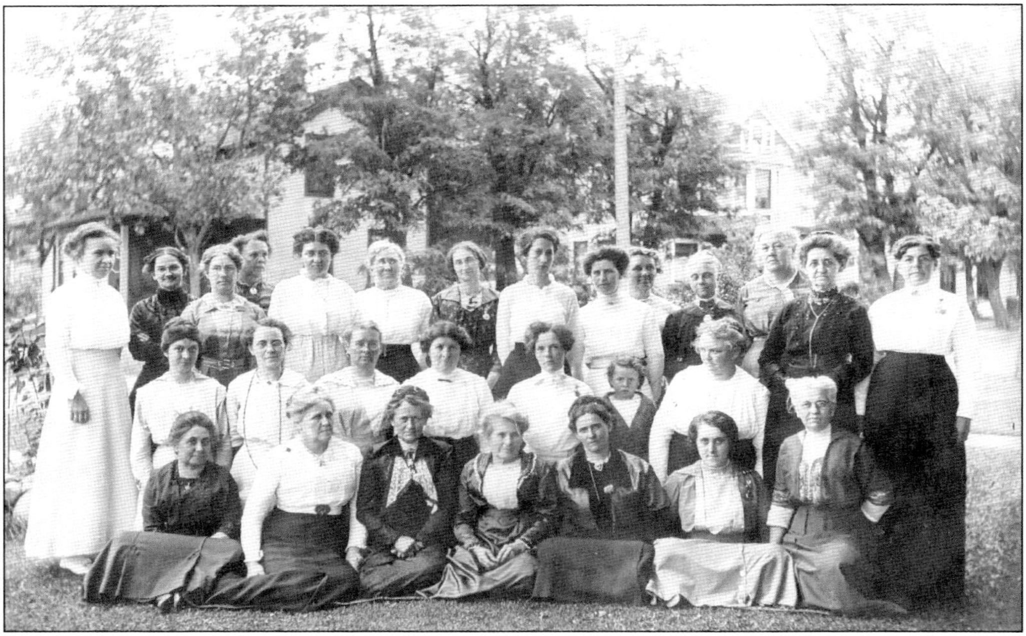

The Lady Maccabees organization was founded in 1890. The sole purpose of the club was to do social and charitable work. Members took care of their own as well if the need arose; if a woman's husband died, each member was asked to give a dime to the widow and her orphaned children. This photograph was taken in 1912 at the corner of Chicago Drive and Franklin Street.

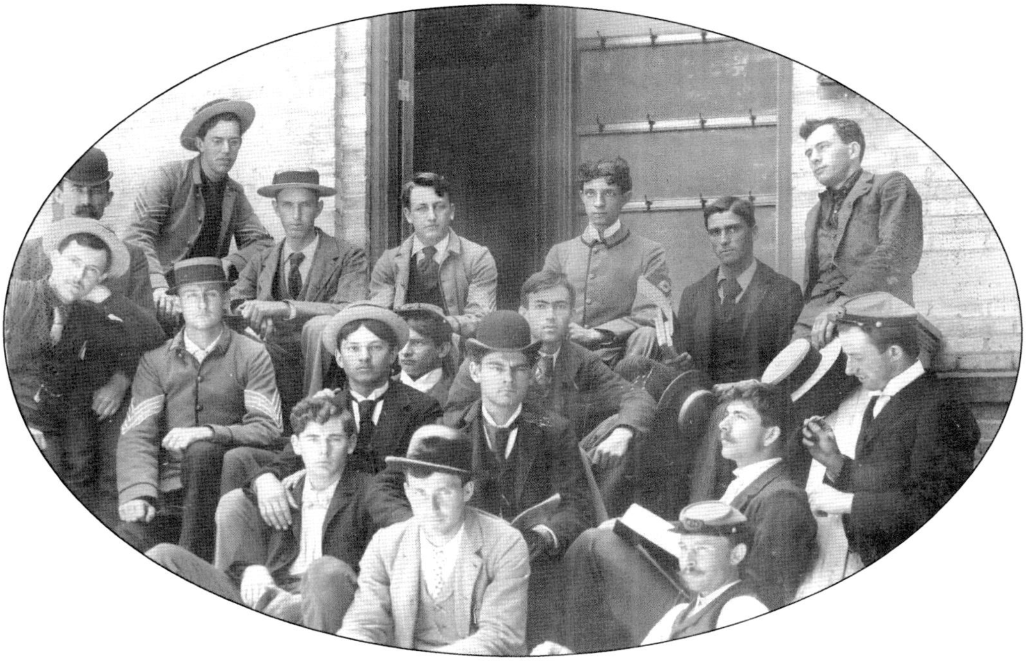

A group of scholarly young men poses for the camera. Note that the clothes they are wearing are a mix of Union soldier coats, hats, suits, and ties.

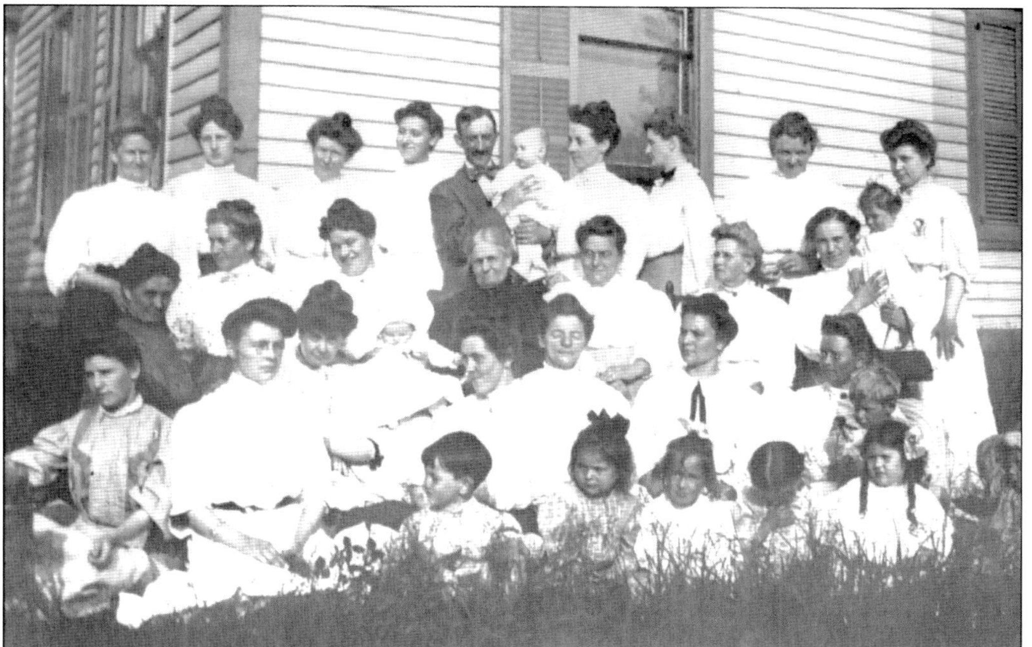

This 1912 photograph shows the Ladies Aid Society. It helped with the World War I effort by raising money and rolling bandages. Ladies' organizations also provided women the occasion to socialize, as raising children and farming was often isolating work. The man in the center, holding the baby, met with the women and was often in charge of giving the Ladies Aid Society direction.

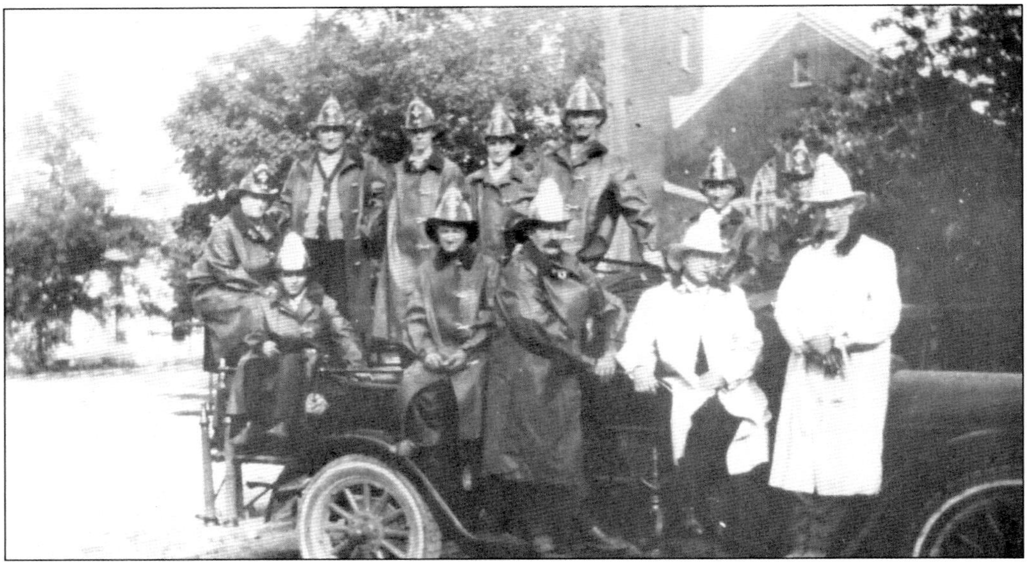

The Grandville Fire Department is pictured here in 1930. From left to right are, (first row) Henry Huizenga, Lotan Hildreth, Laben DeRyke, Henry Bos, Art Moody, and Lyman Hildreth; (second row) Ray Keefer, Al Elders, Carl DePuit, Louis VanderSoors, and two unidentified. Fires were common in Grandville at that time.

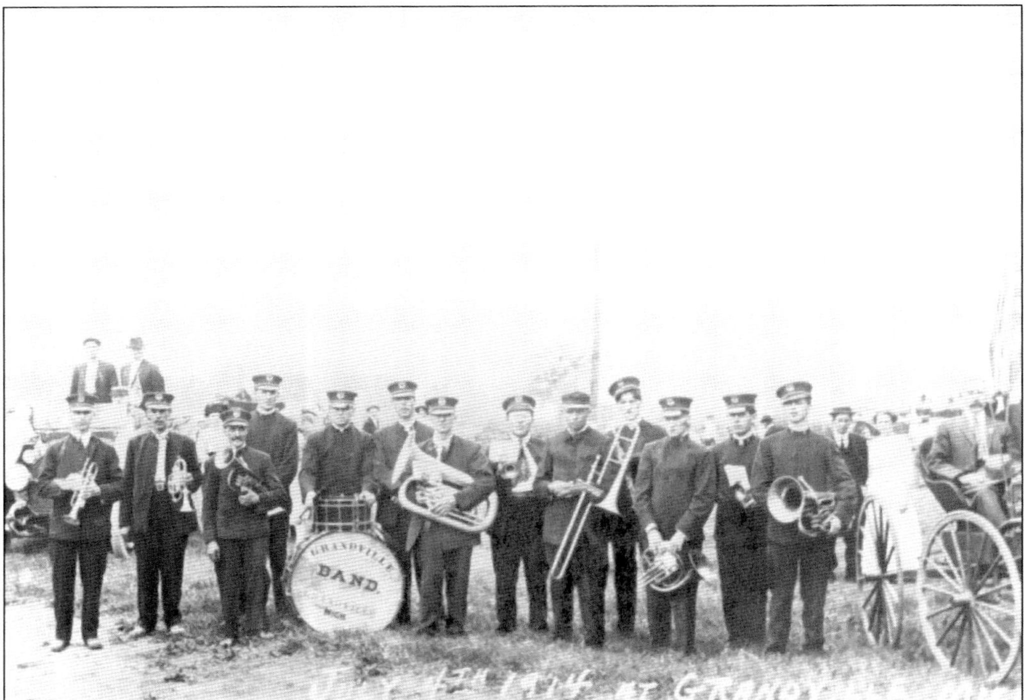

Pictured here on the west side of Wilson Avenue north of the railroad tracks, the Grandville Band pauses during a Fourth of July celebration in 1914.

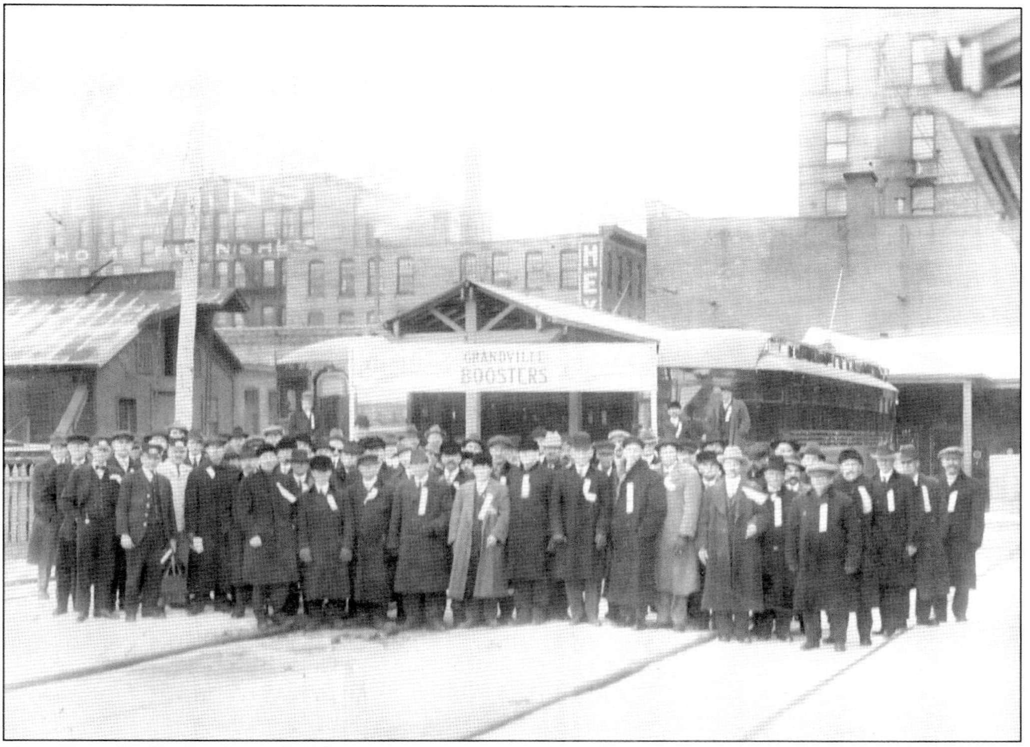

The Grandville Boosters held a convention in November 1914. This image was taken at the interurban train tracks next to the Overland garage in Grand Rapids. The organization's main objective was to promote the village of Grandville and its merchants.

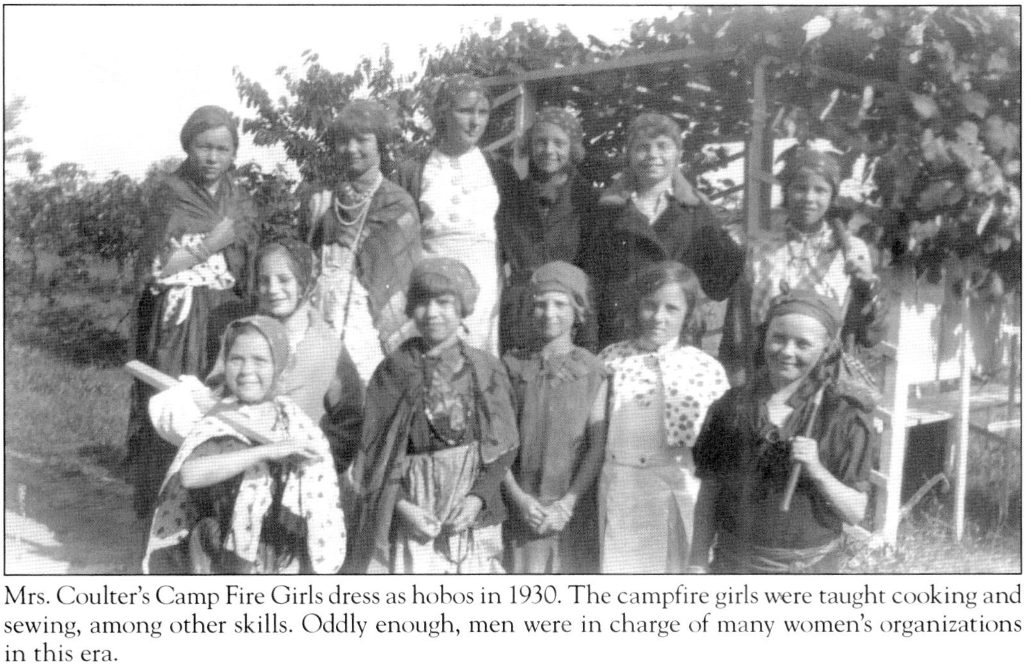

Mrs. Coulter's Camp Fire Girls dress as hobos in 1930. The campfire girls were taught cooking and sewing, among other skills. Oddly enough, men were in charge of many women's organizations in this era.

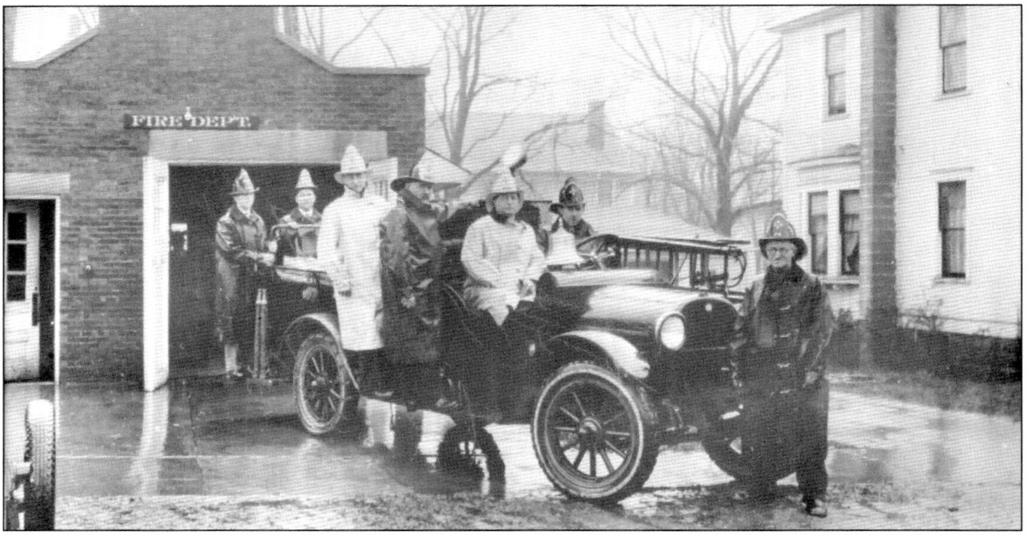

The Grandville Volunteer Fire Department is pictured here in 1932. From left to right are Ed Hoekzema, Carl DePuit, Henry Huizenga, Laban DeRyke, Lotan Hildreth, Lester Grutter, and Henry Bos. Among other fires, the Hammond Building burned down that year. The blaze was caused by oil that was cooking on the stove.

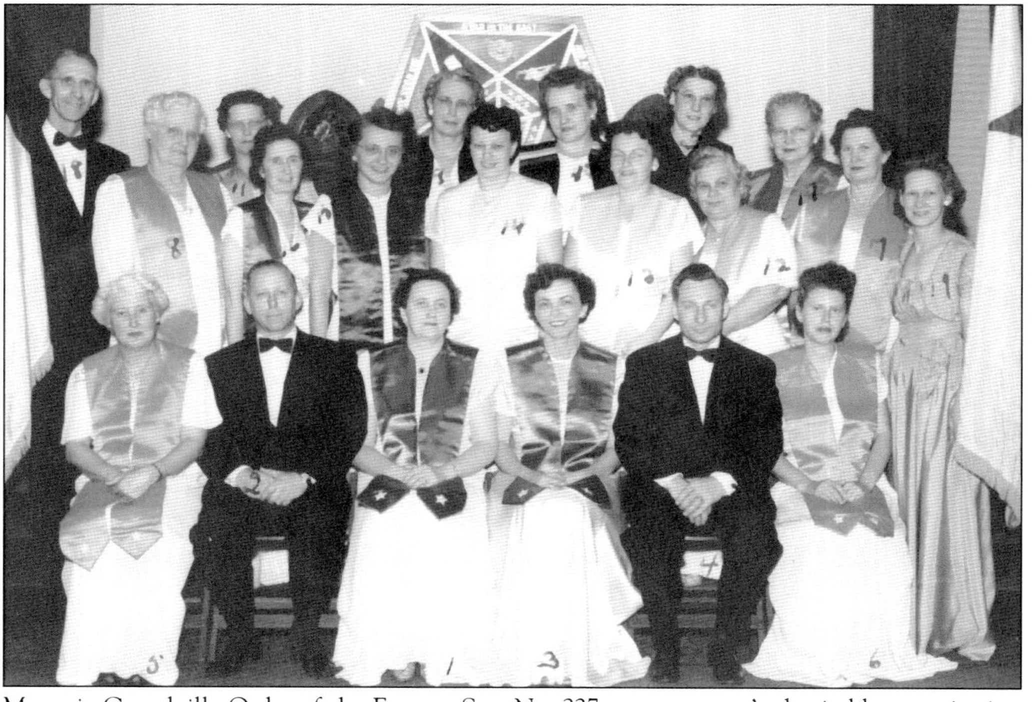

Masonic Grandville Order of the Eastern Star No. 227 was a women's charitable organization built on biblical principles. Founded in 1898, the chapter met in the Grandville Masonic Temple on the corner of White and Franklin Streets until 1968.

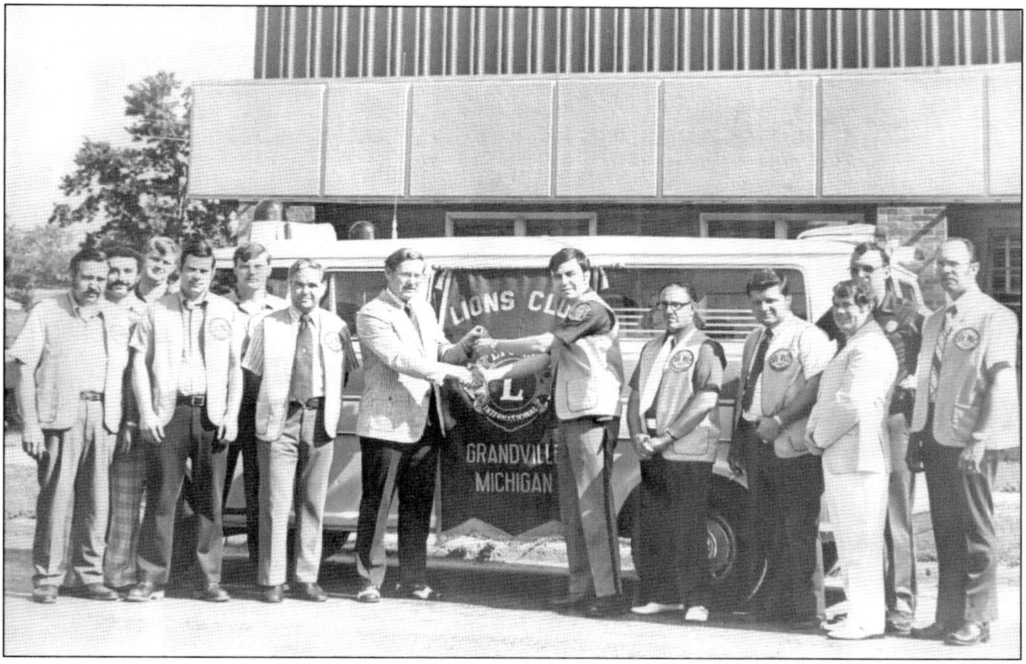

In 1974, the Lions Club, a charitable organization, raised money for a new E-Unit van. Here, Ron Colvin (to the right of the banner) hands over the keys to the new van.

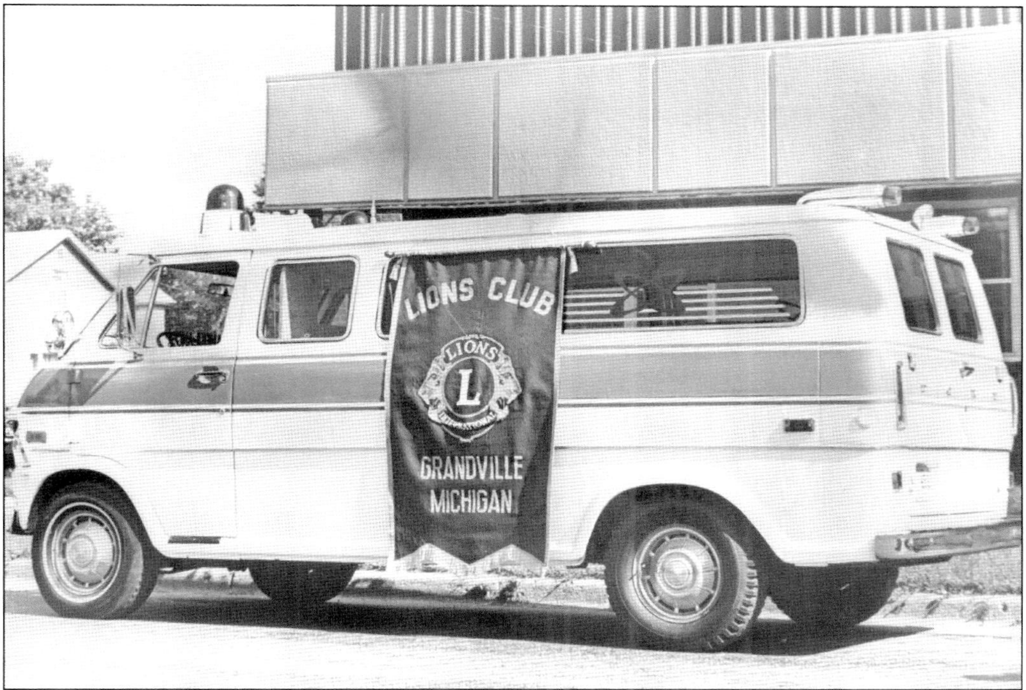

This chair-lift van, along with other modern, medical equipment, was a gift from the Lions Club to the Grandville community. The Lions Club is still very active in the community today.

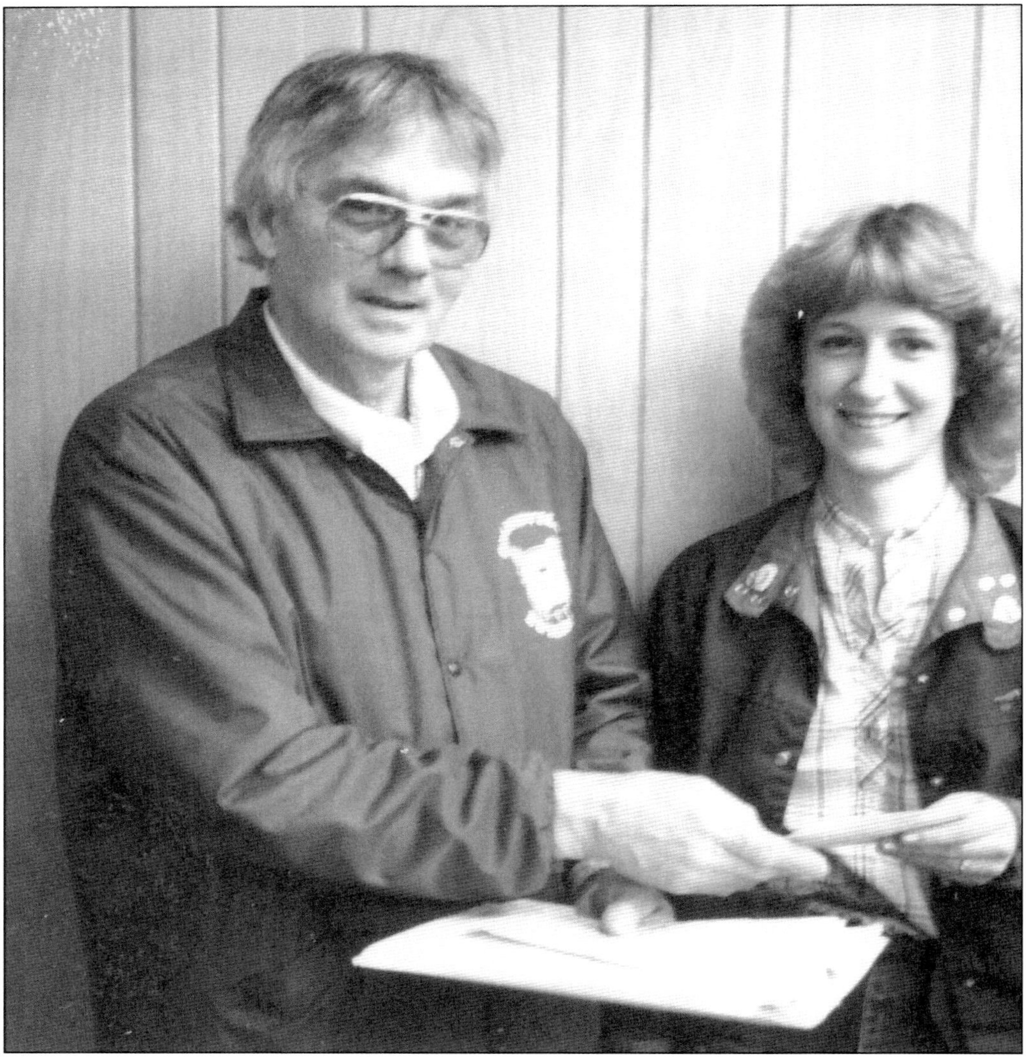

Bill Dudas presents a check to the 1974 Lions Club poster-contest winner. The poster contest funded the new E-Unit van.

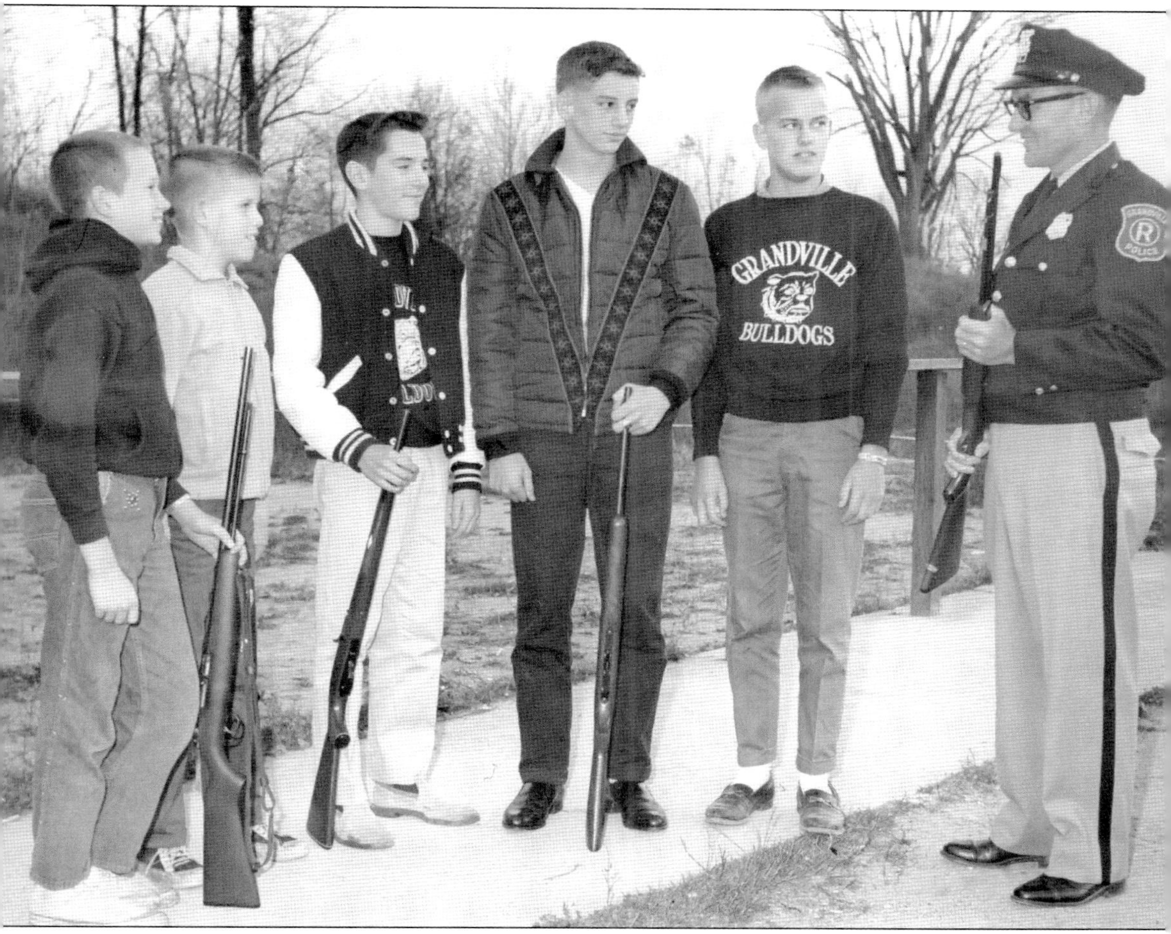

The Grandville Police Department holds a gun-safety class for boys in 1964. Highly involved with community youth, the department held many other programs, including bicycle-safety classes.

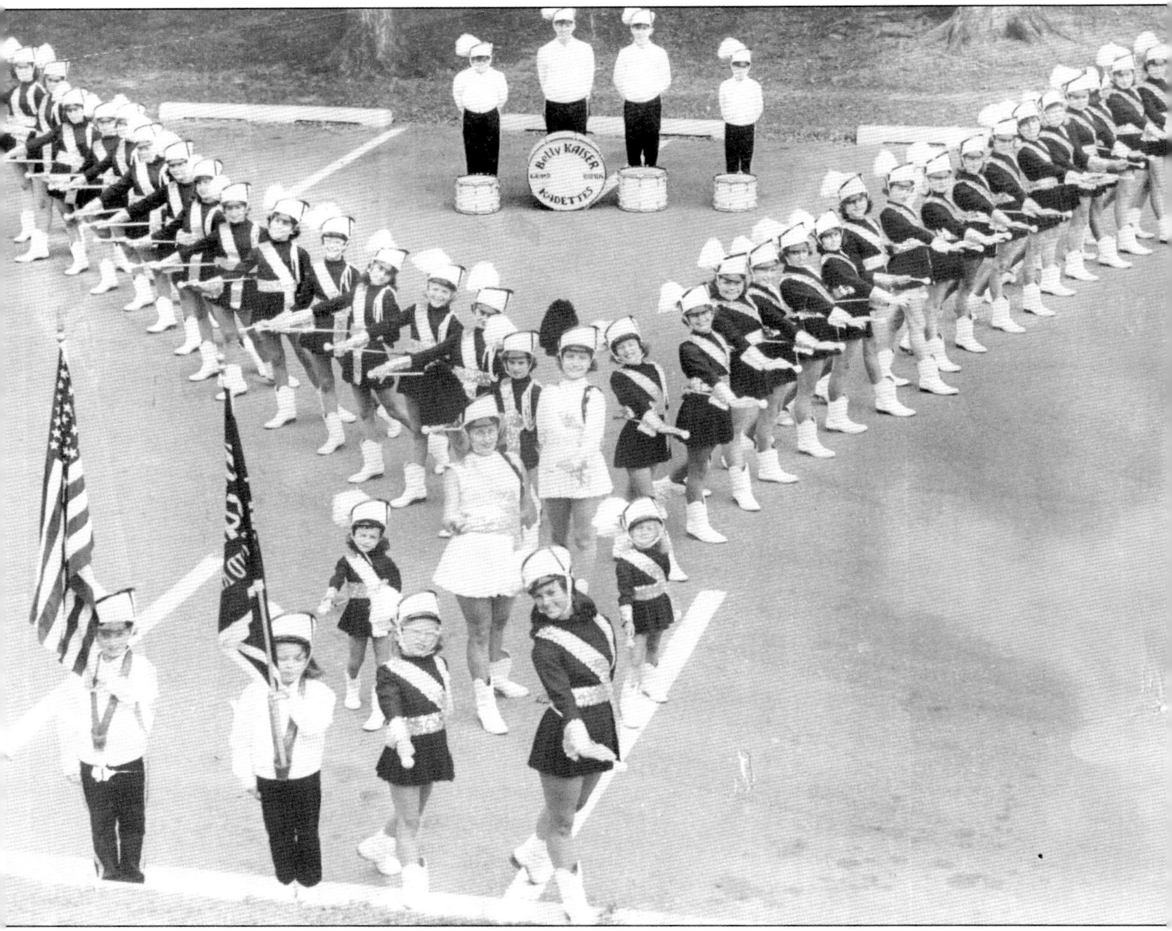

The Betty Kaiser Twirlers, twirling batons and marching to music, performed at many functions, including Grandville parades; there was also another group called the Karen Kaiser Twirlers. The girls often ended up in their school marching band as majorettes.

Five

Baseball Teams

Activities such as school plays and spelling bees were fine social activities of the day, but nothing beat a good baseball game. It seemed that almost all factories, stores, or workplaces had some sort of a ball team. Some teams were so good, they were called minor-league teams and could draw crowds of hundreds on the weekends. Some Grandville ballplayers went on to the major leagues for the Detroit Tigers; Benny McCoy was one of them. Surprisingly, there were quite a few women's teams as well.

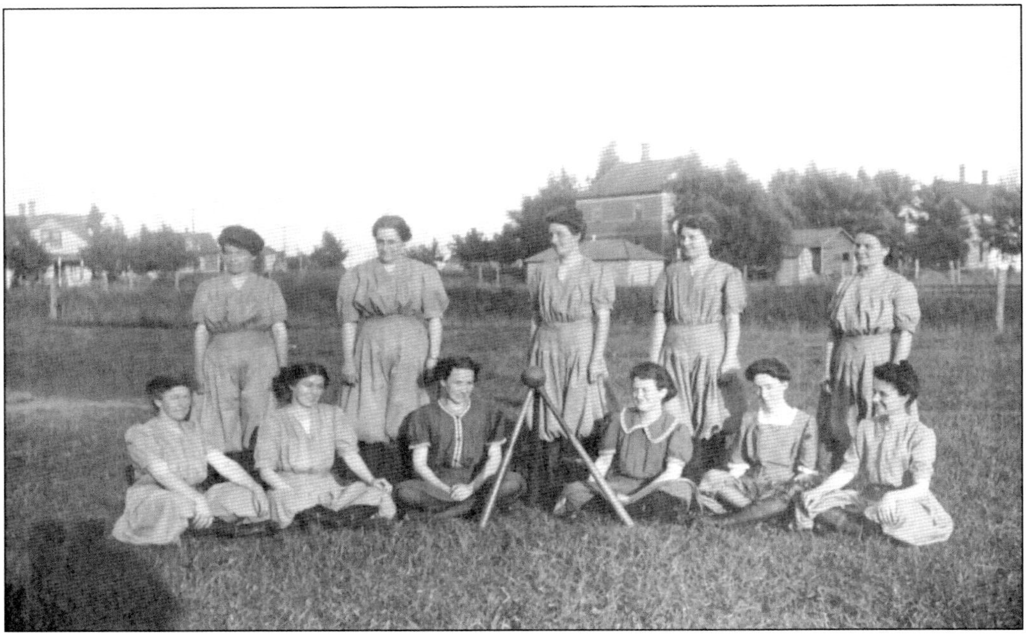

The Grandville Bloomers girls' baseball team won many a game in 1910. Note how the large ball is and the absence of mitts. From left to right are (first row, seated) Minderhout, Hartman, Wright, Glas, Newton, and Pitts; (second row, standing) Ringleberg, Scott, Jewell, O'Rourke, and Caldwell.

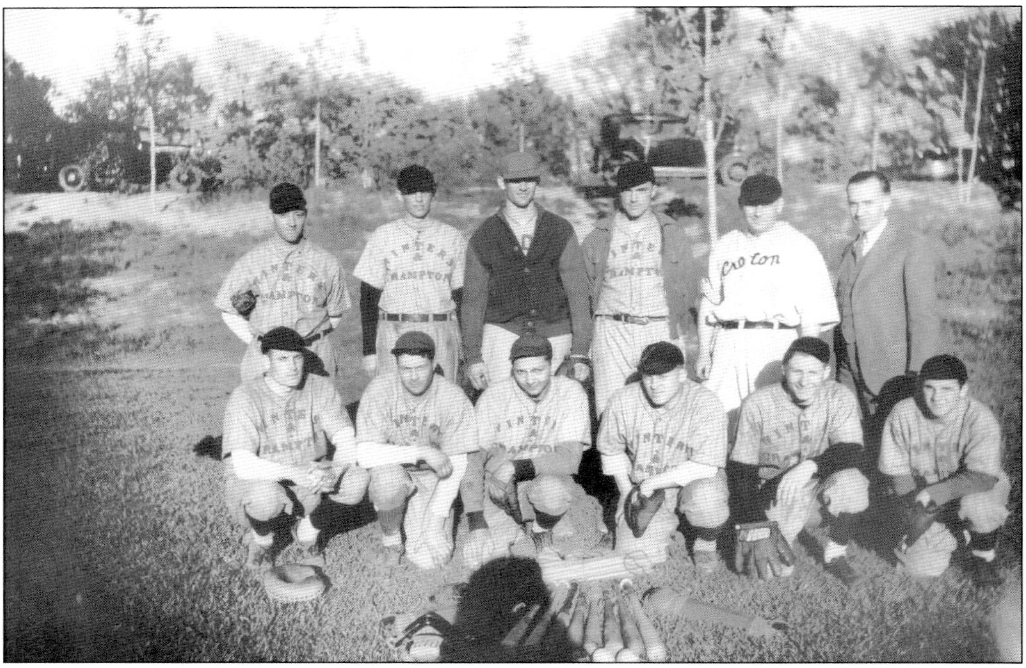

The Winters and Crampton factory sponsored a baseball team in the late 1920s. The team was good, and it played against the Overlands, the Grandville Merchants, and many others in a league. Baseball was a big pastime in those days.

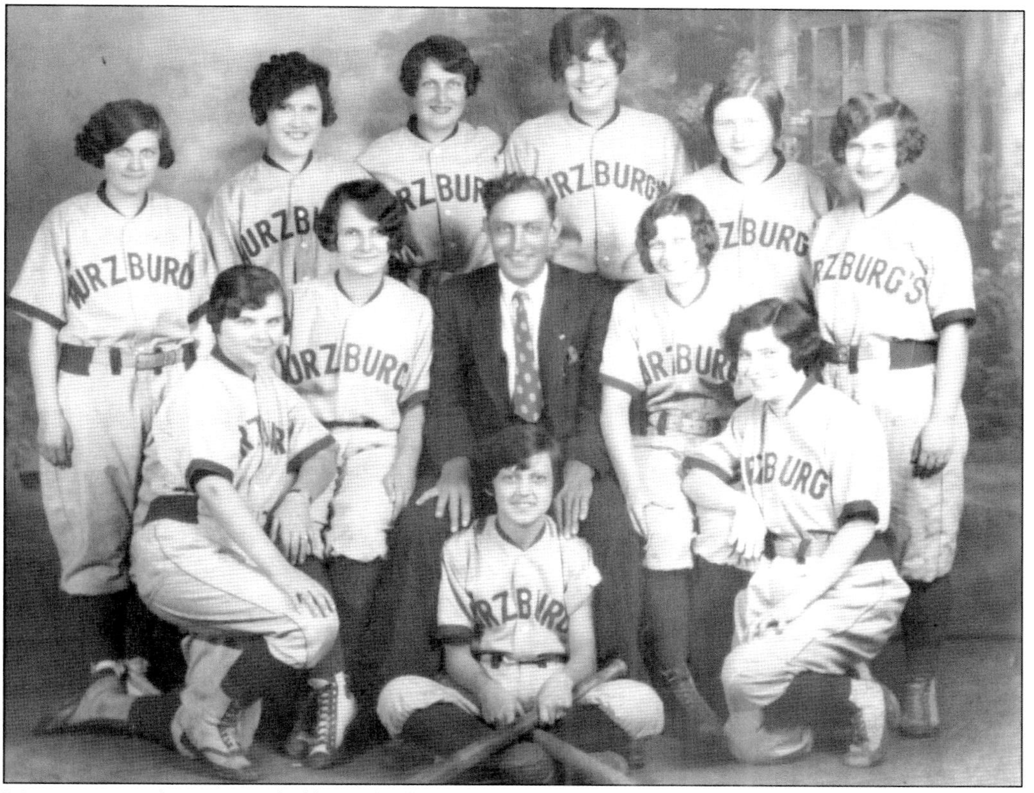

Many women from Grandville worked downtown at Wurzburg's Department Store and played on the ball team at one time or another. This team was a winner in 1926. People went to downtown Grand Rapids to go shopping at Wurzburg's, which was one of the largest stores in the area at that time.

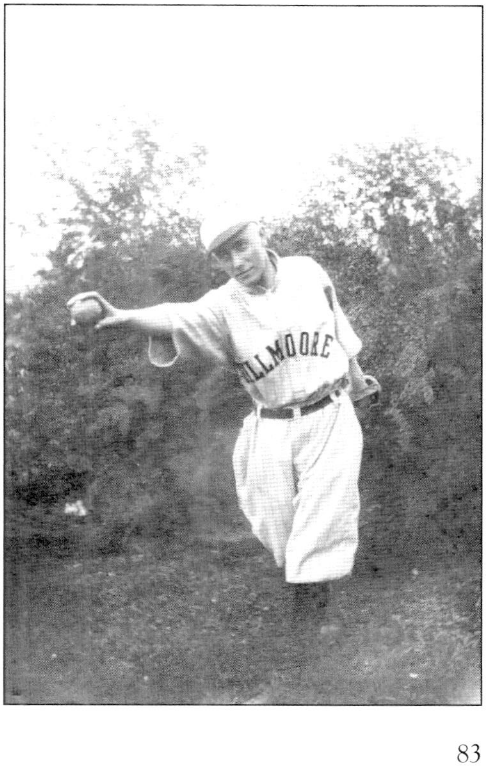

A pitcher for the Filmore team strikes a pose. Many players went on to greater things after being discovered in these "minor leagues." Grandville boasted more teams than most of the surrounding cities.

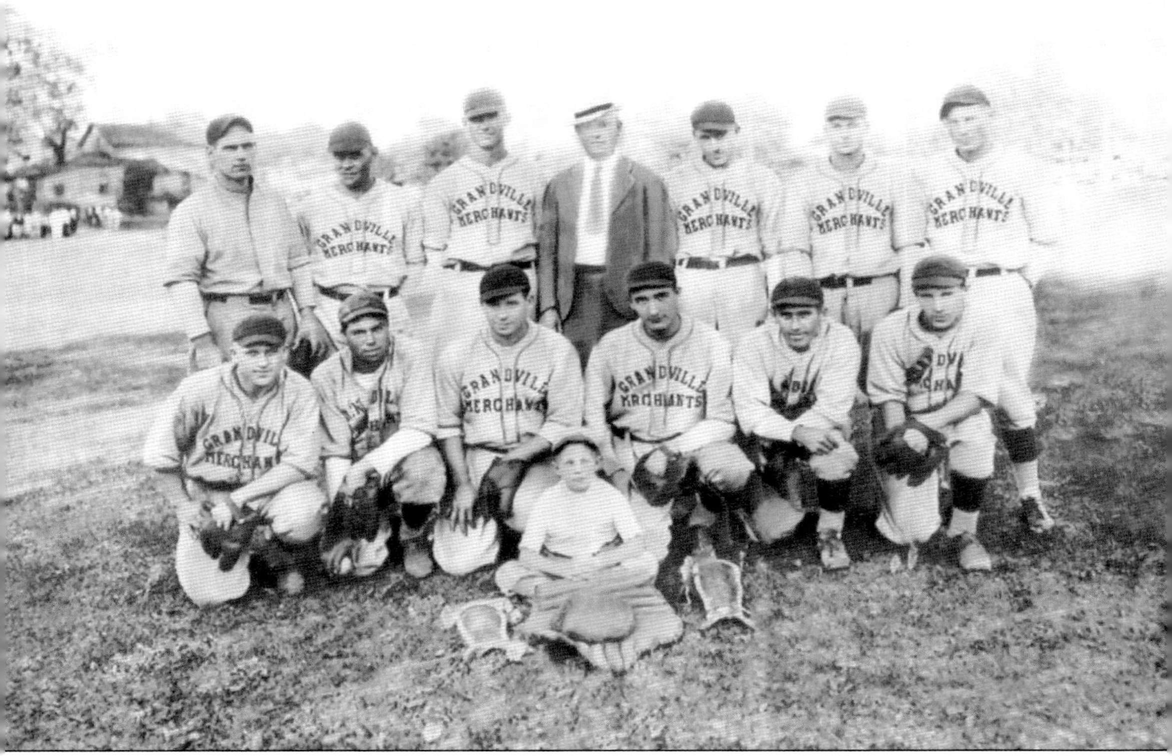

Pictured here in 1935, the Grandville Merchants baseball team was sponsored by businesses in Grandville. Manager Elmer McCoy had many sons on the team. The sixth player from the left in the back row, son Benny McCoy, was picked up by the Detroit Tigers and went on to have a wonderful career in professional baseball. Grandville even designated a "Benny McCoy Day" in August 1939, with a parade and celebration in his honor. The batboy seen here is Bob Bolt.

Six

DISASTERS

From boats sinking in the Grand River to interurban wrecks, Grandville has had its share of natural and man-made accidental disasters. There were major floods in 1838, 1852, 1883, and 1904. The 1883 Grand Rapids flood washed whole cities downriver, creating a logjam that took out every bridge from Grandville to Grand Haven. In 1904, Grandville neighborhoods were destroyed by another flood, which caused residents to rebuild a little farther from the river. When the expressway was built, it pushed the town even further from the water.

Grandville has also had its share of tornados, which hit the area in 1956 and 1965. Some very severe storms have also come through, and at the time, because warning systems were still in their infancy, there was mass destruction and much loss of life.

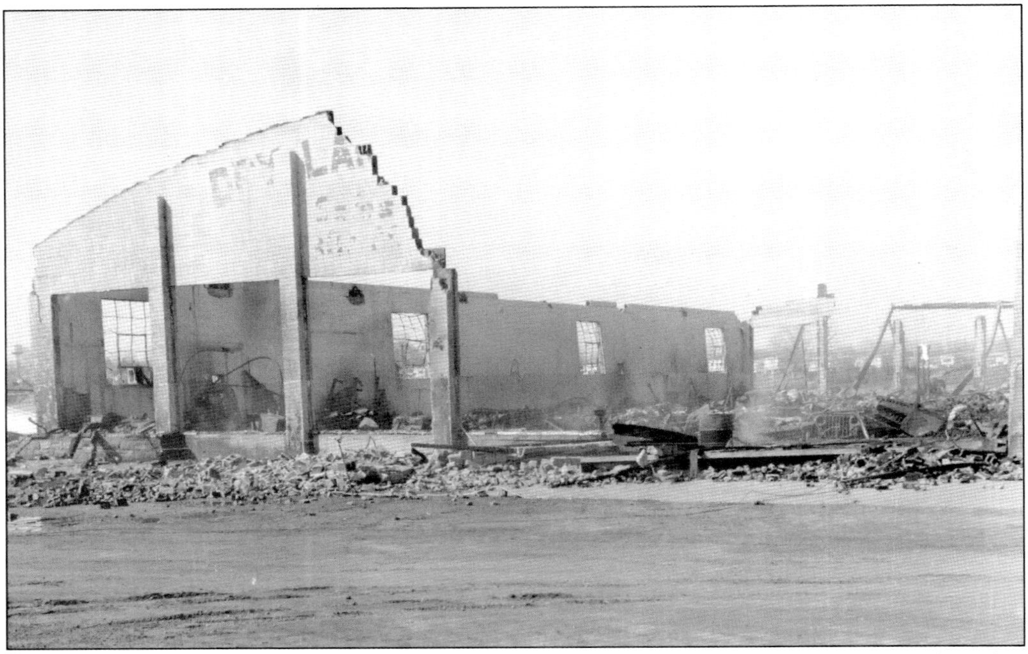

On Palm Sunday in 1965, a tornado tore through the area, leaving devastation for miles. This was considered one of the worst storms in Grandville history.

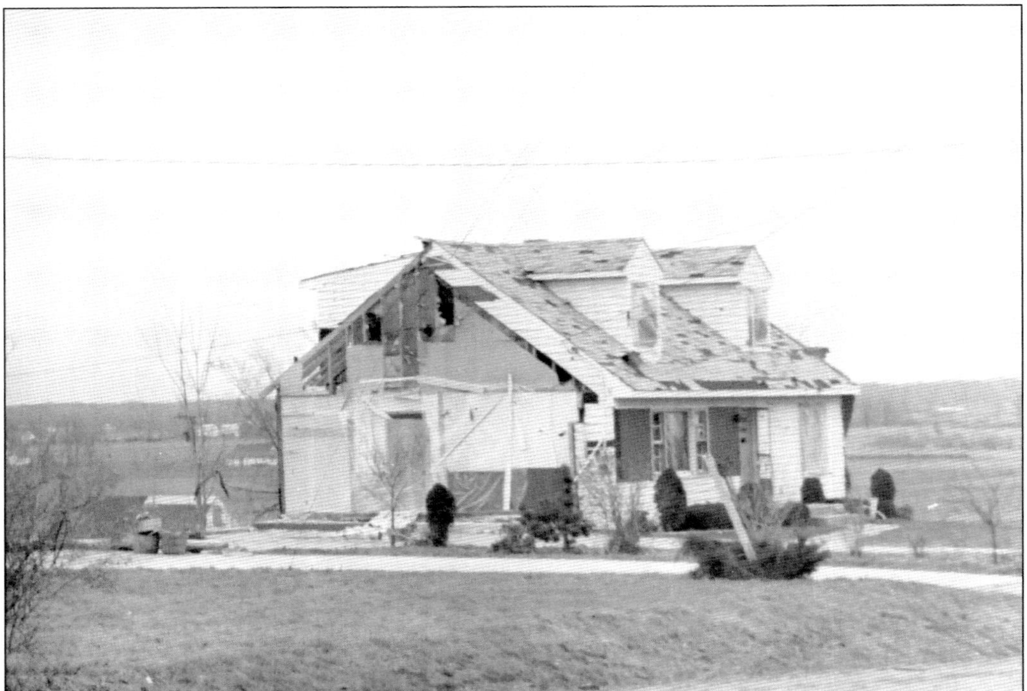

This house did not make it through the 1965 tornado. Many more neighborhoods looked just like this, with devastation stretching for miles. Many people lost everything.

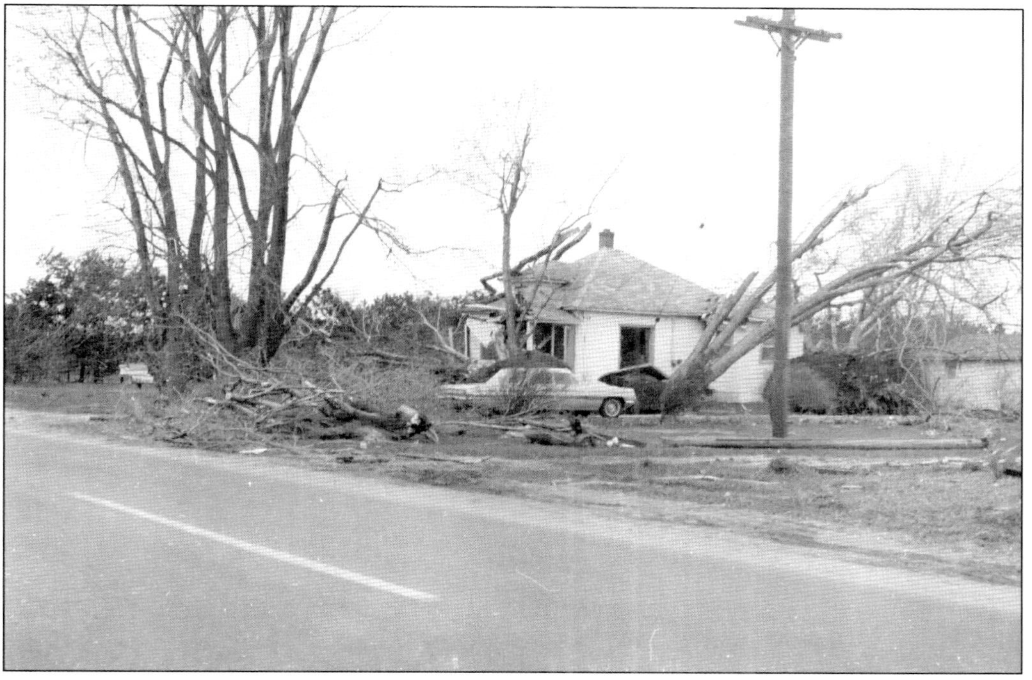
Trees were uprooted, and houses were torn apart. Several people were killed in the storm.

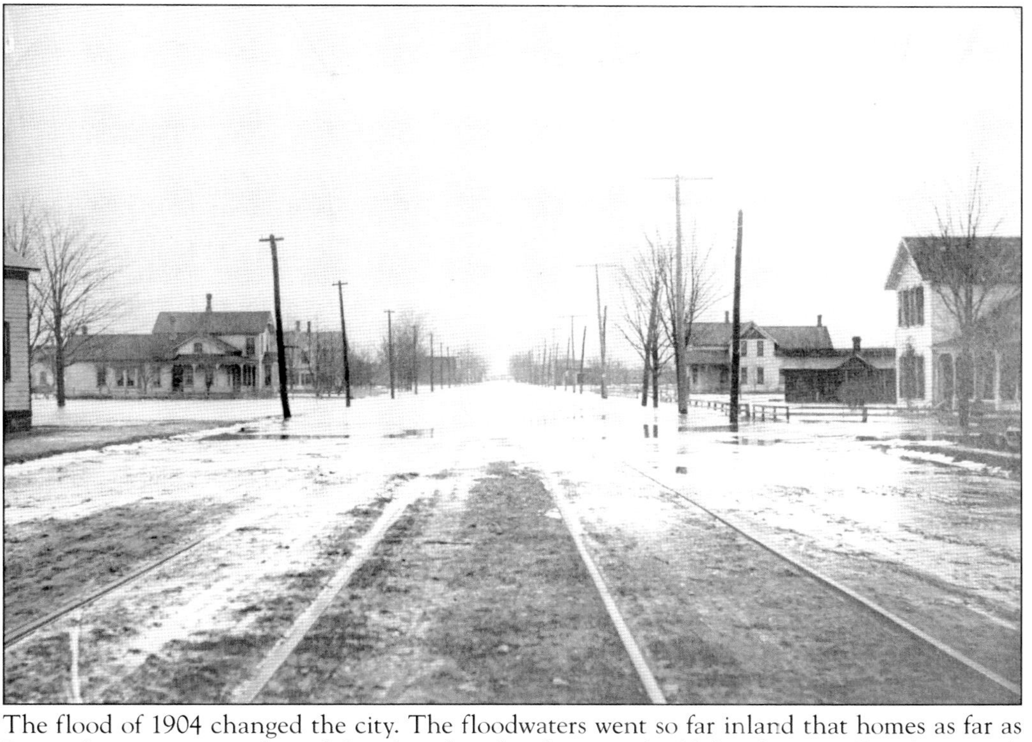
The flood of 1904 changed the city. The floodwaters went so far inland that homes as far as Prairie Street were waterlogged. People rethought where to rebuild their houses. This photograph shows Chicago Drive to the west, looking out of town.

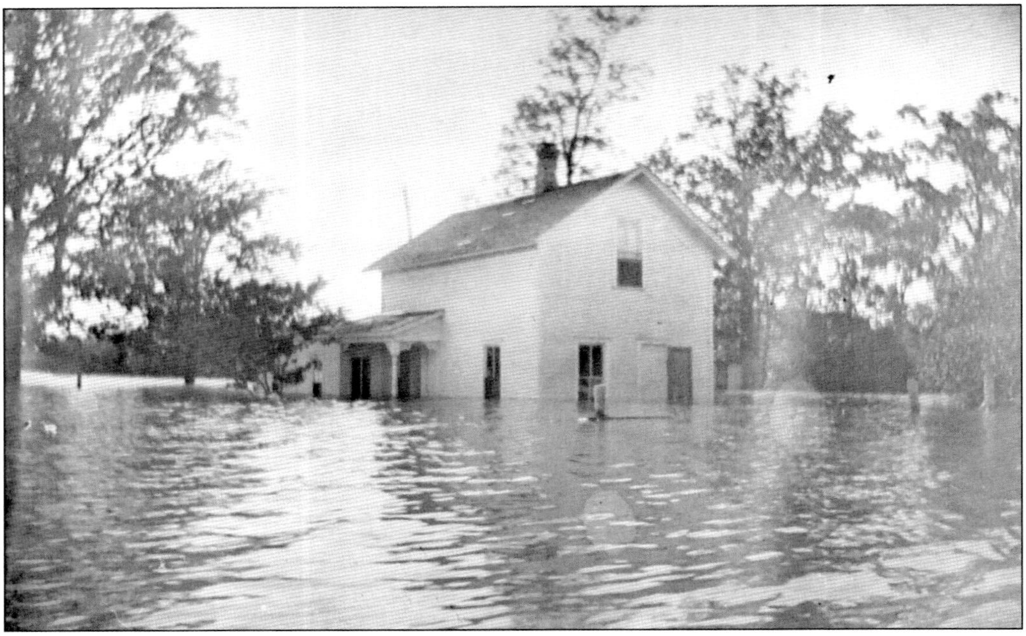

Pictured here during the flood of 1904, the McHoskey house was located on Wilson Avenue where the post office is located today. The river continued to rise for days, and some people were stranded in their houses with no food or water.

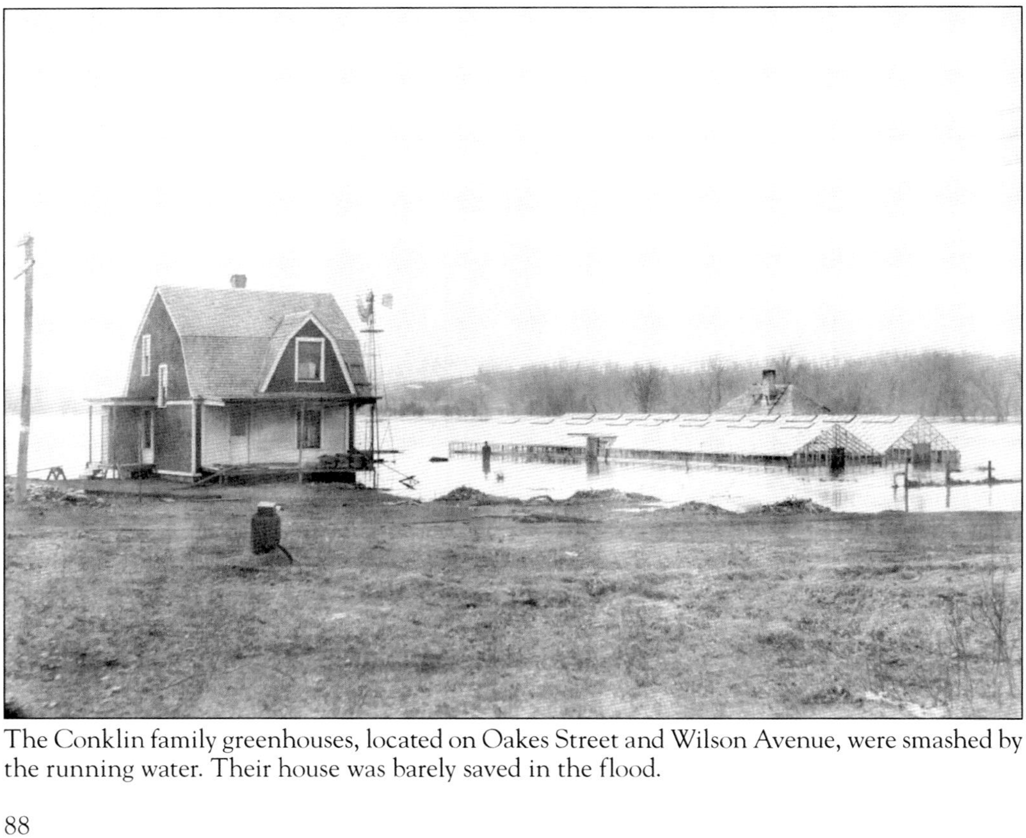

The Conklin family greenhouses, located on Oakes Street and Wilson Avenue, were smashed by the running water. Their house was barely saved in the flood.

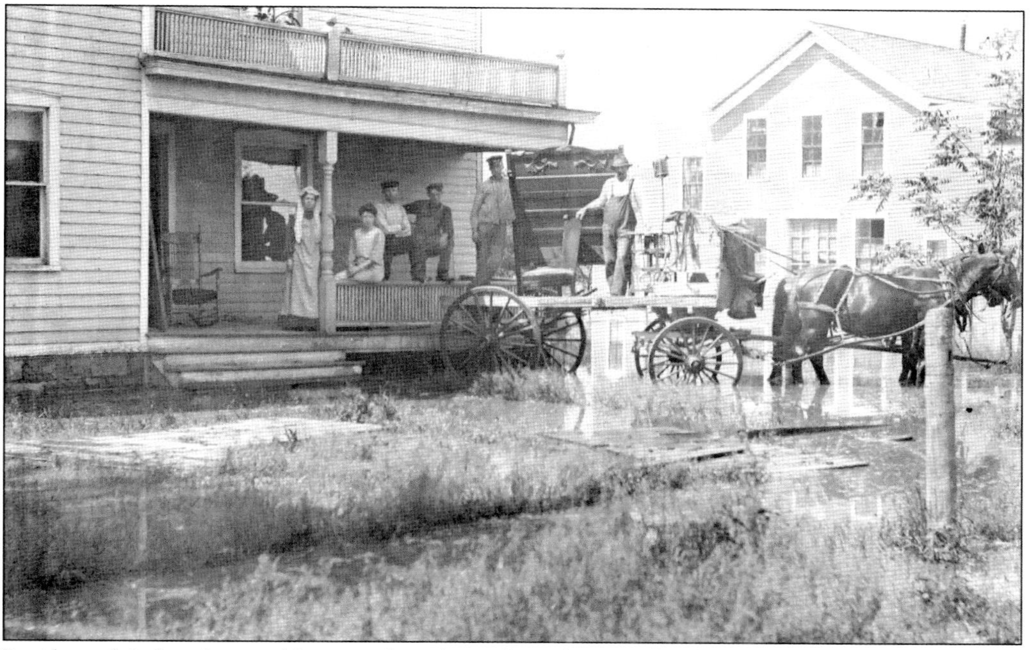

Residents did what they could to save their things from the 1904 flood. Some people loaded up wagons with furniture, which they took to higher ground. Insurance was not available in those days.

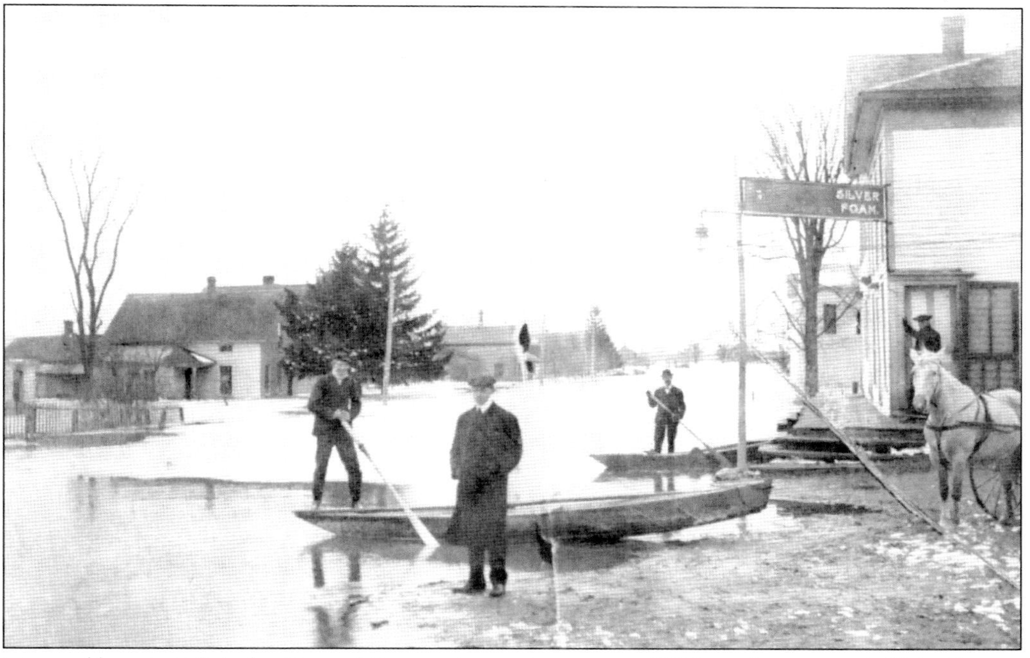

Pictured here in 1904, the Osgood Tavern sits on the corner of Wilson Avenue and White Street. To the west, the devastating flooding is visible down Wilson Avenue. The tavern served Silver Foam Beer made by the Grand Rapids Brewing Company. The Congregational church also met here. The man standing in the boat is Jake Mastenbrook, the owner of the hotel next door. The man in the trench coat is Lloyd Getman.

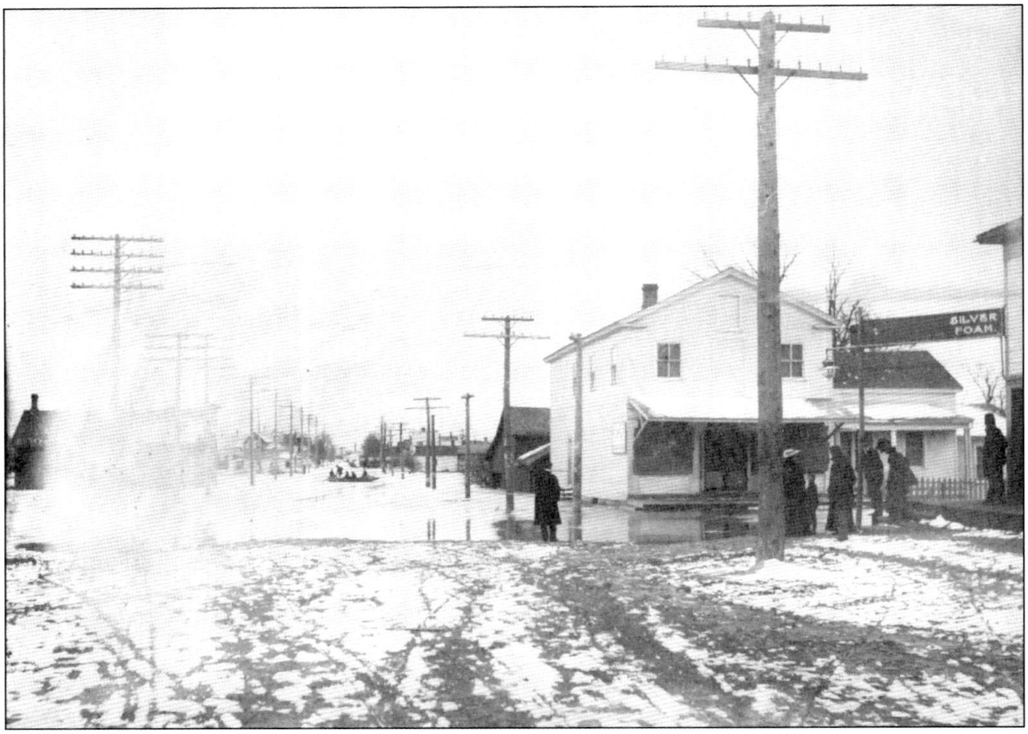

This is the corner of Wilson Avenue and White Street showing the flood from another angle.

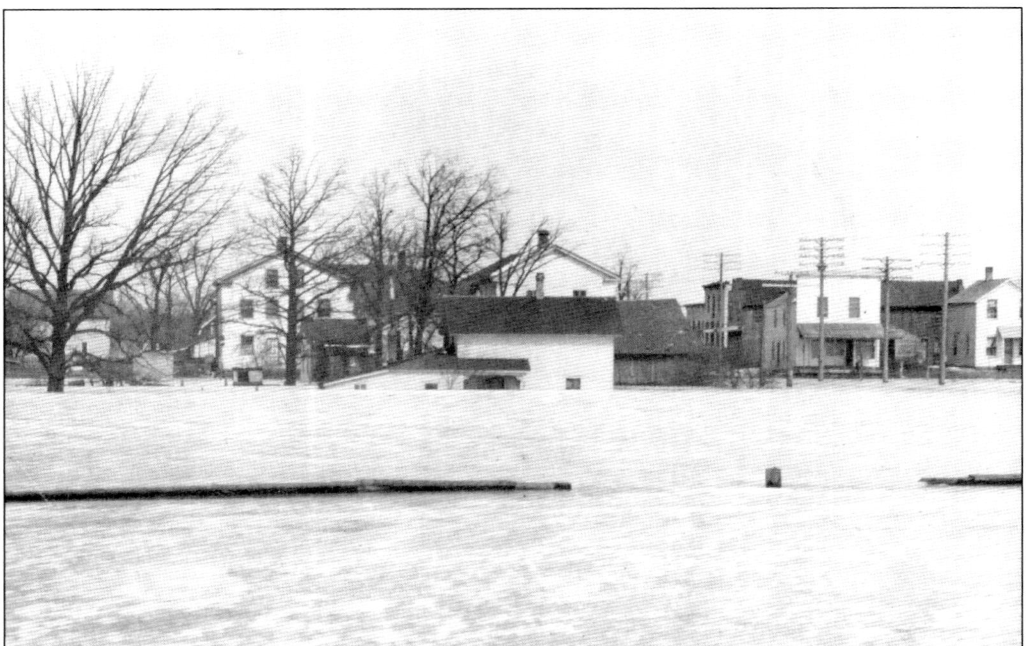

Chicago Drive is seen here underwater. The street in the middle facing north is Wilson Avenue. In this area, only boats were able to traverse the deep floodwaters.

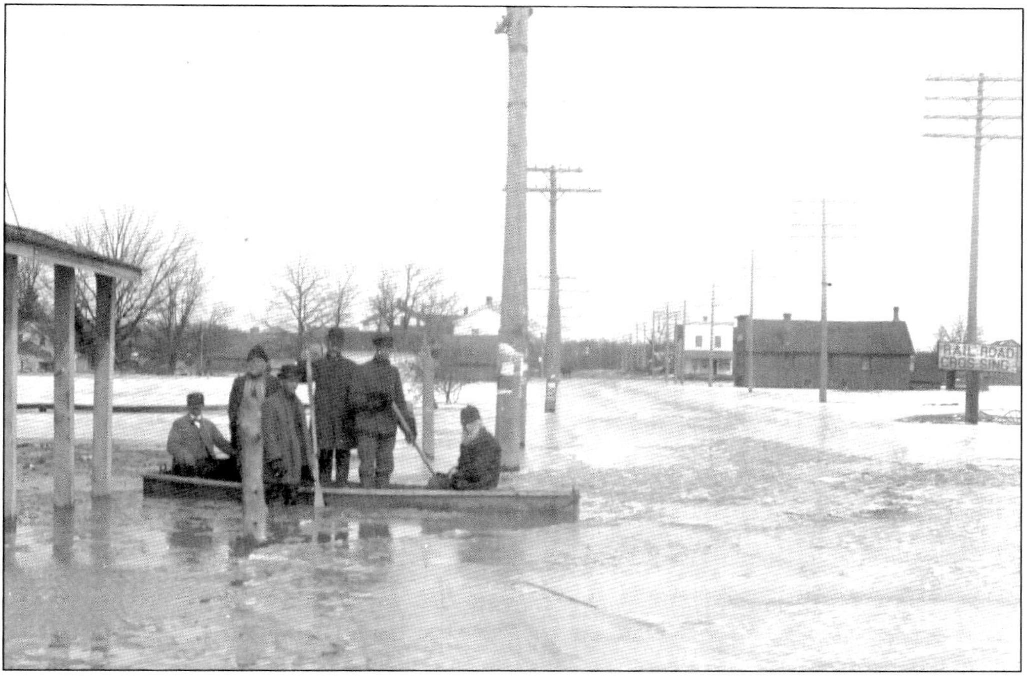

On Wilson Avenue, boats were used to cross the ice-laden water in 1904. After this flood, the city of Grandville was rebuilt farther away from the river.

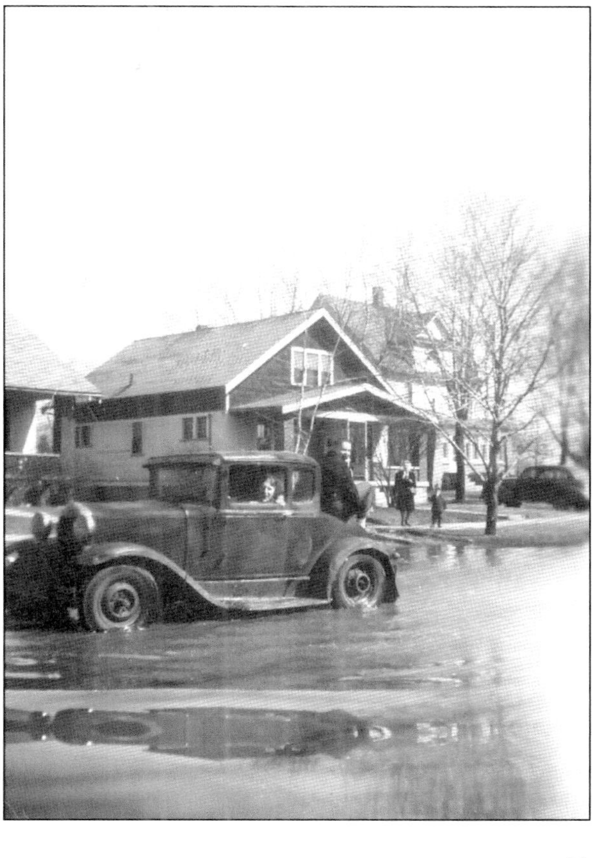

Pictured here in 1947, this is the front of John and Gert Gort's house.

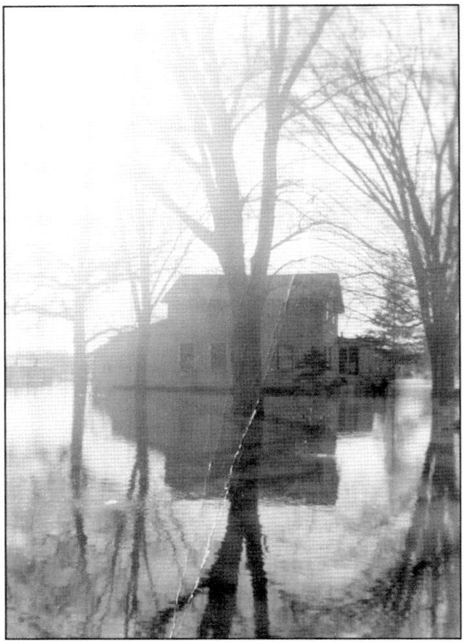

This is another view of the flood on White Street.

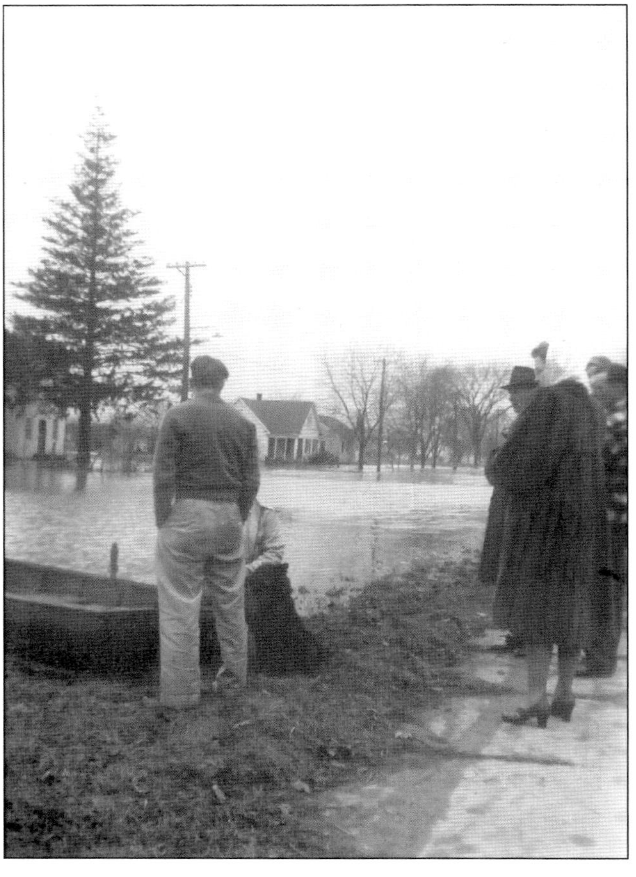

In certain areas, residents were completely stranded by the flood. The police may have operated boats in order to transport residents to work or to get food. Some residents had no heat or water.

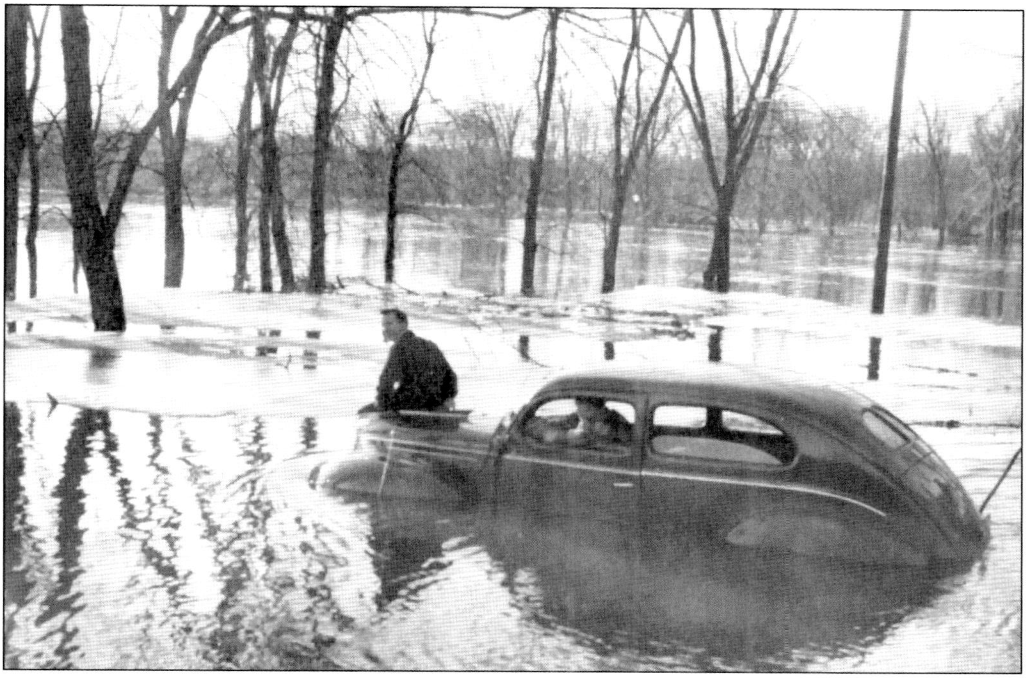

In the 1947 flood, a motorist is stranded. Some people drove down by the river to watch the rising waters only to find they could not get out.

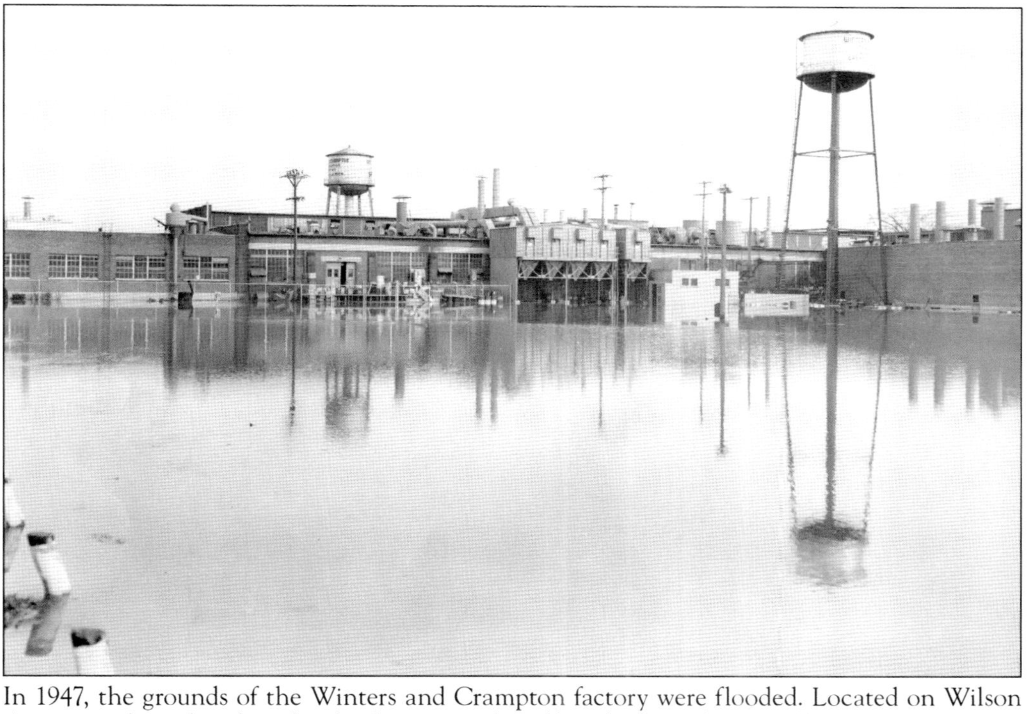

In 1947, the grounds of the Winters and Crampton factory were flooded. Located on Wilson Avenue at the railroad tracks, the factory employed hundreds, making small metal parts. This is the back of the building.

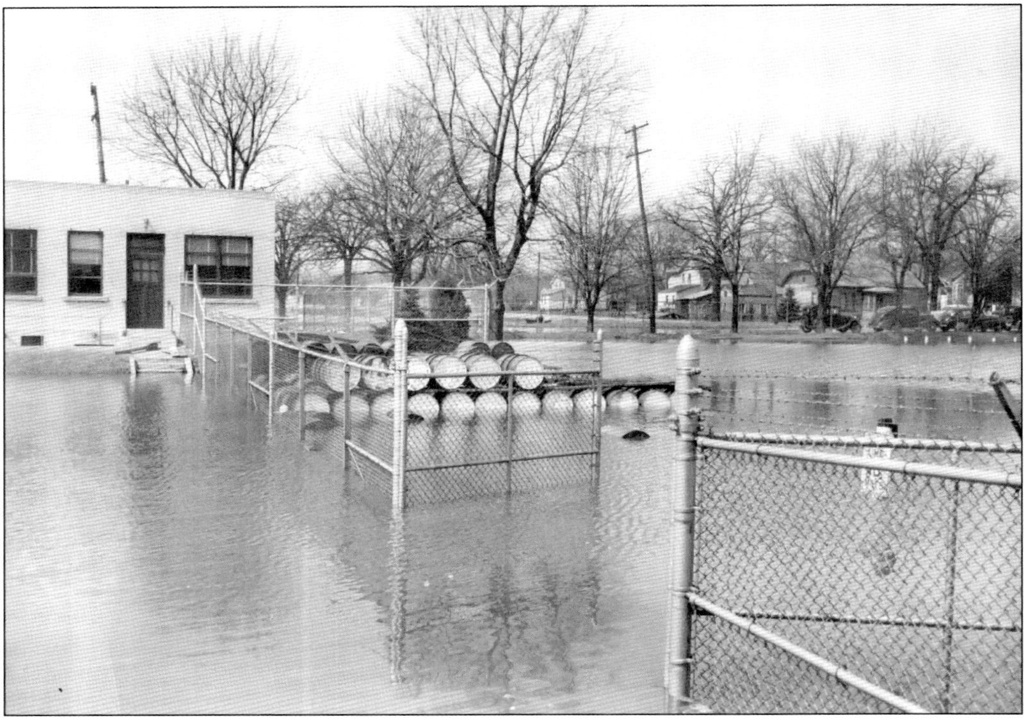

This is another view of the flood at the Winters and Crampton factory.

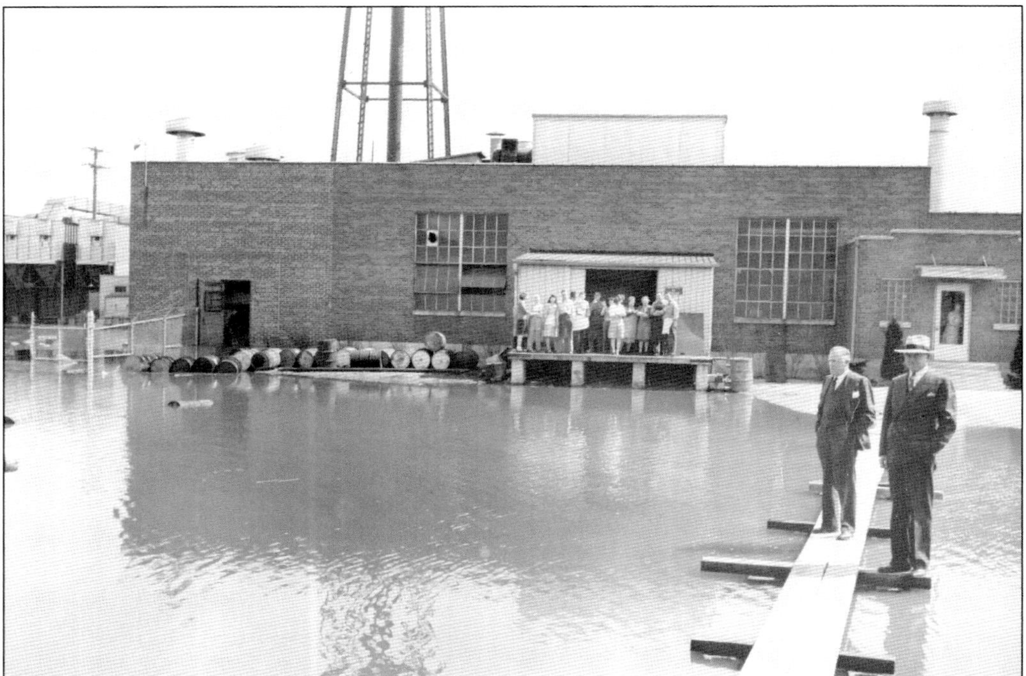

It was business as usual for Winters and Crampton in 1947, as it did not shut down operations during the flood.

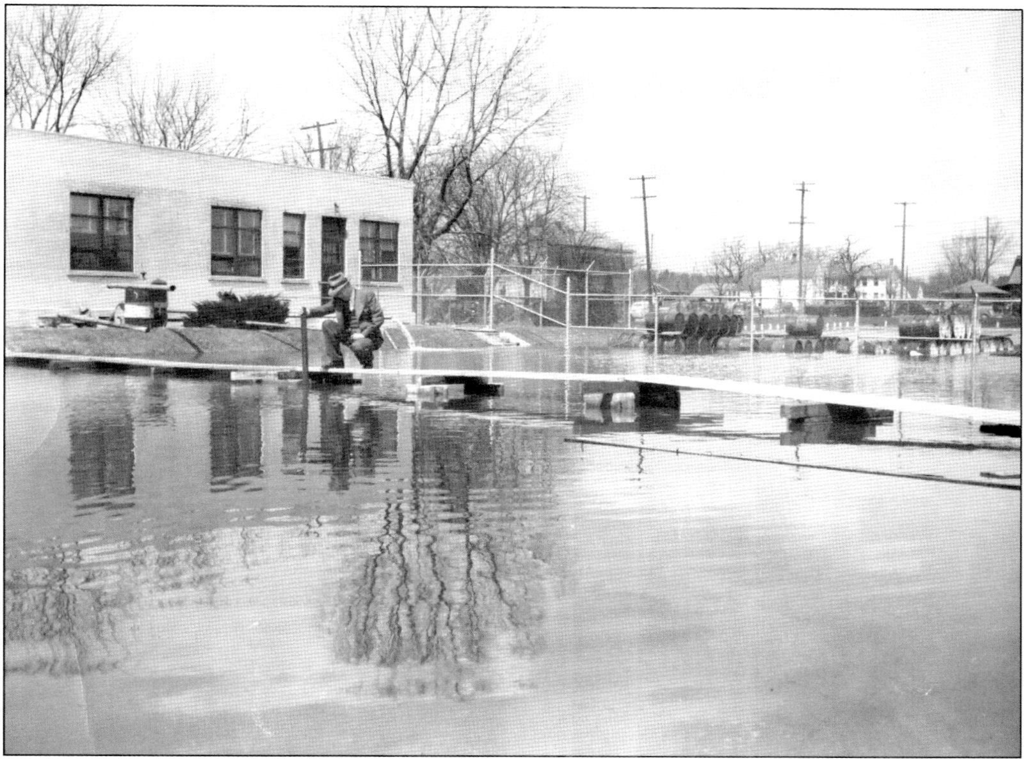

Here, the depth of the water is measured outside the Winters and Crampton building. In the parking lot, the water may have exceeded six feet.

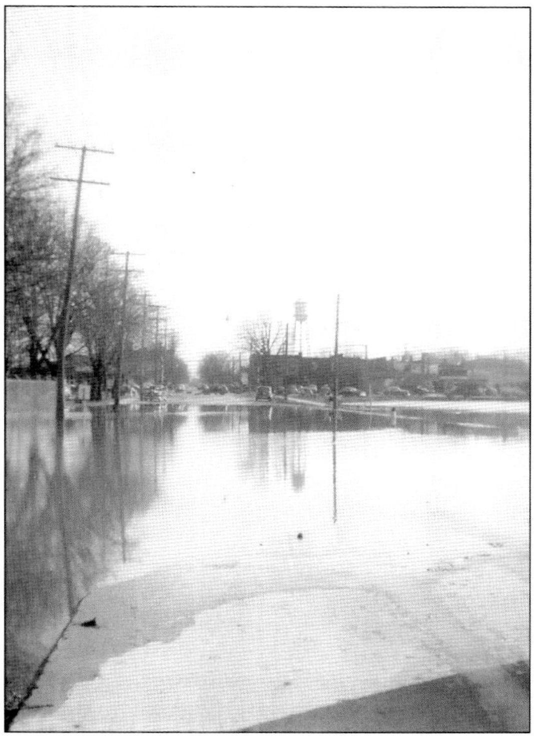

This is Wilson Avenue Street leading into Winters and Crampton.

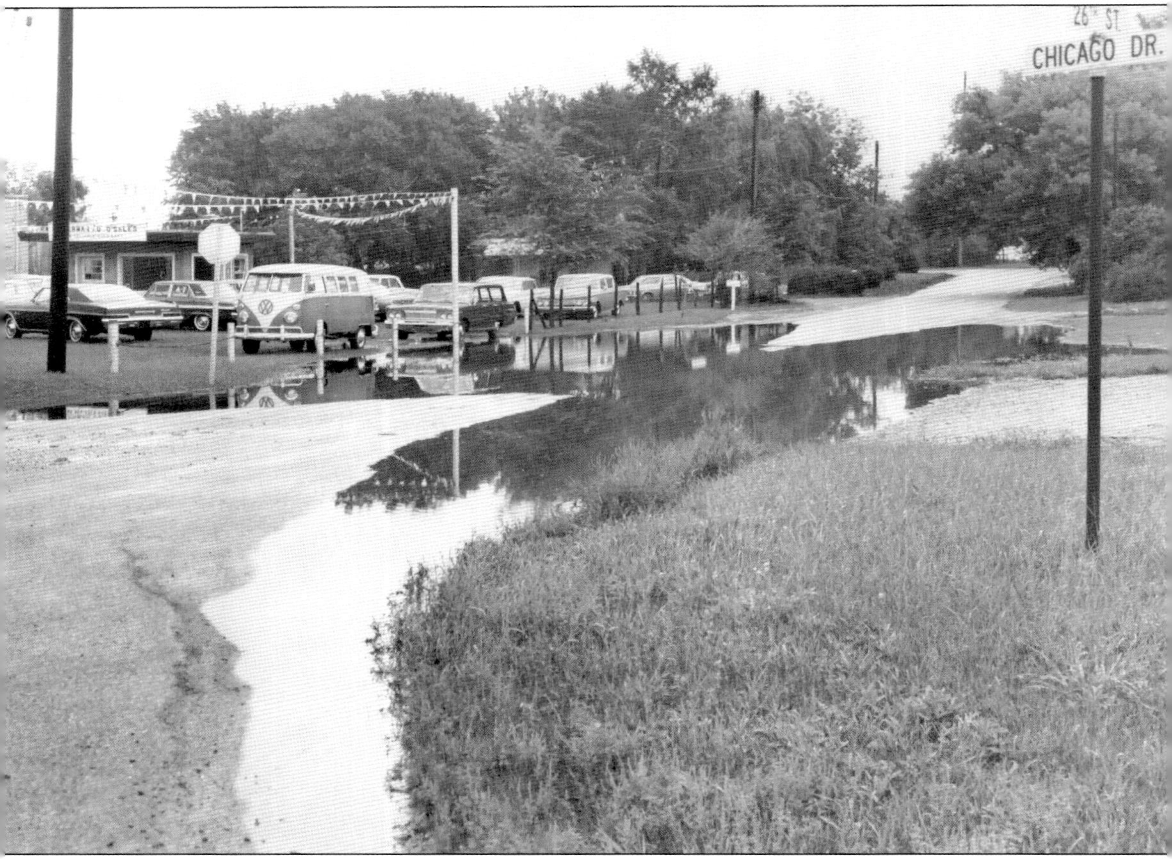

Over the years, Grandville experienced many floods. Pictured here are rising waters at an automobile lot on the corner of Twenty-sixth Street and Chicago Drive. The Grand River flooded a little every year, so residents in a sense were used to it. Only when flooding stopped traffic and business did it become a nuisance.

Seven

Parks

Grandville boasts many parks. Henry Johnson Park provides scenic views of the Grand River and has a sledding hill that to this day still thrill all who take it on. There is Wedgwood Park on Wilson Avenue, created on land given to the city by Dr. Llewellyn Wedgwood in 1939. It was finally made into a park in the 1970s. Heritage Park on Canal Avenue has a man-made pond that was dug during excavation for the I-196 expressway, but the insurance was too expensive to turn the pond into a swimming lake. Then, the historical society moved the No. 10 one-room schoolhouse to the park, where it served the community as a museum. Finally, Calvin Crest Park on Ivanrest Street is Grandville's hidden gem.

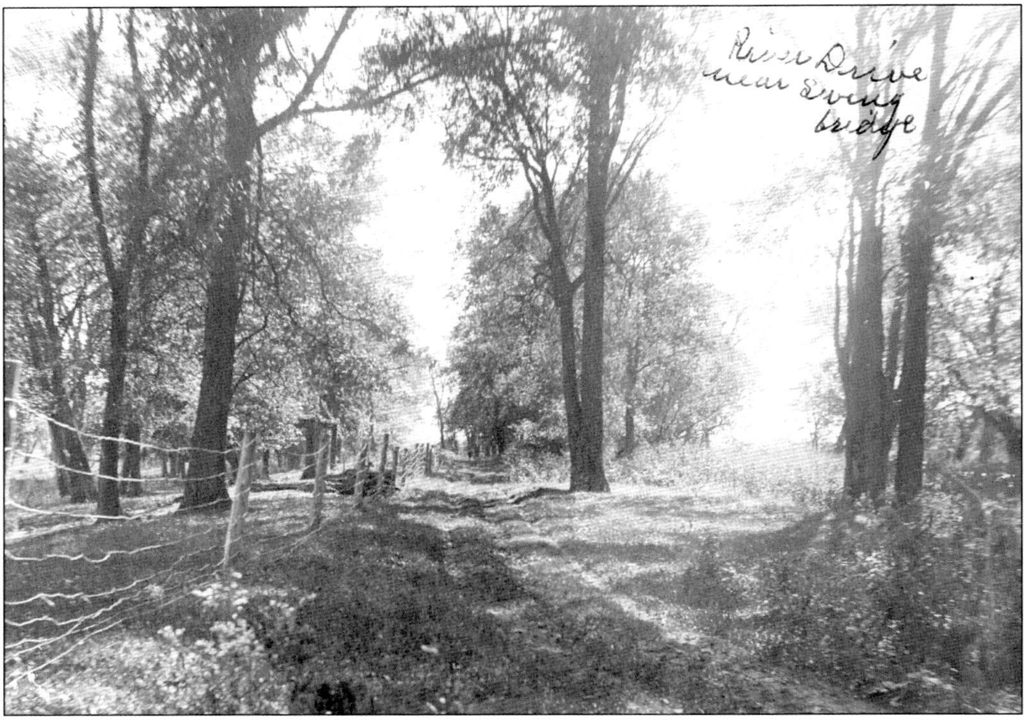

Pictured here in the early 1900s, this is Johnson Park Drive in Henry Johnson Park on the Grand River. The drive was beautiful but primitive; this scenic river road goes to the top of the hill in the park and is still in Grandville today.

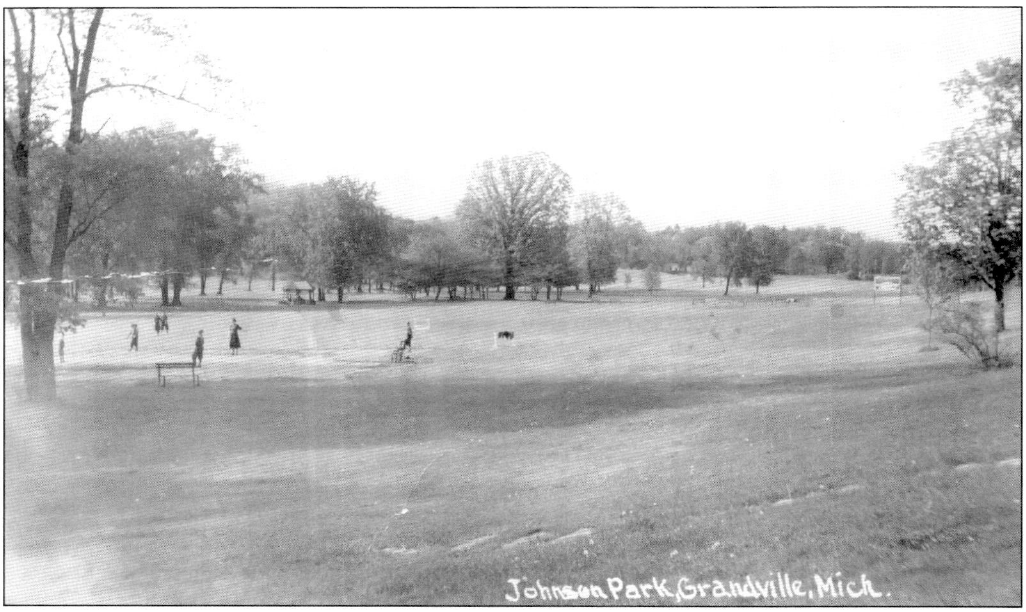

Henry Johnson Park is located along the Grand River. This photograph was taken near the park entrance in its early years, but not much has changed today. It is still a widely used park, popular for the Grandville High School cross country races, family picnics, hiking, and sledding.

Henry Johnson Park is pictured here along the banks of the Grand River in the early 1900s.

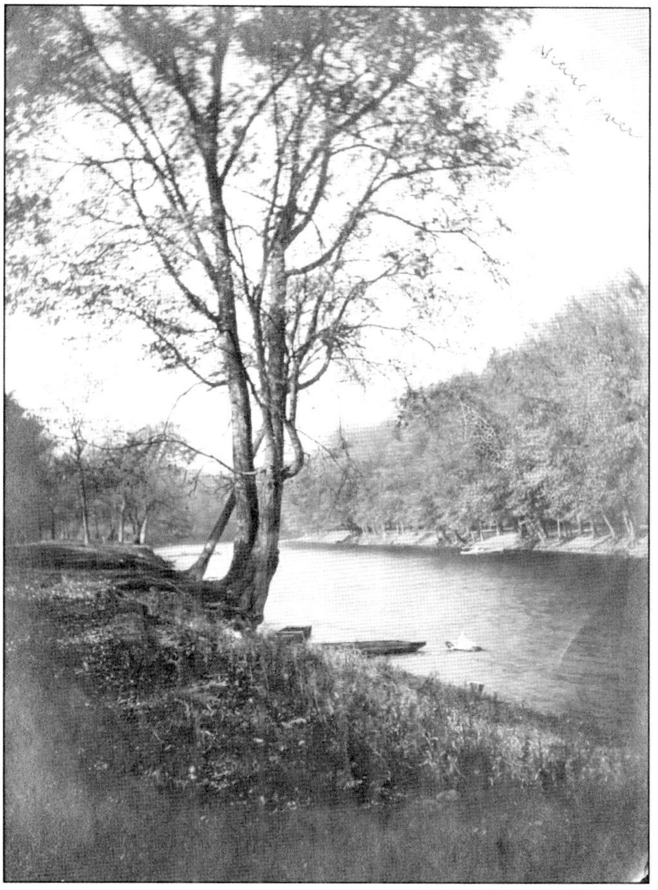

Sledding was popular at the Henry Johnson Park hill in the 1960s. Often, a bonfire was made at the top while children spent the day taking trips down. This photograph shows a good wipeout! Today, the steps are gone, as is the toboggan run, but the hill is still used for sledding.

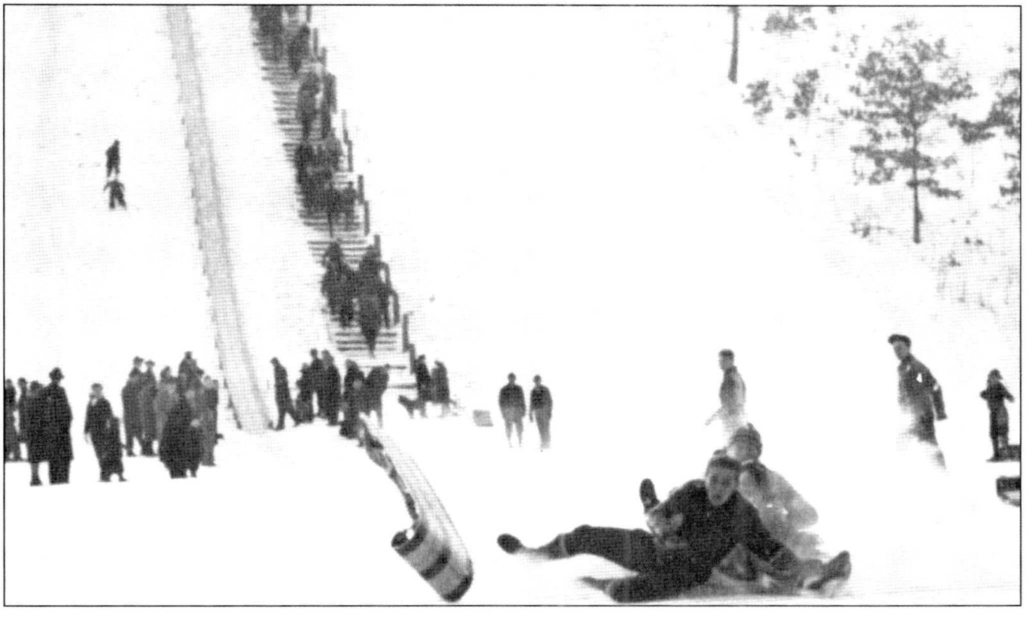

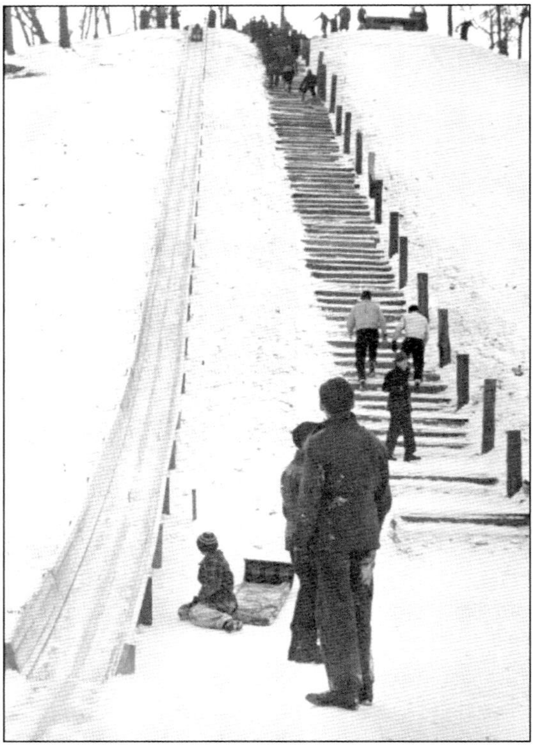

Pictured here is the toboggan run at the Henry Johnson Park hill in the 1960s.

Grandville is very proud of its parks, including Wedgwood Park, Calvin Crest Park, and Heritage Park. This is the ground-breaking ceremony for Wedgwood Park, established in 1973 on Wilson Avenue at Buck Creek. City dignitaries are pictured here with shovels; among them are James Buck, Evelyn Guy, Ted Zondervan, Harold Becker, and Howard Nyenhuis.

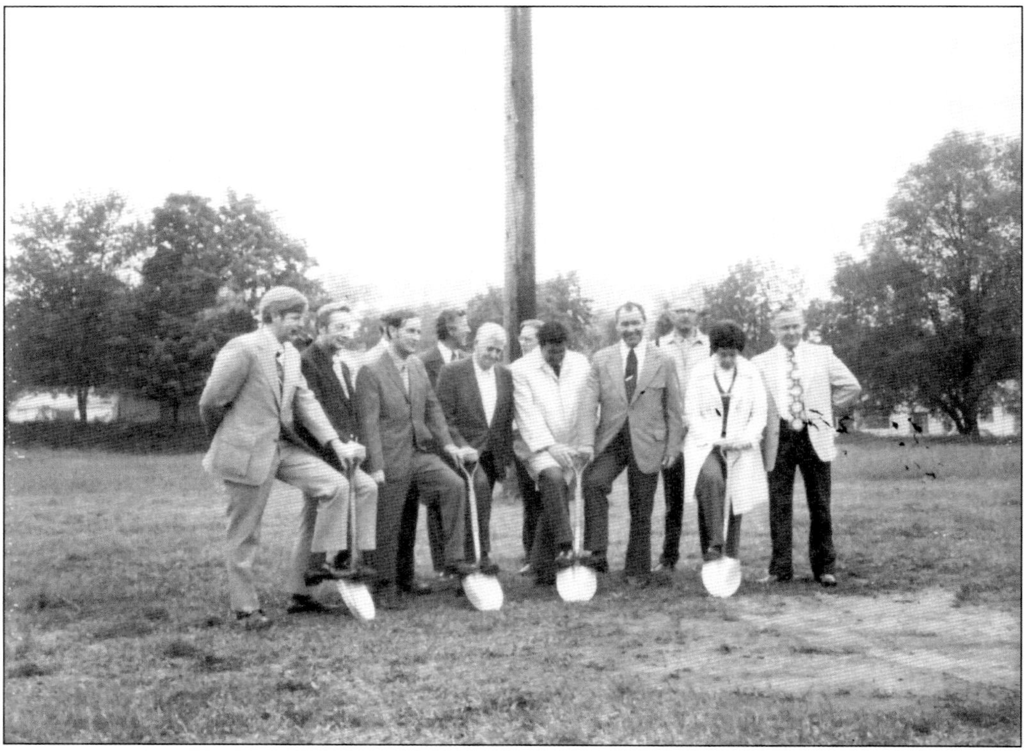

Here, the Versluis Playground Memorial is being made for Wedgwood Park in 1974. Playground equipment was added, making the park more kid friendly. This park is still used today for activities such as biking, hiking, and picnics along the creek. The park is connected to Grandville Middle School by a bridge over Buck Creek.

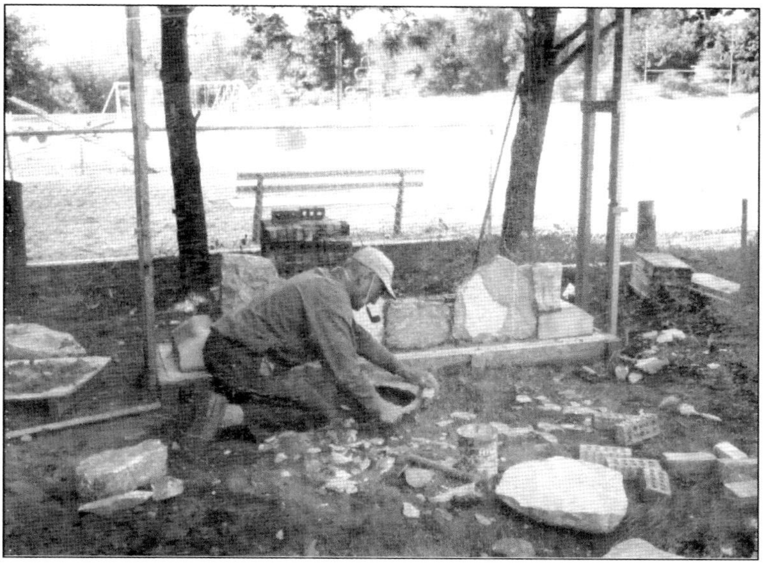

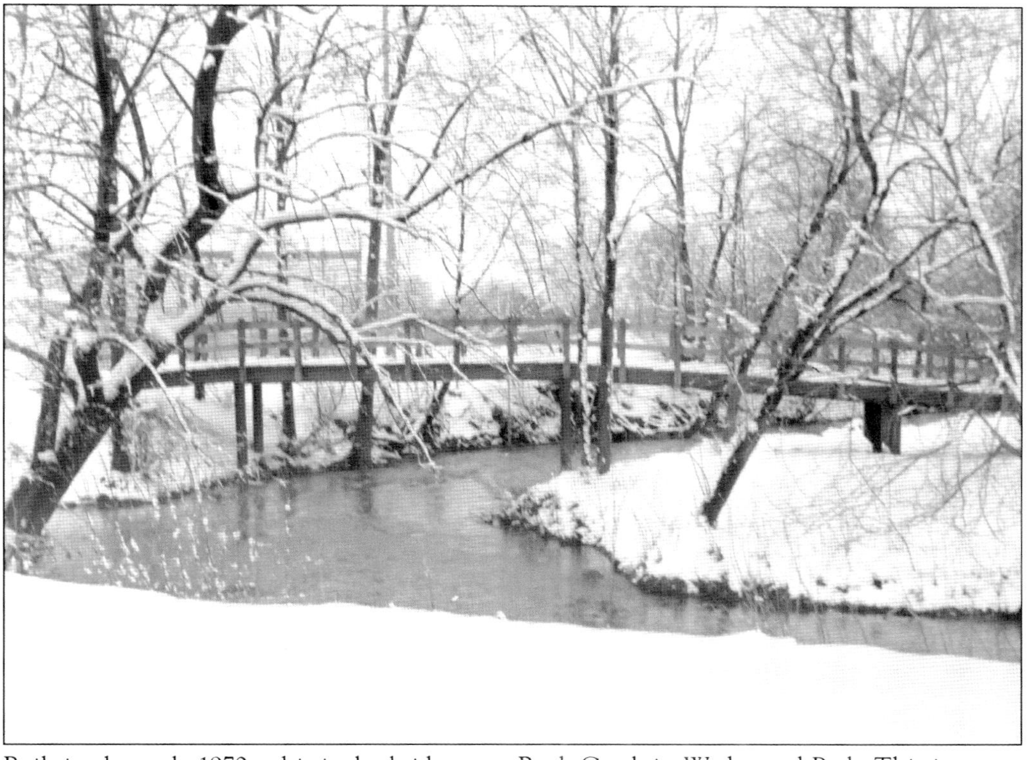

Built in the early 1970s, this is the bridge over Buck Creek in Wedgwood Park. This is a very beautiful park with the creek running through it and plenty of ducks to feed. The park also has ball fields and soccer fields. It was named after Dr. Llewellyn Wedgwood.

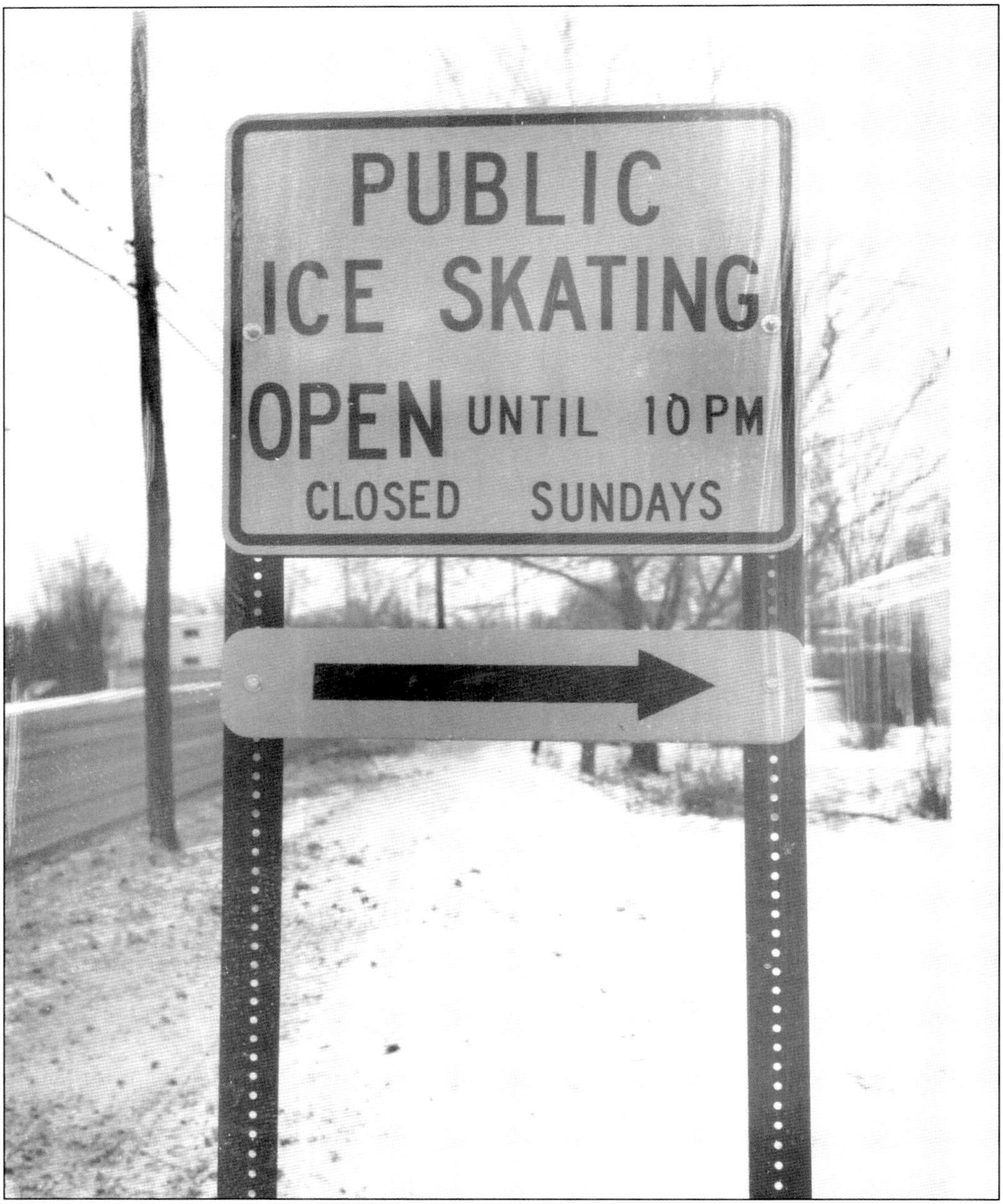

Public ice-skating was popular at Wedgwood Park. The field was flooded and frozen every winter, and a warming house with bathrooms was built in the 1970s. A person could rent ice-skates there for a nominal fee.

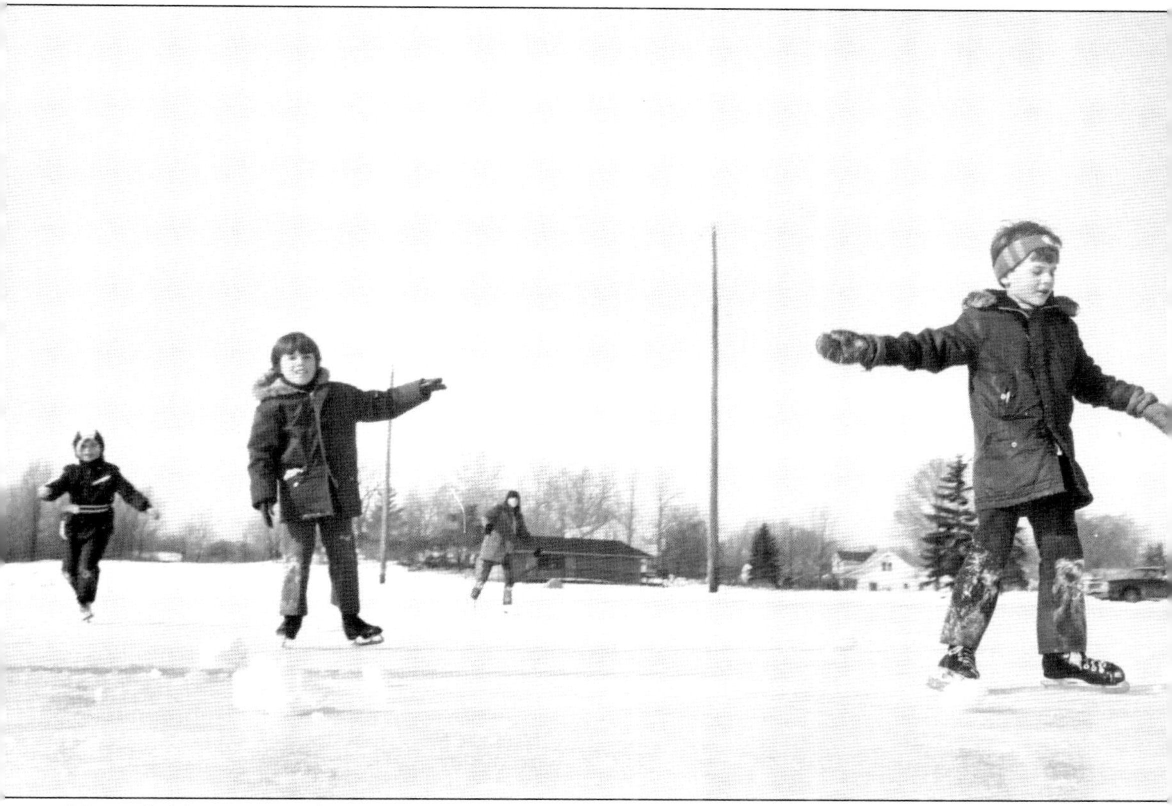

Here, children are ice-skating at Wedgwood Park in 1975. The warming house still stands in the park, although ice-skating is no longer practiced there.

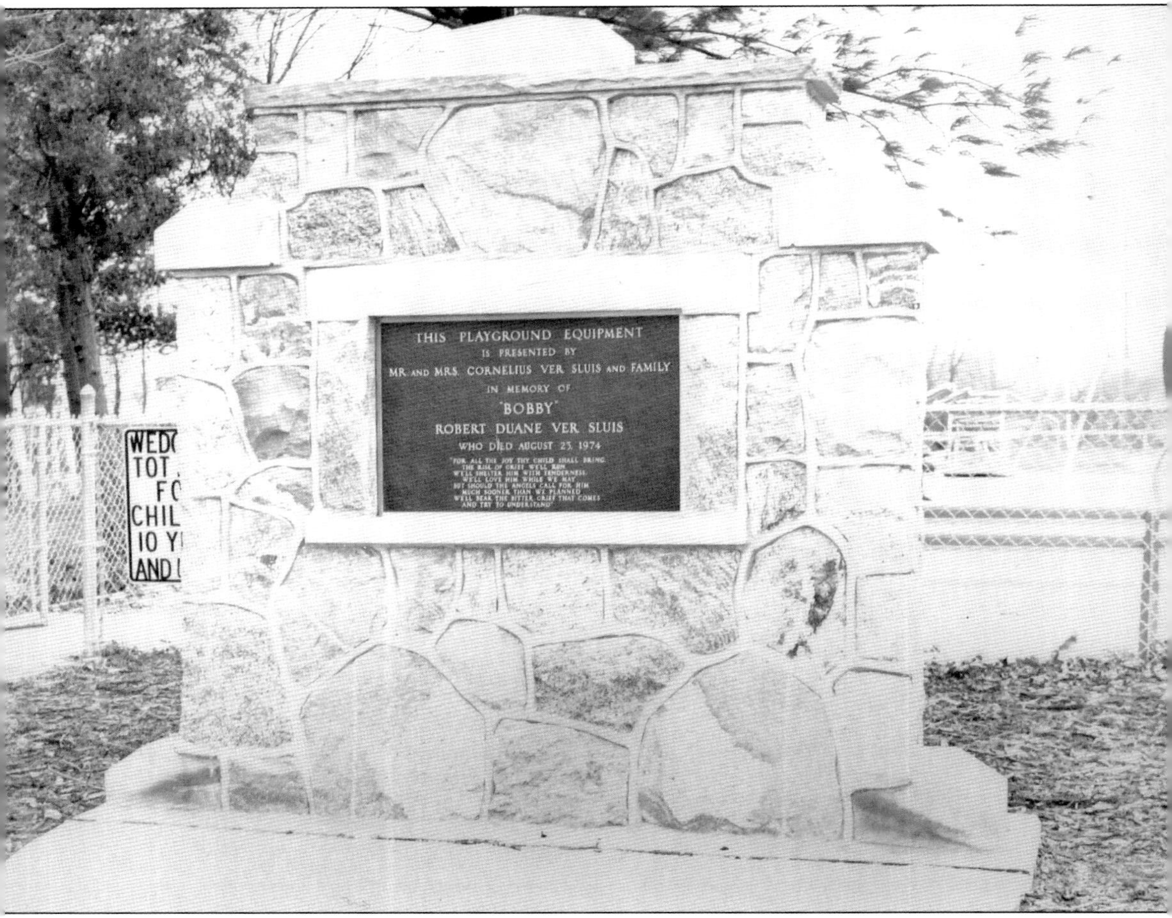

The finished Versluis Playground Memorial stands in front of the playground in 1974. The equipment has been upgraded many times since then, and the park is well maintained.

Eight

Celebrations

Evidence that Grandville has enjoyed Fourth of July has been found as far back as the 1880s, when people on the banks of the Grand River decorated boats for the occasion. Music and speeches were given by politicians on steamboats, which were enjoyed by people onshore. Dancing and parties also accompanied the holiday. Today, Grandville has one of the best and most wonderfully organized Fourth of July celebrations around, including fireworks, craft shows, and ball games.

Grandville had its share of churches, but it also had its share of saloons. The city closed a saloon on the Grand River because too many people would get drunk and walk off the dock in the back, resulting in a few drownings.

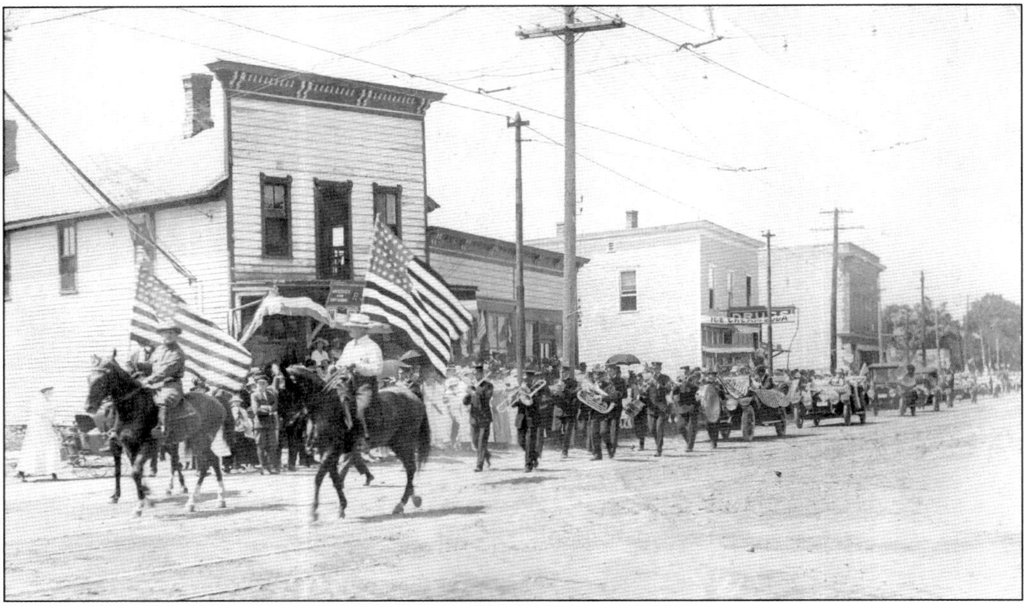

In 1914, Fourth of July was celebrated with a parade down the middle of Chicago Drive; the cross street is Wilson Avenue. Horses, decorated wagons, and homemade costumes can be seen here.

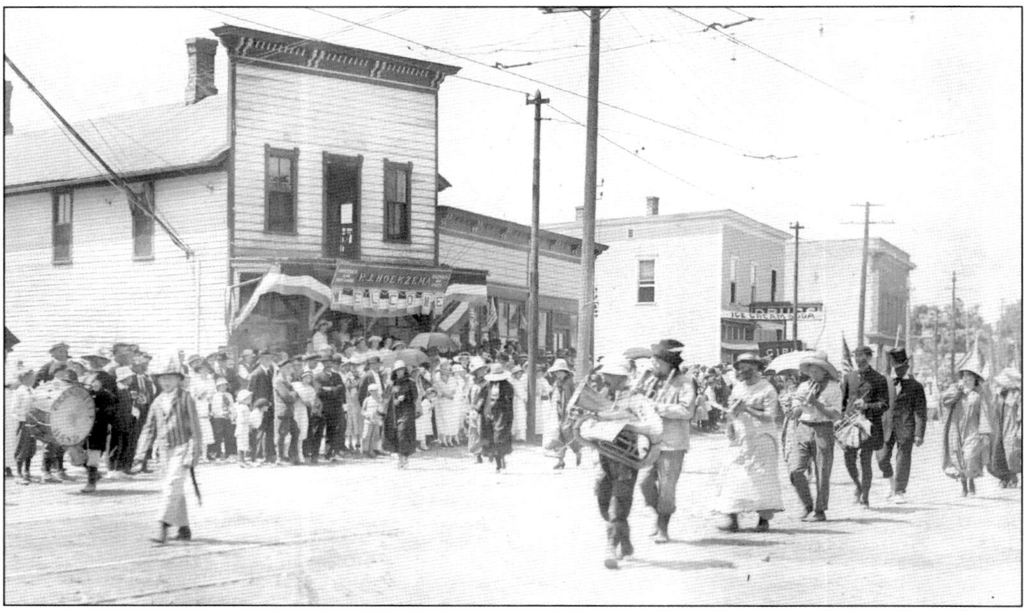

This is the rest of the parade going down Chicago Drive in 1914. Hoekzemas Drug Store is on the corner (left). Dr. Llewellyn Wedgwood's office was located above the drugstore.

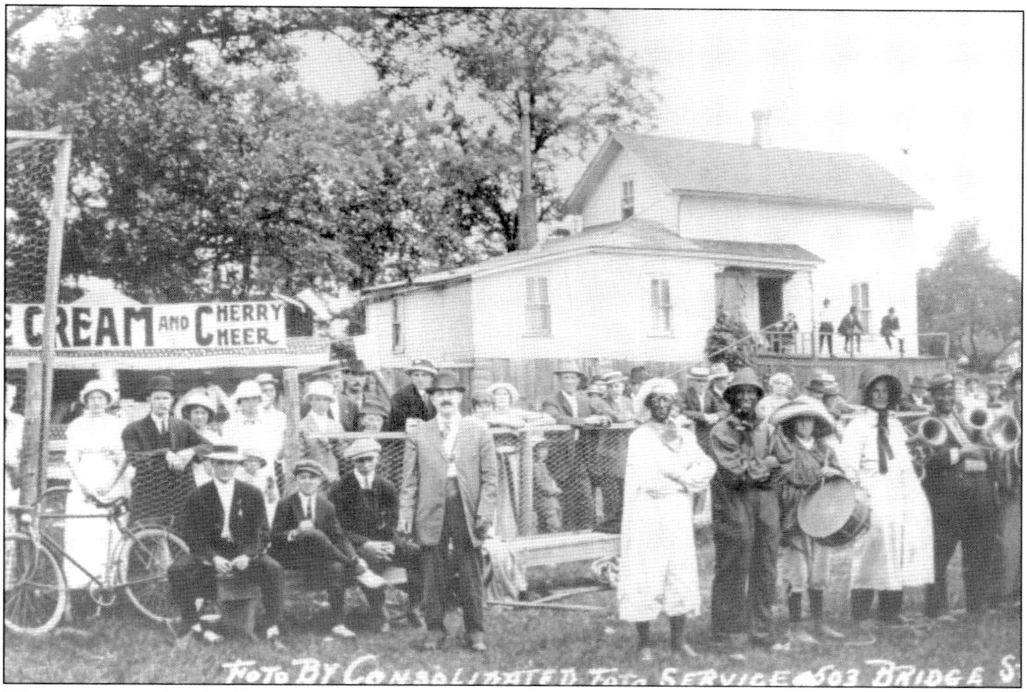

The 1914 Fourth of July celebration continued into the afternoon with a ball game and ice cream. This photograph was taken on the west side of Wilson Avenue by the railroad tracks, where the post office is located today. Members of the Rube Band are dressed in costume.

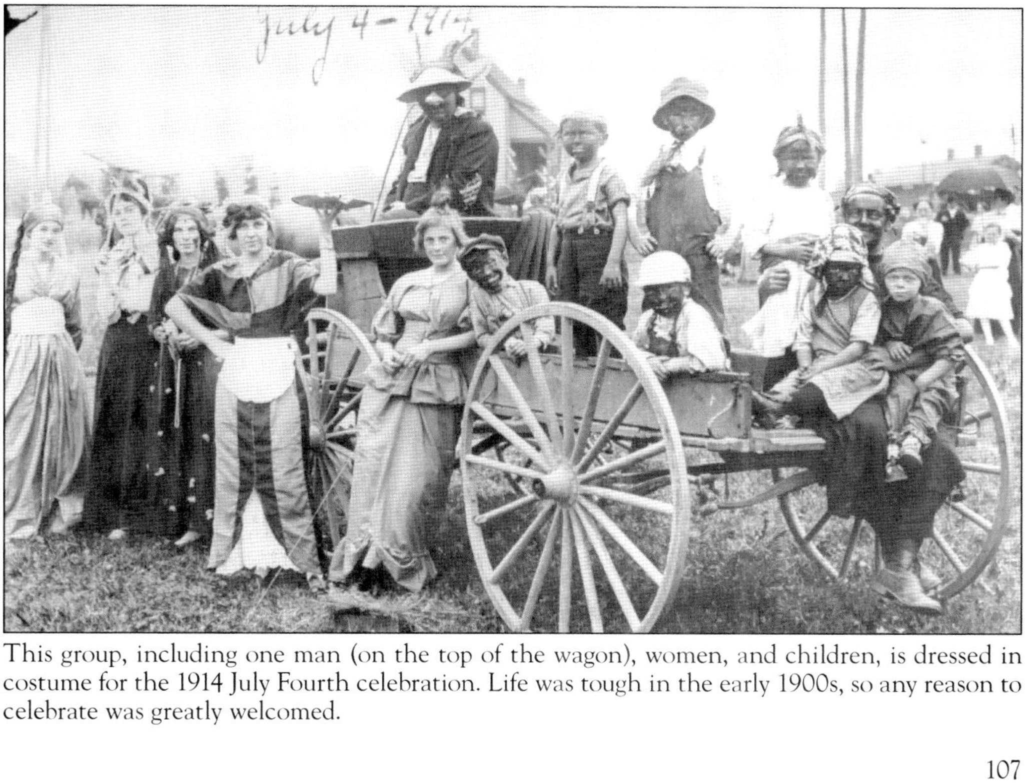

This group, including one man (on the top of the wagon), women, and children, is dressed in costume for the 1914 July Fourth celebration. Life was tough in the early 1900s, so any reason to celebrate was greatly welcomed.

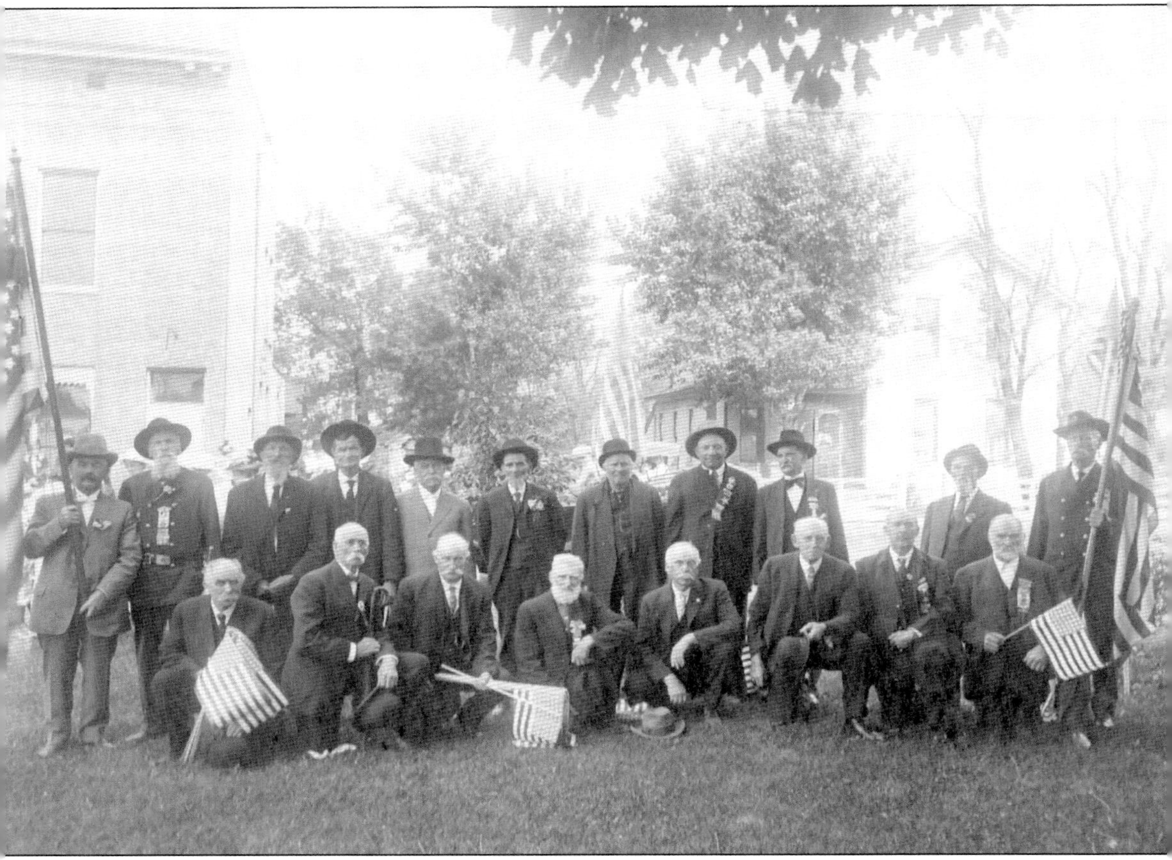

The 1914 Fourth of July parade was attended by Civil War veterans from the surrounding area, who were celebrated for their patriotism and bravery. Capt. Henry Preston (front row, sixth from the left) was General Grant's bodyguard when General Lee surrendered at Appomattox to end the war. Preston lived at the corner of Franklin and Maple Streets, where the Grandville Library stands today. His daughter Mae Preston married widower Dr. Llewellyn Wedgwood, who had two small daughters from a previous marriage.

The Boy Scouts began the Memorial Day Parade by saluting the flag in Wedgwood Park in 1981. The monument seen here was created by Charles Kaiserlian, who sized up every piece of fieldstone and determined how it should be chipped to fit into a foundation.

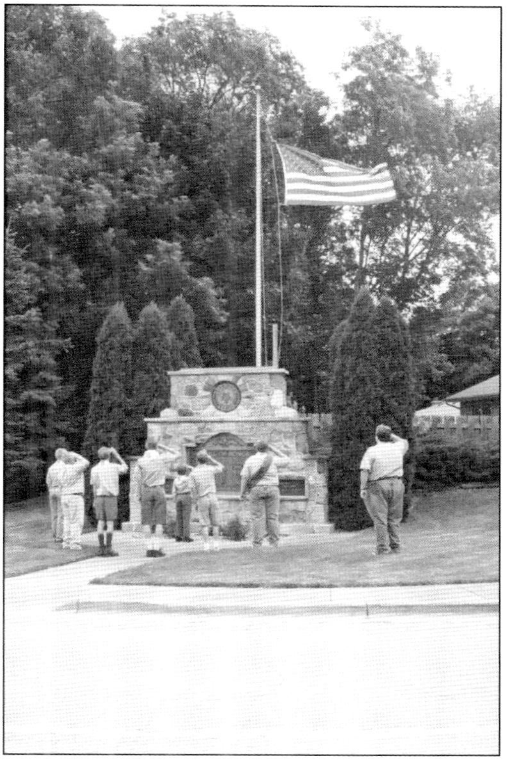

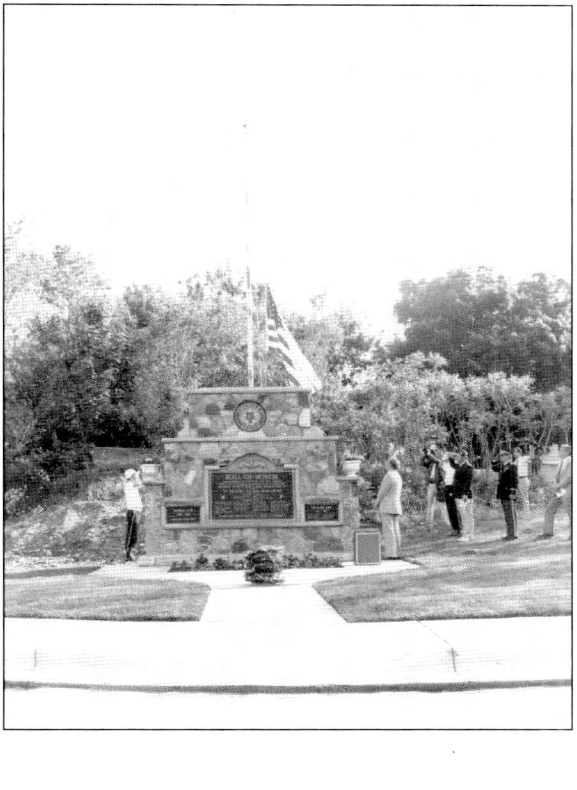

City officials pay their respects on Memorial Day in 1981. They then joined the parade that went from Wedgwood Park, down Prairie Street, and ended in the Grandville Cemetery underneath the Civil War monument. There, soldiers would lay the wreath.

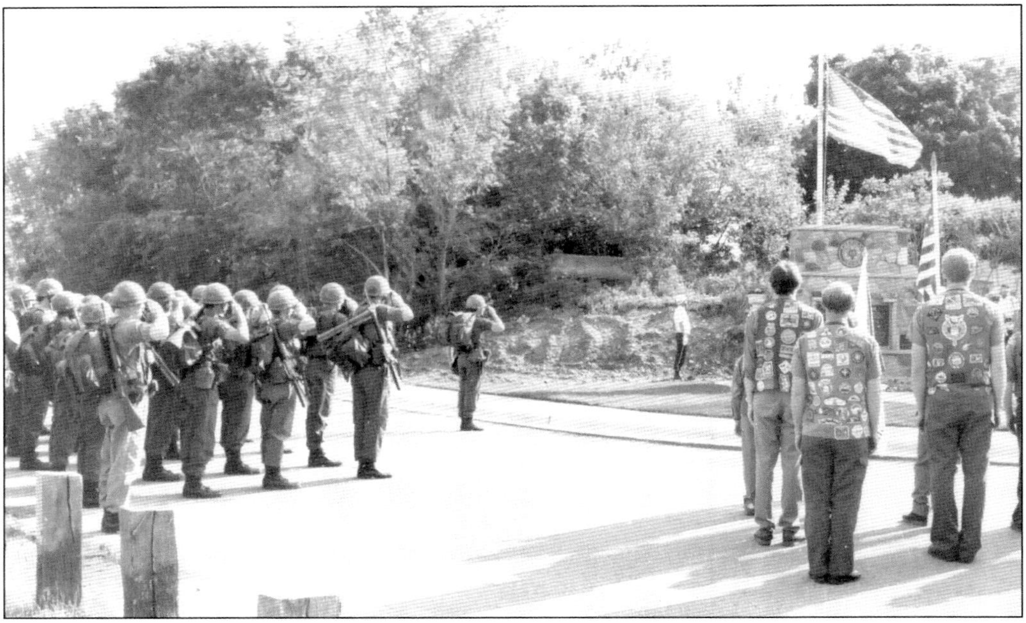

Soldiers pay their respects on Memorial Day 1981 in Wedgwood Park. This memorial lists the names of the Grandville fallen on the city's Roll of Honor. It includes the names of the men from Vietnam and the Korean War. This monument replaced the one torn down that stood at Chicago Drive, and the names on the World War I plaque were added to this memorial.

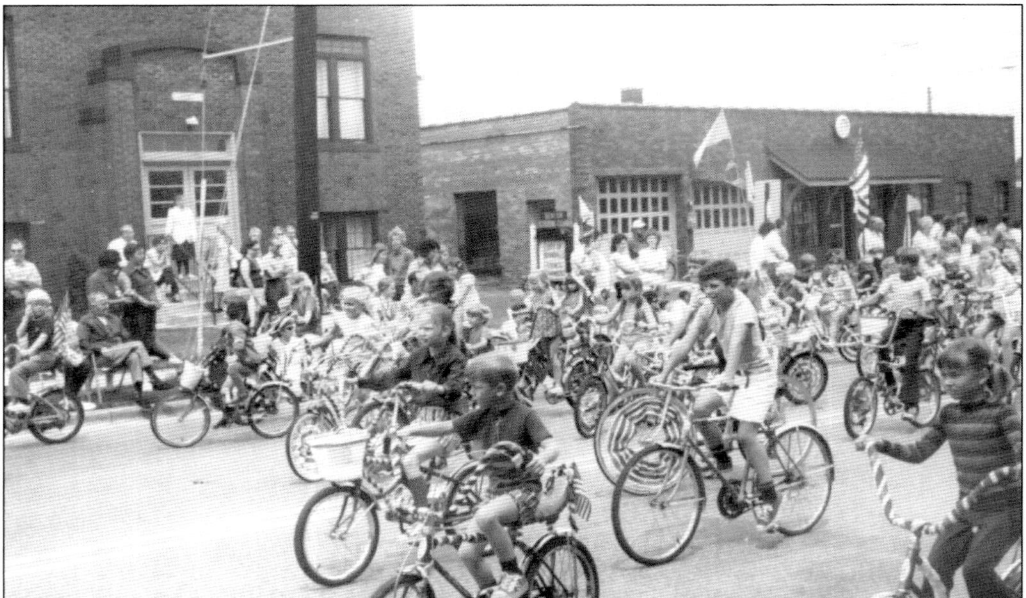

On July 4, 1973, children are pictured with decorated bikes for the parade. The former parade route started at the school, went west down Prairie Street, turned south on Wilson Avenue, wound around Big Spring Lake, and ended in the high school parking lot on Wilson Avenue. This was north of Prairie by the old fire barns.

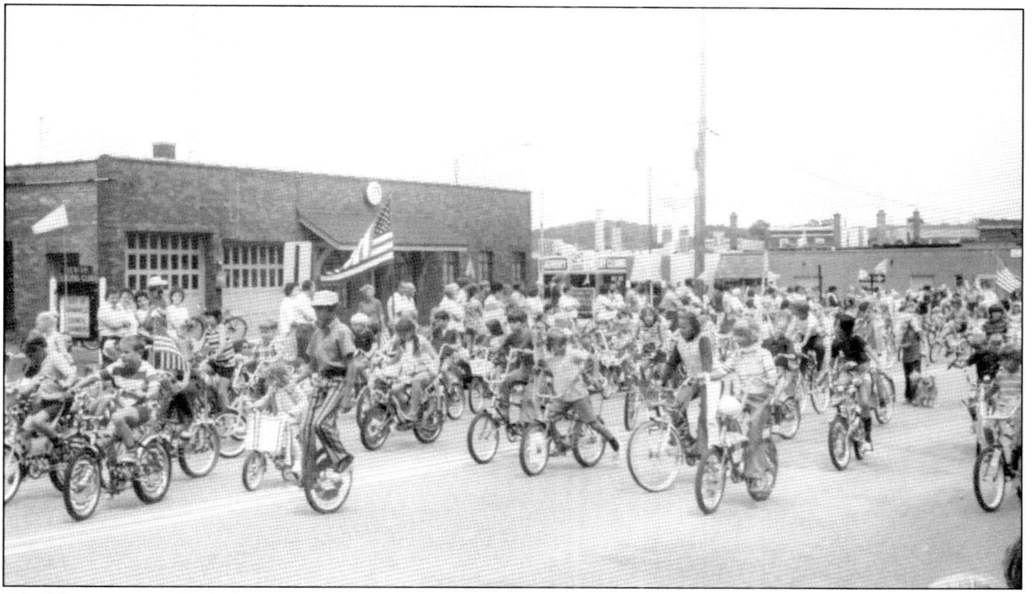

Children enjoy the bike parade going down Wilson Avenue on July 4, 1973. In those days, there were many floats in the parades, and anyone could join in. The Grandville High School Band led the parade.

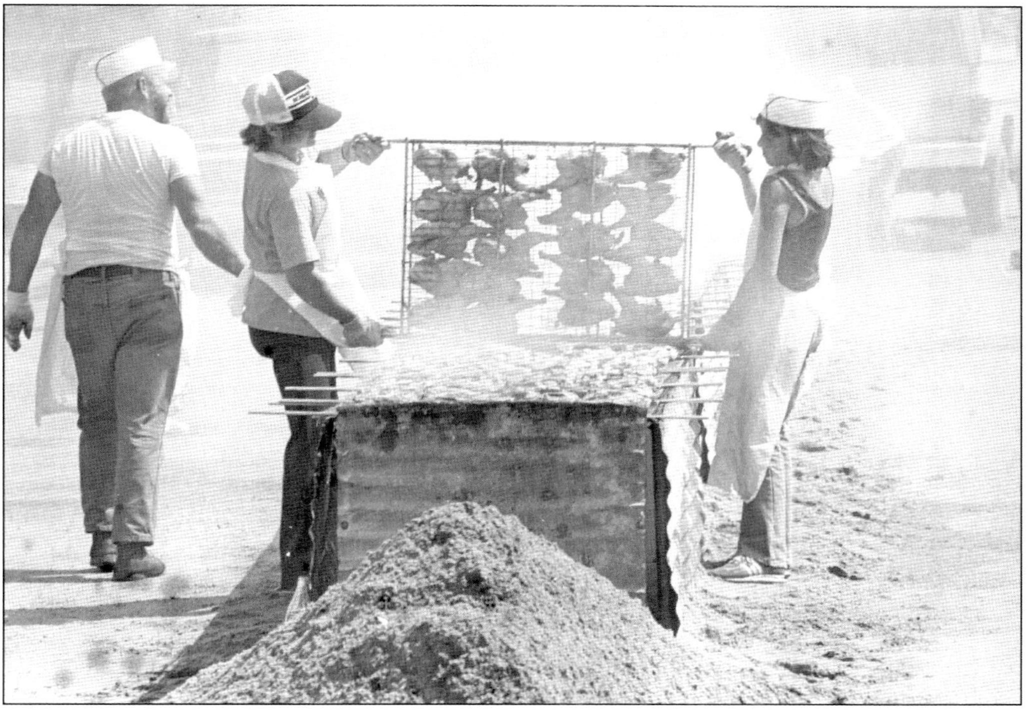

The streets were cornered off, and the chicken barbeque was set up on July 4, 1979. For many years, it was tradition to have a chicken barbeque. First, it was the parade, then a craft show, and then games were held at Wedgwood Park. The day was filled with baseball games, concerts, and skydiving and ended with fireworks from the Grandville Football Field.

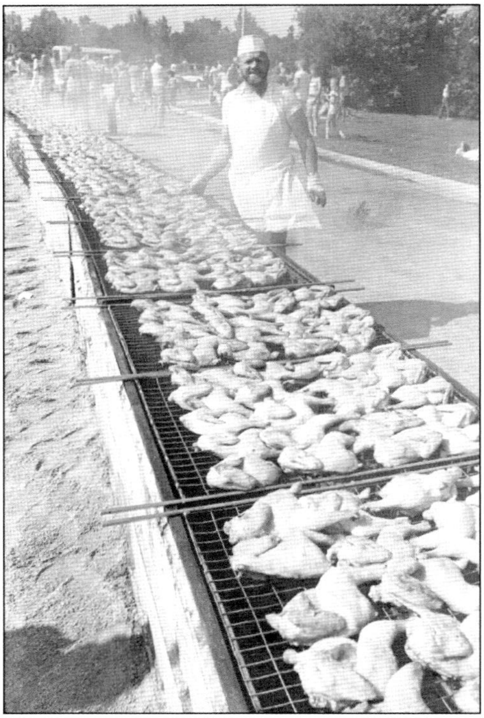

It was a tall order in 1979 to feed everyone at the Fourth of July celebration in Grandville. Eating was just one of the many activities. In addition to the chicken barbeque, there was a hole-in-one tournament to win an automobile and music in the park.

The police department put on a bicycle-safety class every year. Officers taught children how to watch out for automobiles and cross streets safely. Even a little bike maintenance went a long way. Every year, bike licenses were purchased so that if a bicycle was ever lost or stolen, the police could identify it when located.

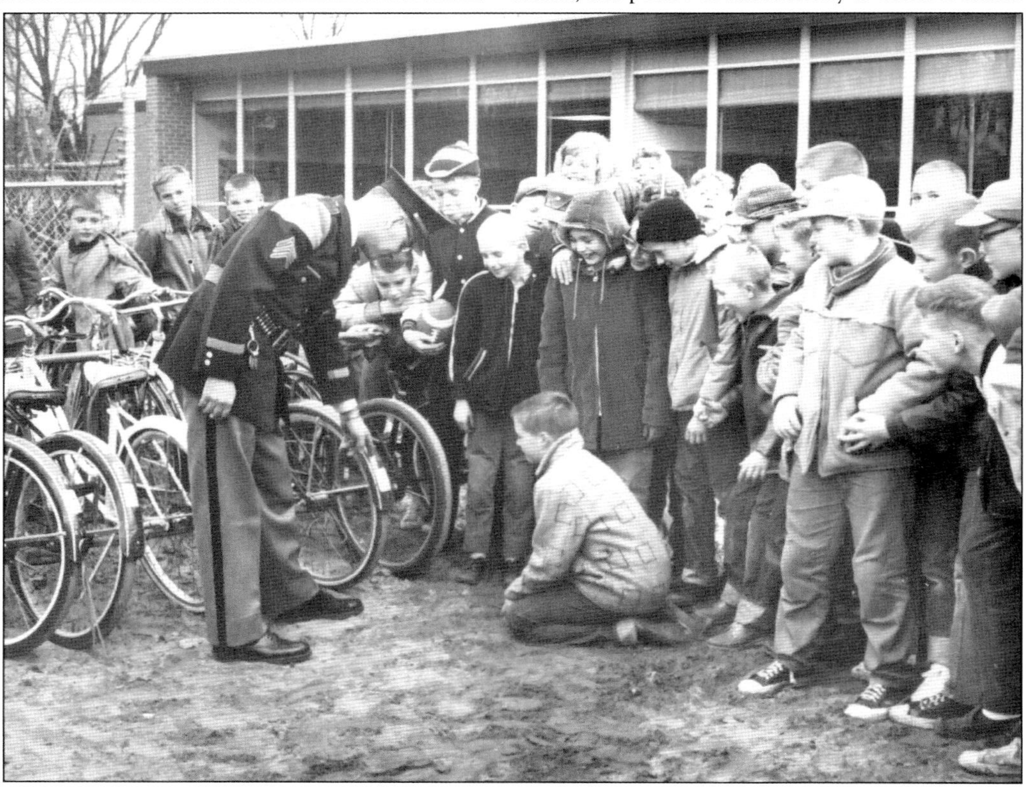

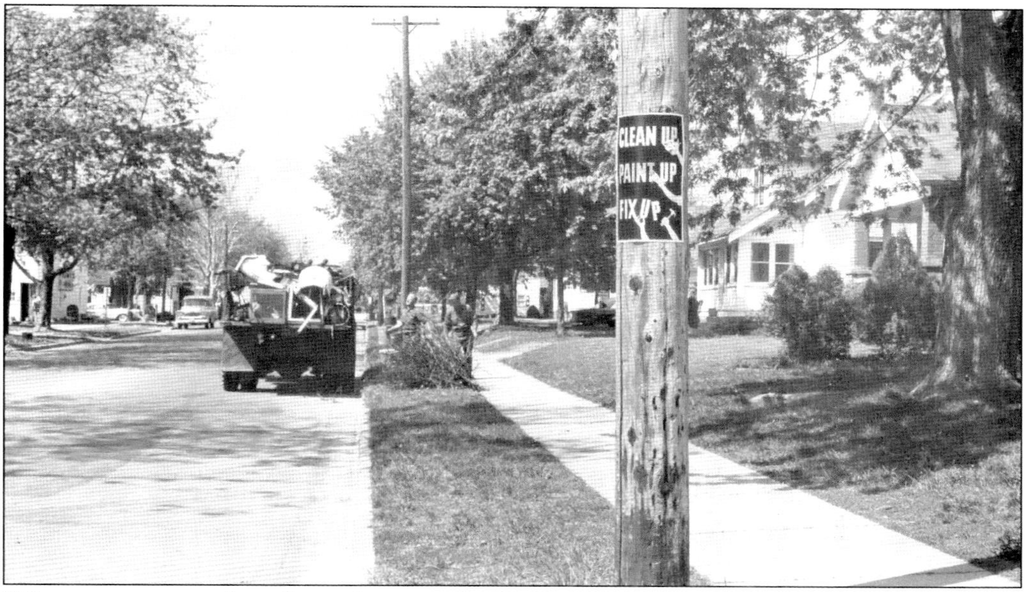

"Clean up, paint up, fix up" was the motto for the city in 1963. "As we stated before, I feel this is a wonderful venture for a community to take part in. It stimulates civic pride and has everyone working for a common cause. A clean community in turn makes a healthier community that is wealthier and wise," said general chairman Fred Devries in preparation for the event.

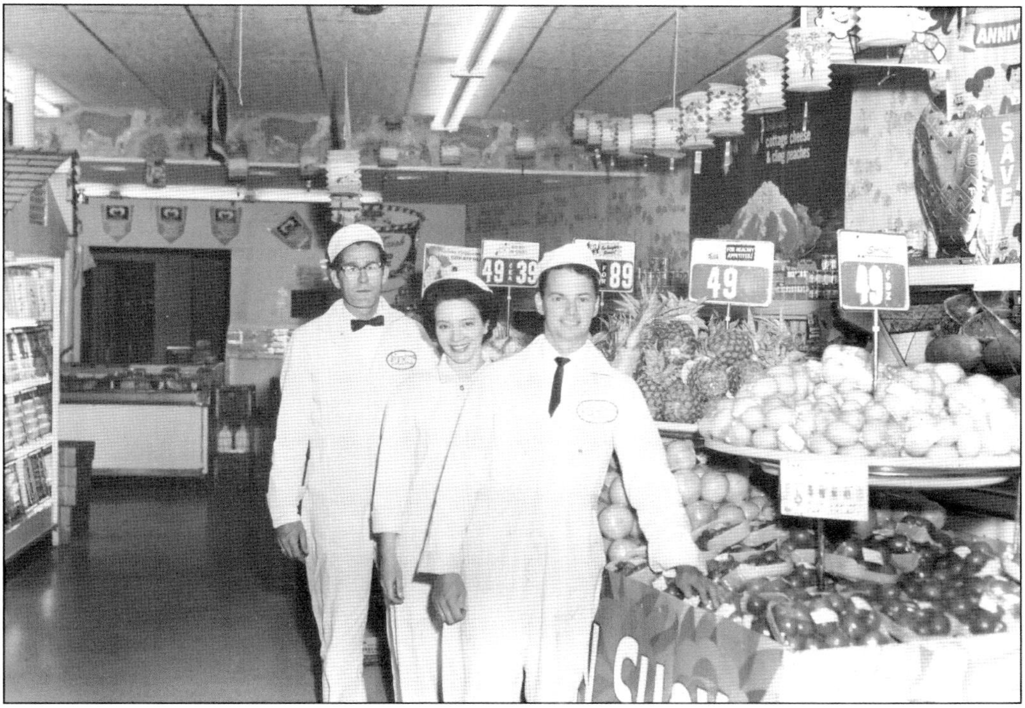

Local stores helped with the cleanup days by supplying children with boxes. Every business owner was given circle patches to sew onto their employees' clothes stating, "Clean up, paint up, fix up."

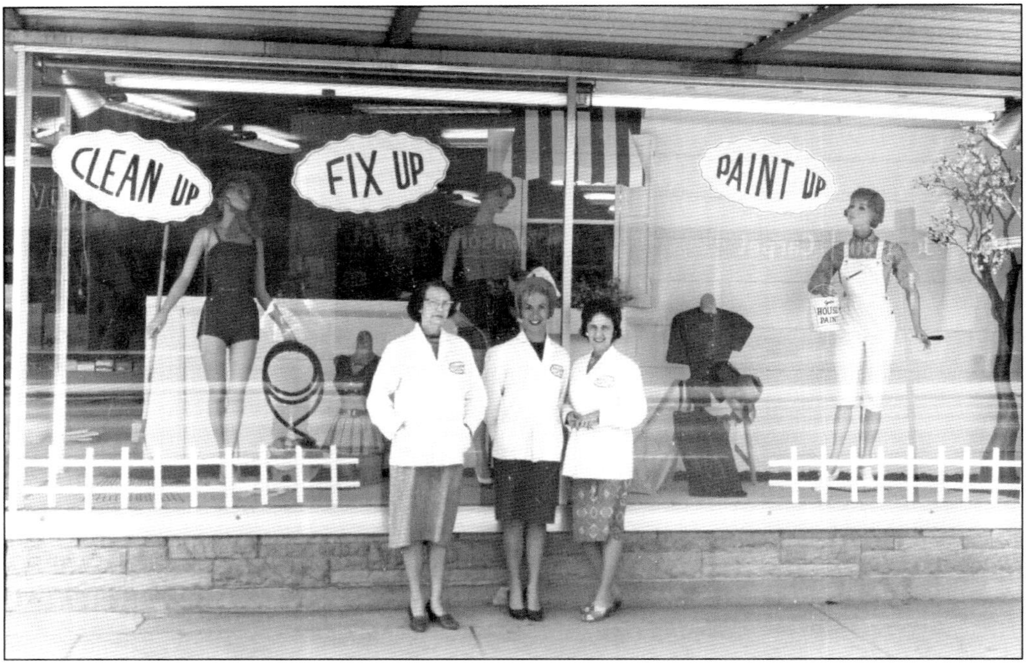

Here, three employees stand outside the store wearing white smocks with "cleanup" patches on them. Everyone got into the act one way or another to promote cleanup week. People painted storefronts and made signs to put in the windows of businesses.

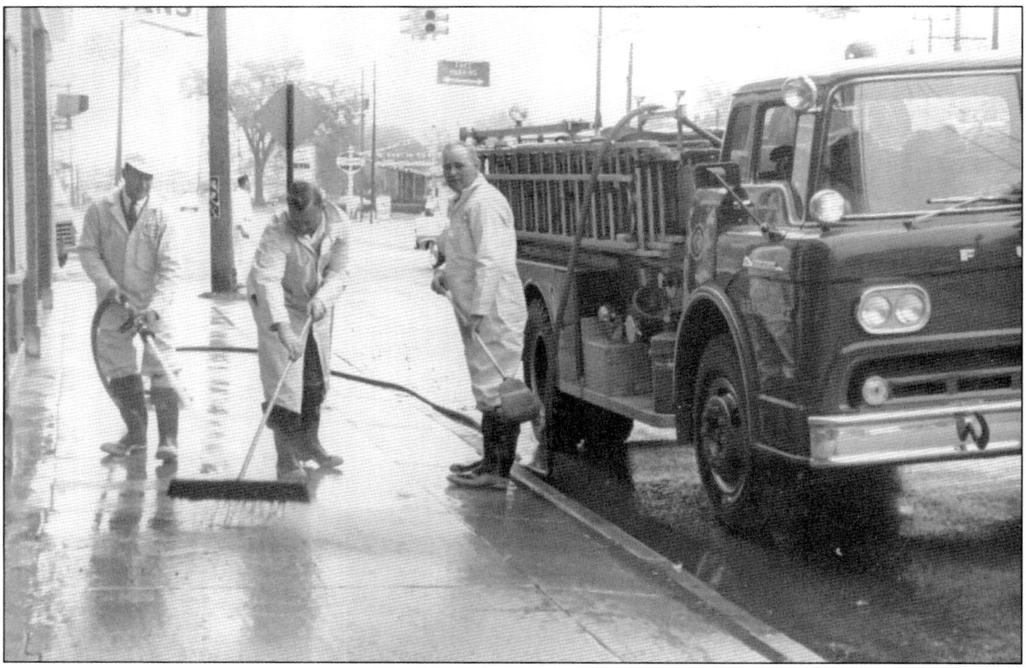
A fire truck was used to hose down the streets. Everything in Grandville in 1963 was going to be clean. These men may have even washed the fire truck. Note the "cleanup" patches on their white smocks.

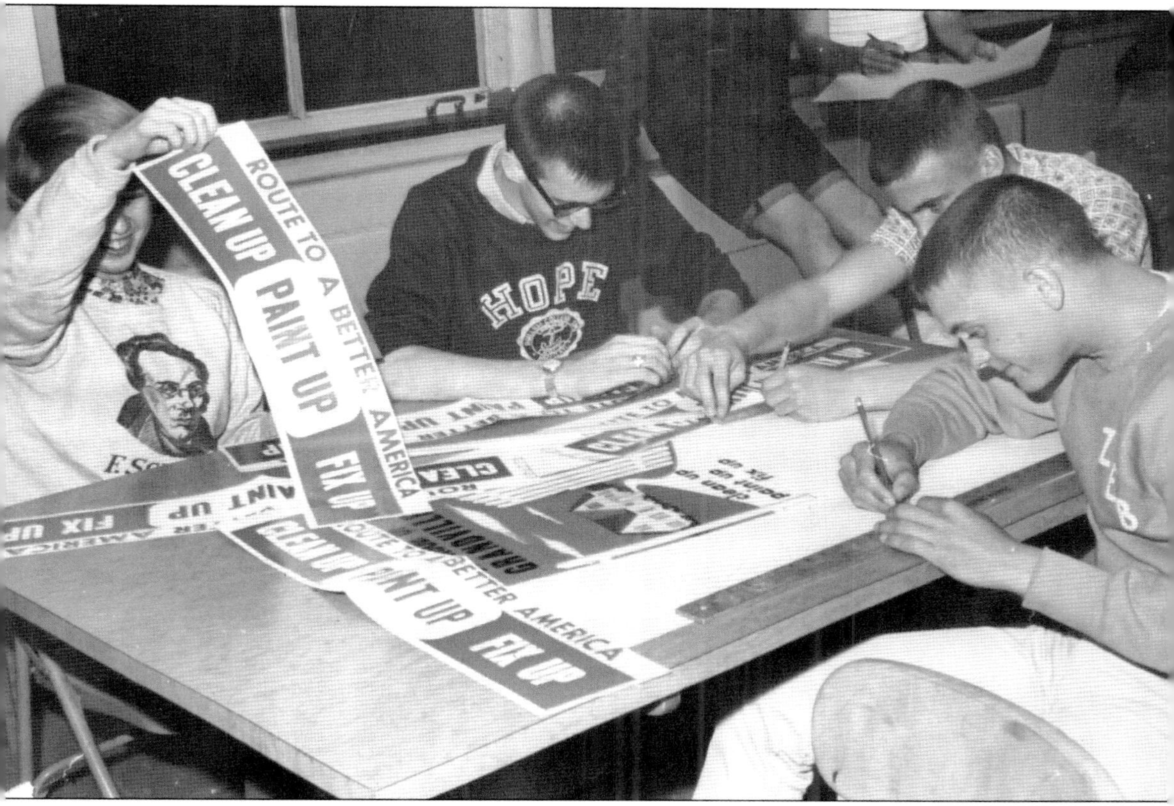

Students at Grandville High School also participated in cleanup week. They worked on locker clean outs, floats, and signs to be used in the community. The student council was in charge of organizing the students. The whole school got involved in one way or another.

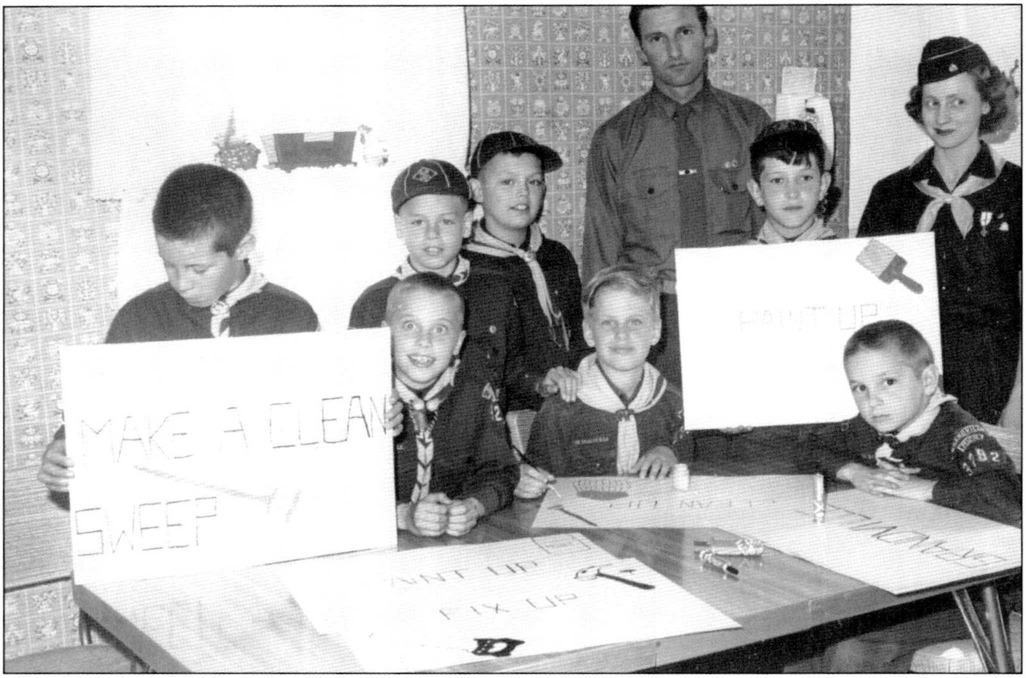

Cub Scout Pack 3292 made posters for the 1963 cleanup week. From left to right are Skip Kenyon, Terry Start, Doug Hop, Dan Dreyer, Mike Polavin, Bob Dreyer, Dean Davis, Joe Harlette, and Mrs. Start.

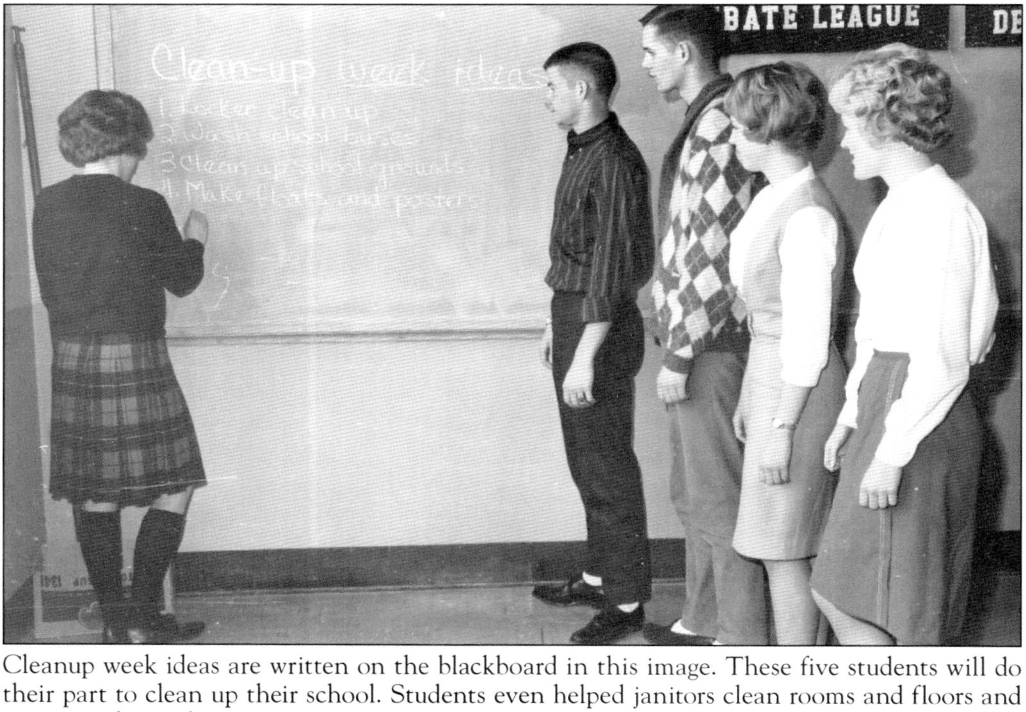

Cleanup week ideas are written on the blackboard in this image. These five students will do their part to clean up their school. Students even helped janitors clean rooms and floors and carry out the trash.

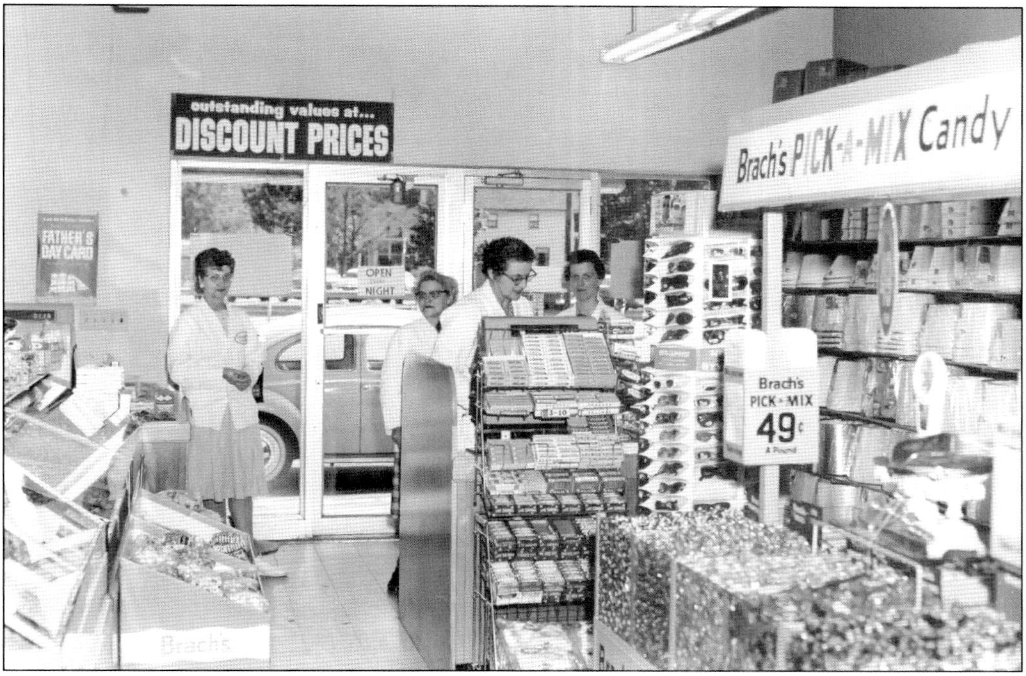

Drugstore workers wear white smocks with "cleanup" patches.

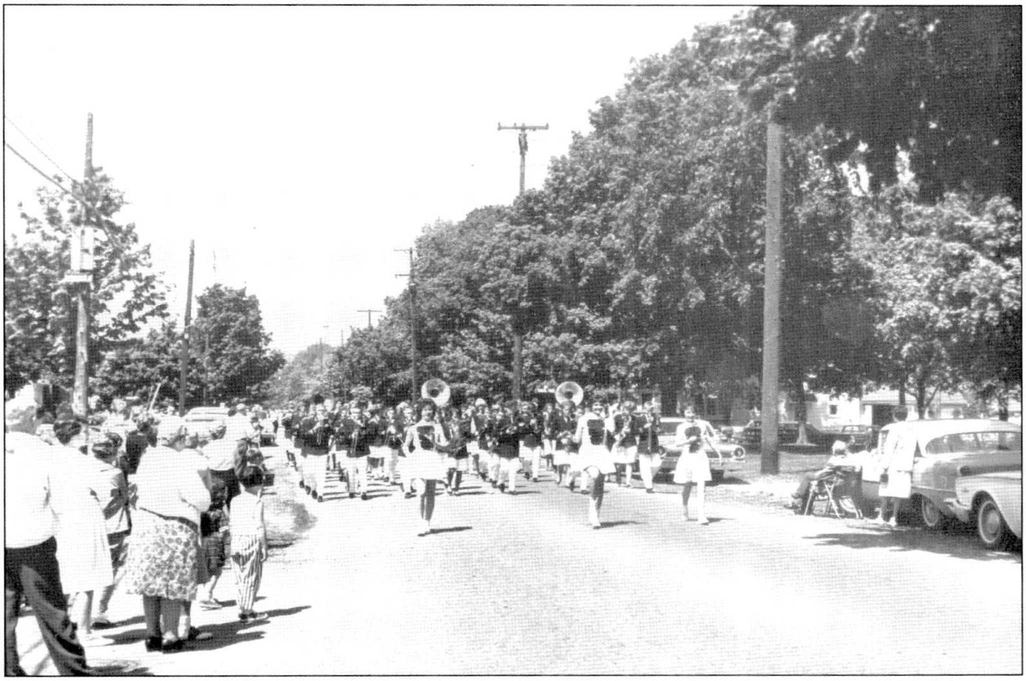

This photograph shows the cleanup parade. The parade was one of the biggest and best in Grandville's history. Entries even came from outside the city. Merchants donated vehicles, and high school students made the floats. The cooperation was wonderful. The churches were outstanding, in particular, with their floats. Here, the Grandville Band is coming down the street.

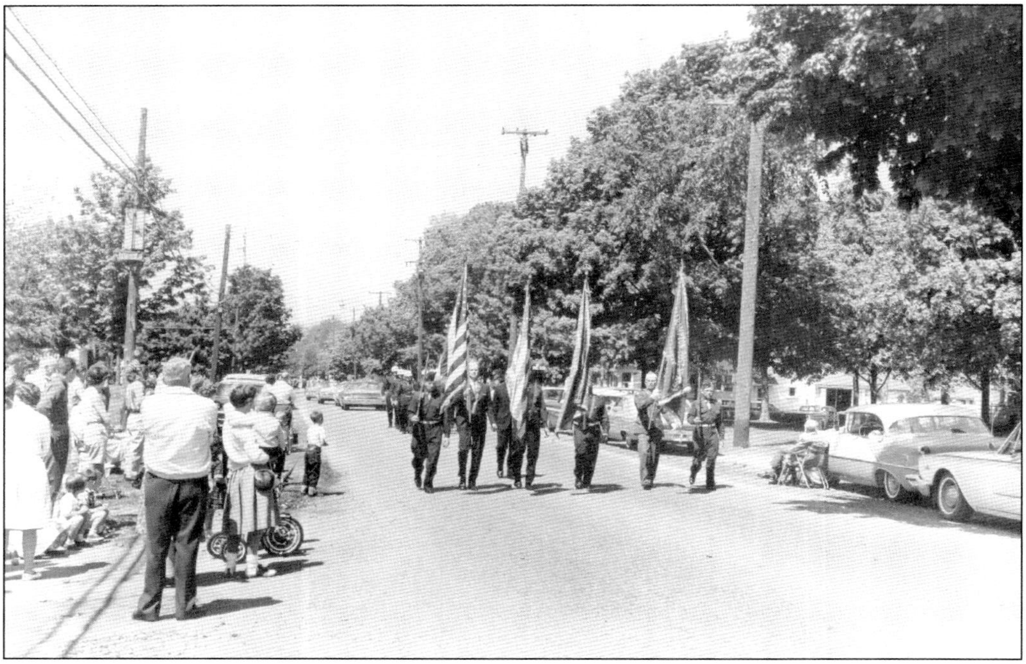

Pictured here with flags, even the veterans helped with the 1963 cleanup. The parade represented just about every organization, with everyone coming together for a common cause.

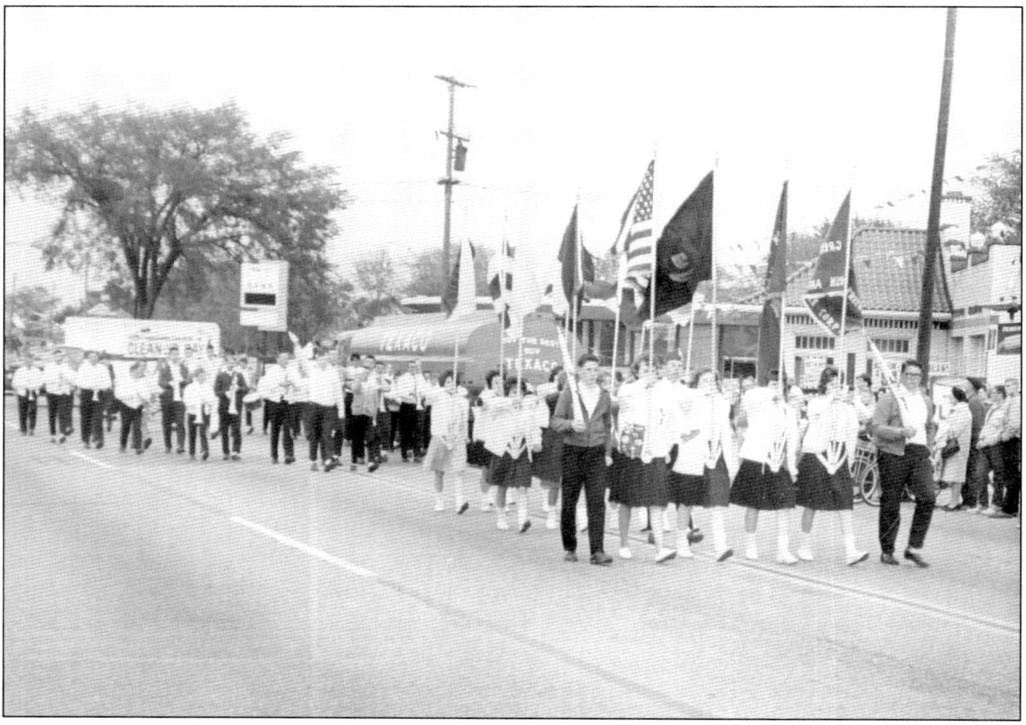

Even the Grandville Junior High Band got to march that day. Everyone was marching and working towards a goal of a clean city.

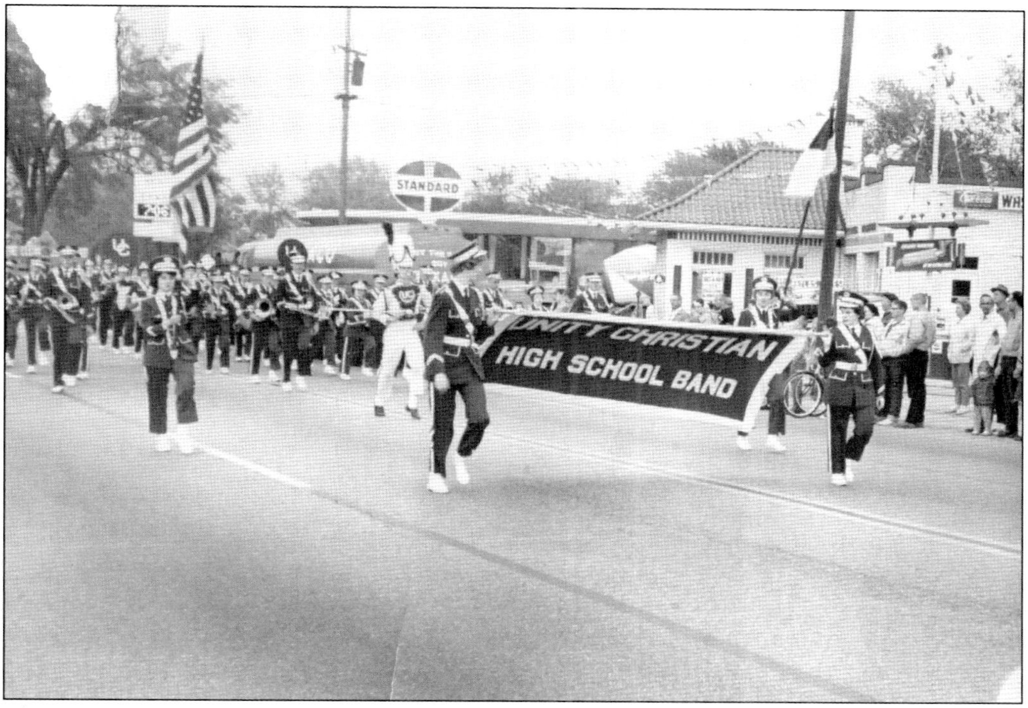

The Unity Christian High School Band was in full uniform at the 1963 cleanup-day parade. It was one of several bands partaking in the celebration that day.

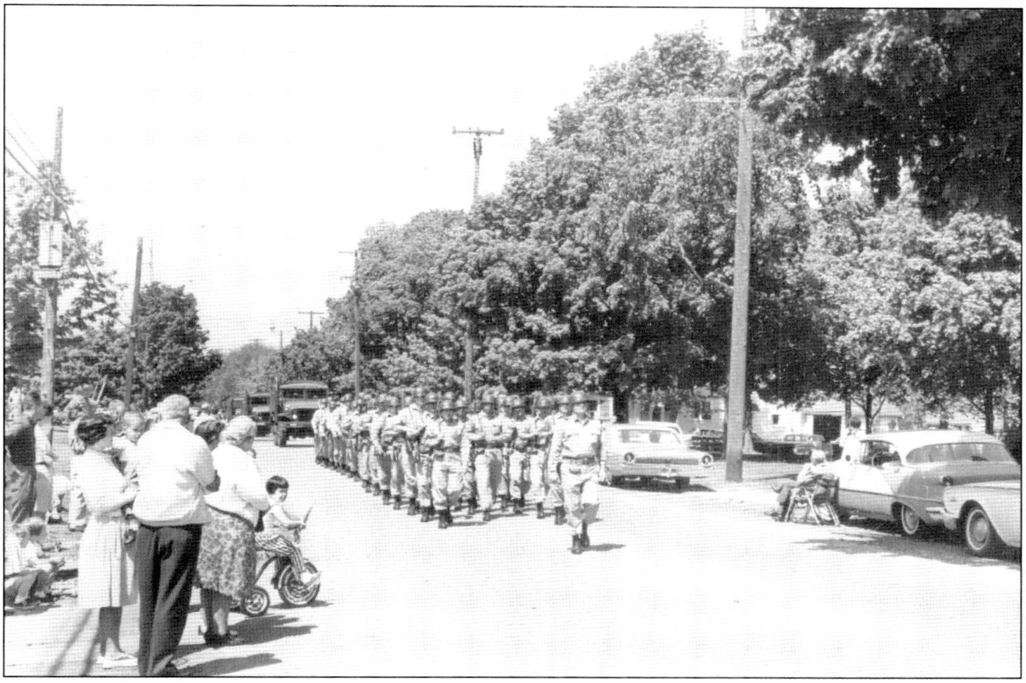

The Army was there to support the cleanup-day parade in 1963 with the motto "To serve, protect, and clean."

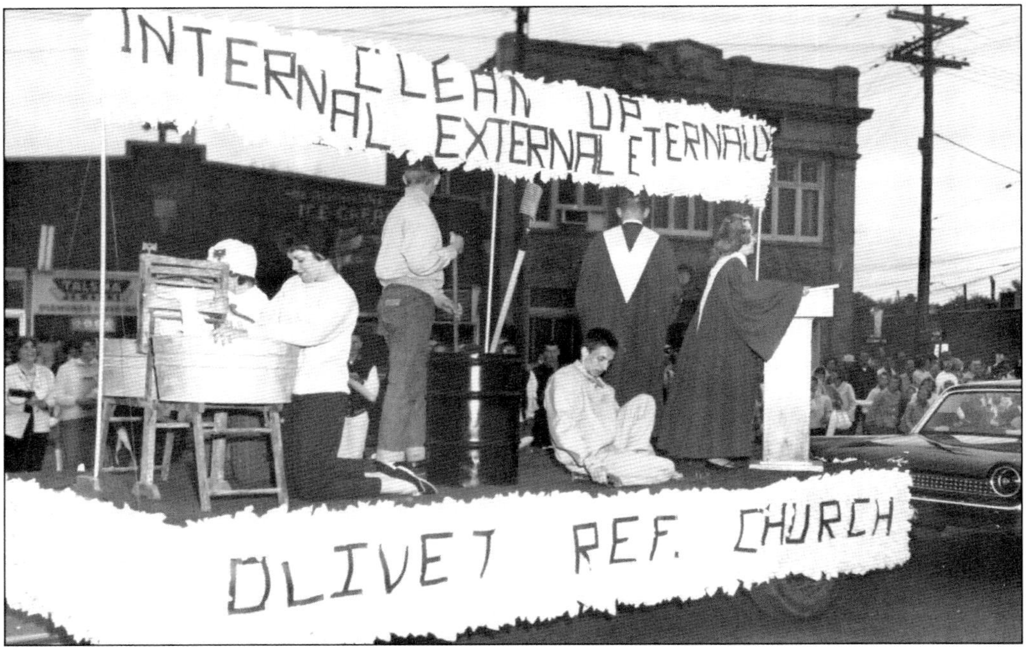

External and internal cleanup was the theme of the float of the Olivet Reformed Church. Another church emphasized the need for a new library on its float. In 1964, the library was on the ballot.

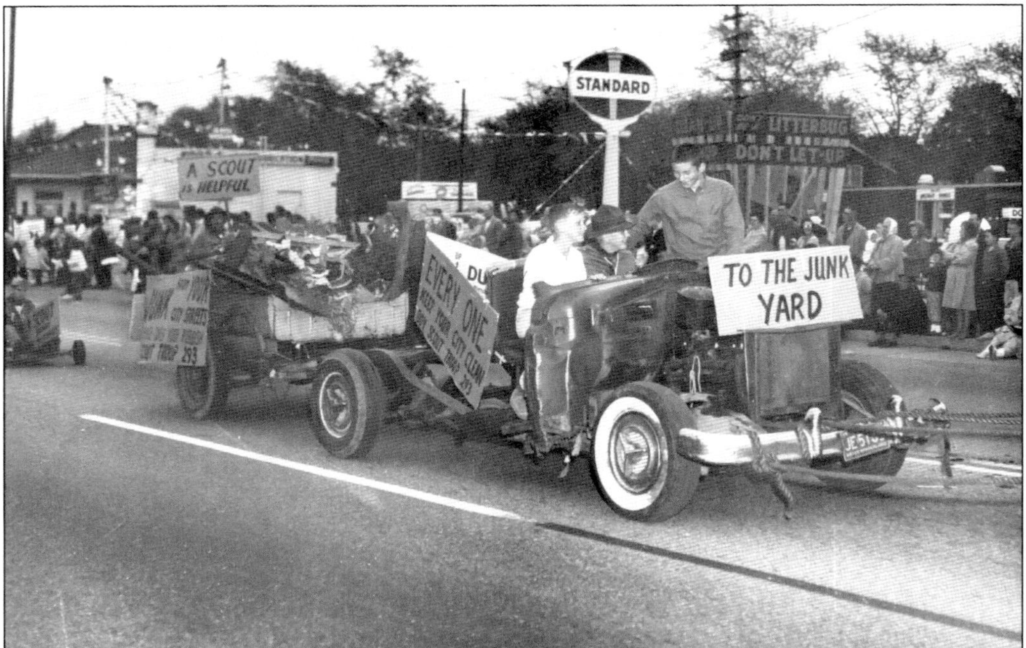

Boy Scout Troop 293 had an automobile wreck for a float. The Boy Scouts pitched in with cleaning up Grandville roadways that week—no trash was left on the ground. The parade ended, but the cleanup did not.

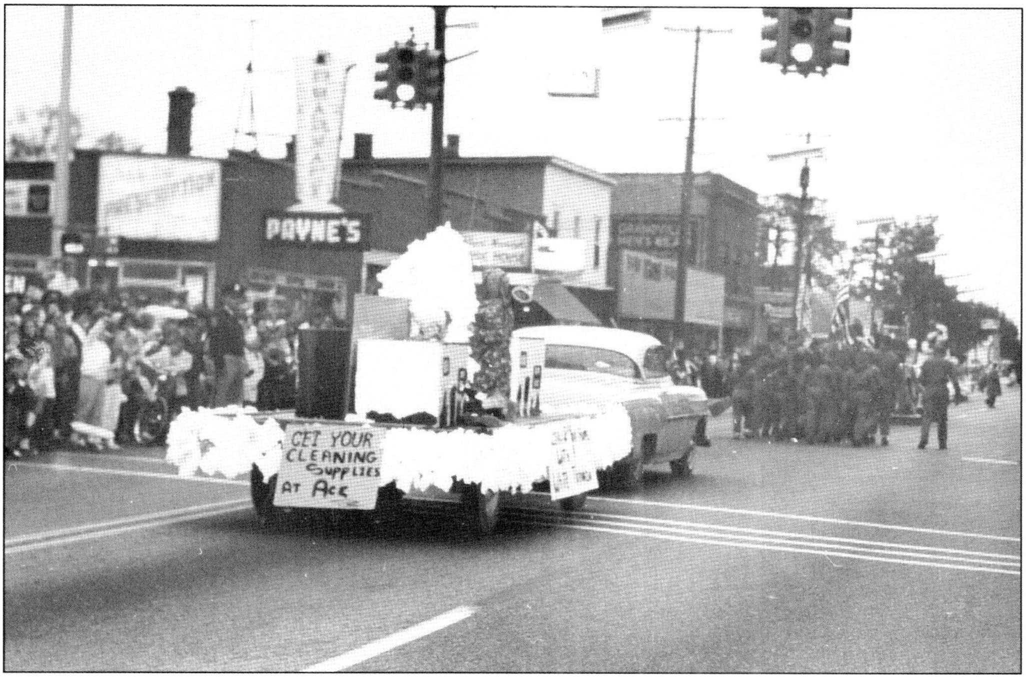

This is a float from Ace Hardware advertising cleaning supplies.

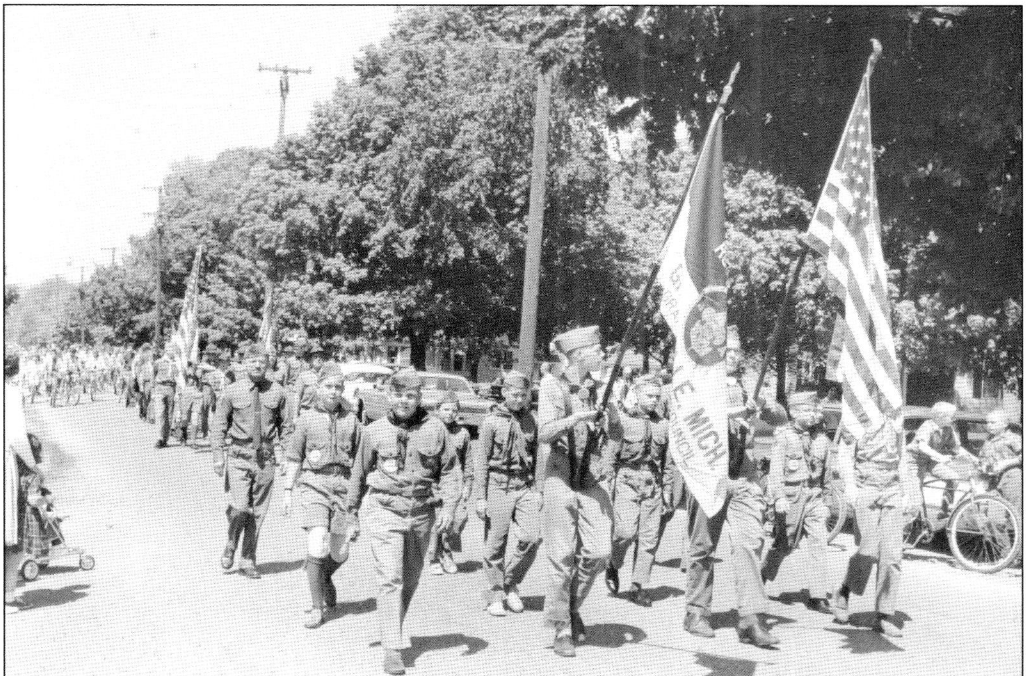
This is another Boy Scout troop in full dress uniform.

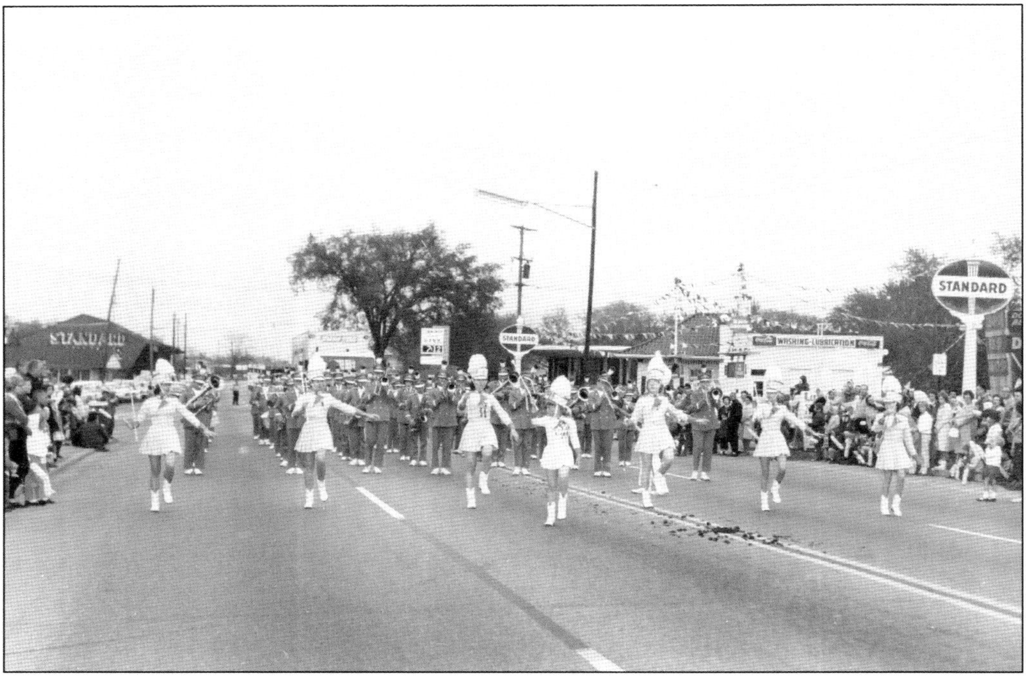

Here is the Grandville Marching Band on cleanup day.

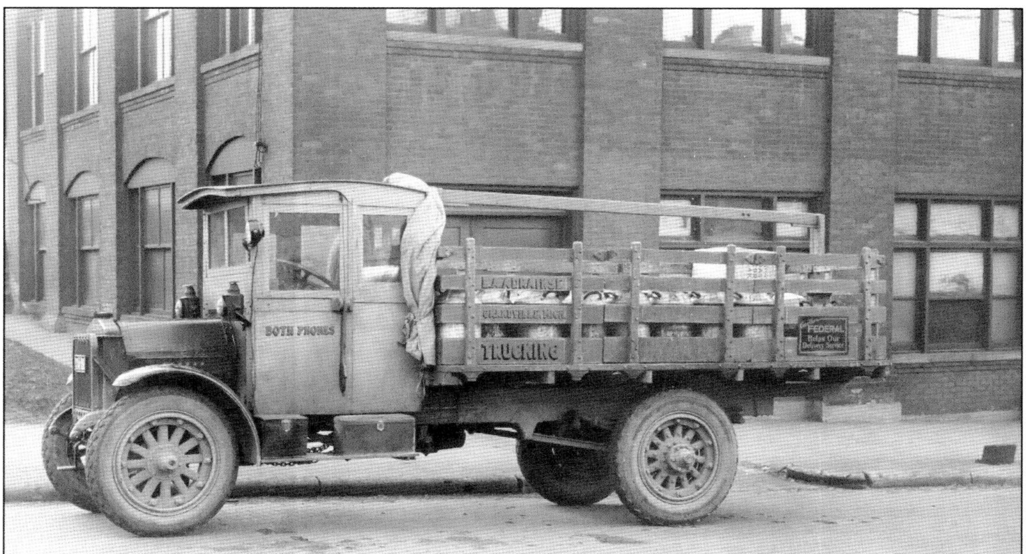

A relic in its time, this milk truck owned by Gene Adrianse was put to use in the cleanup.

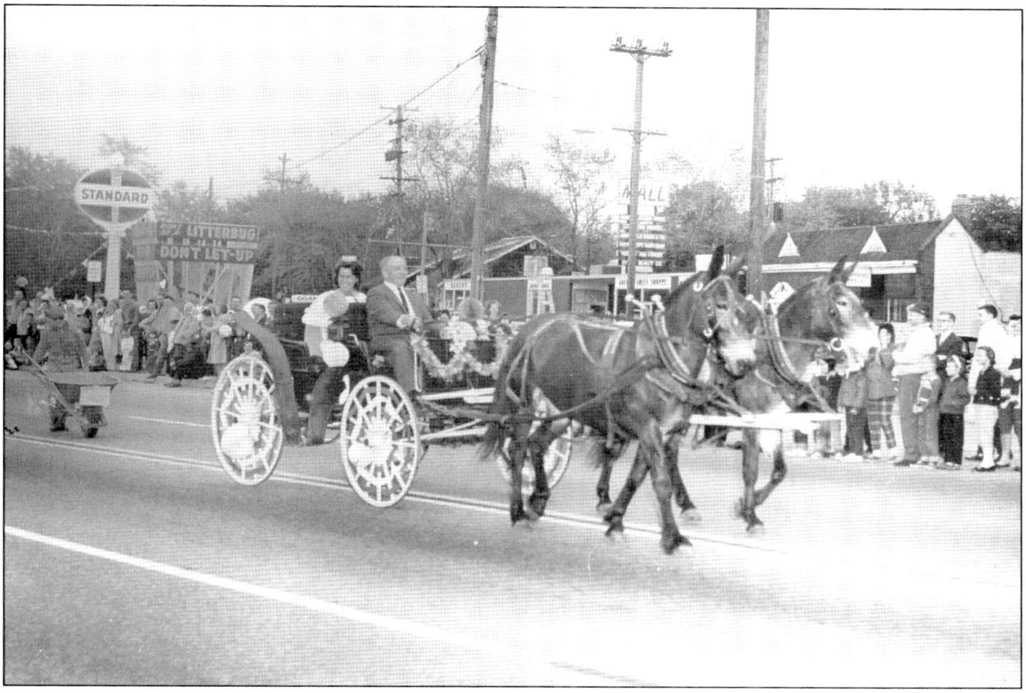

Dorothy Weaver, the queen of the cleanup parade, rides here in a carriage. She was also Grandville High School's homecoming queen in 1963. The parade wound its way down Chicago Drive, ending at the edge of town.

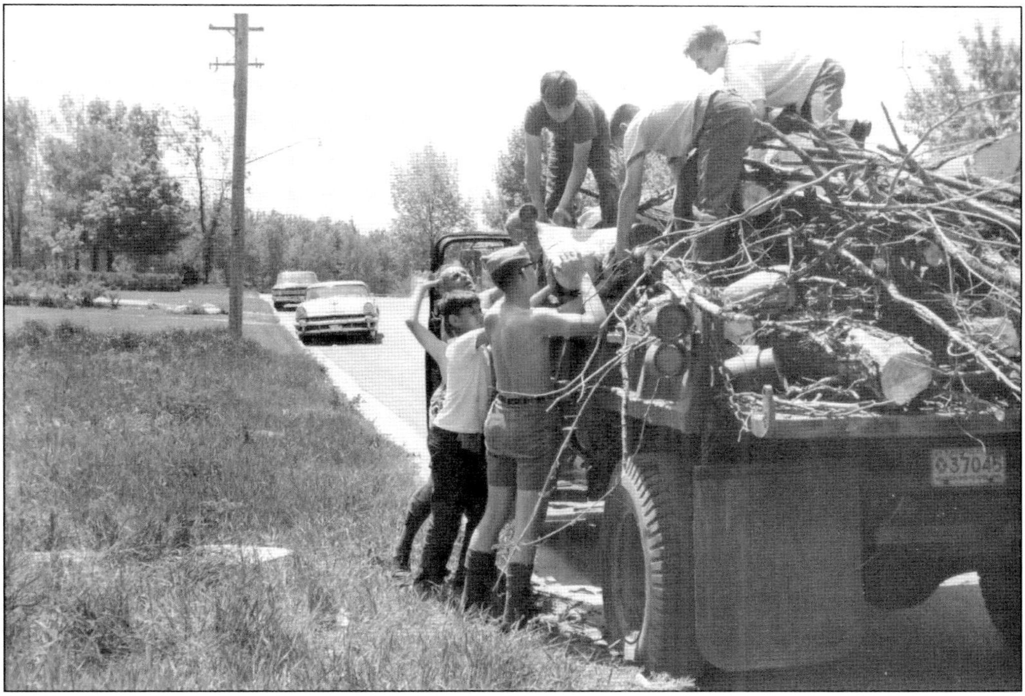

Here, Boy Scouts clean the roadways. Truckloads of debris were picked up along the road.

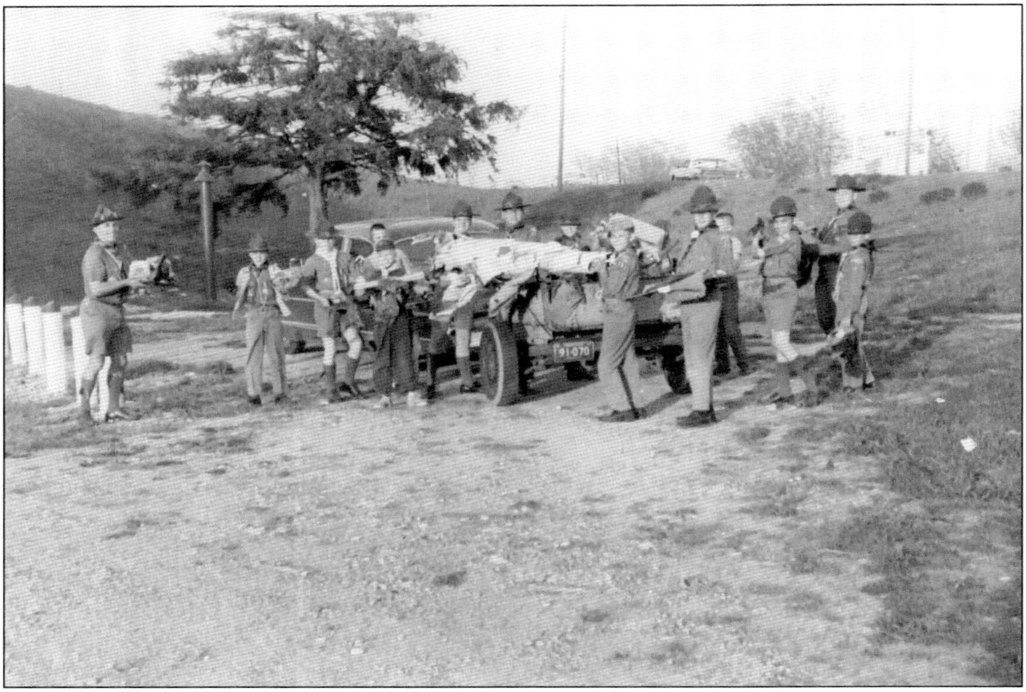

Led by Dusty Smith, members of Boy Scout Troop 293 were the unsung heroes. Here they are cleaning up the area under the viaduct of Twenty-eighth Street and Chicago Drive.

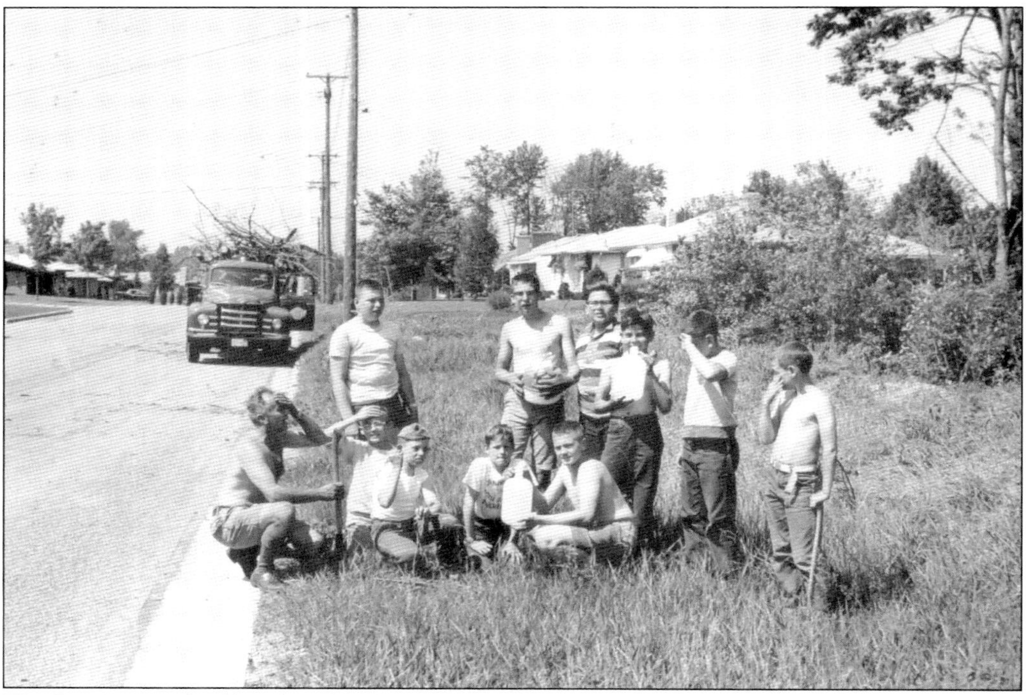

The Boy Scouts finally take a break after a long, hard day at work. Note the water jugs and the truck behind them that is filled to the top.

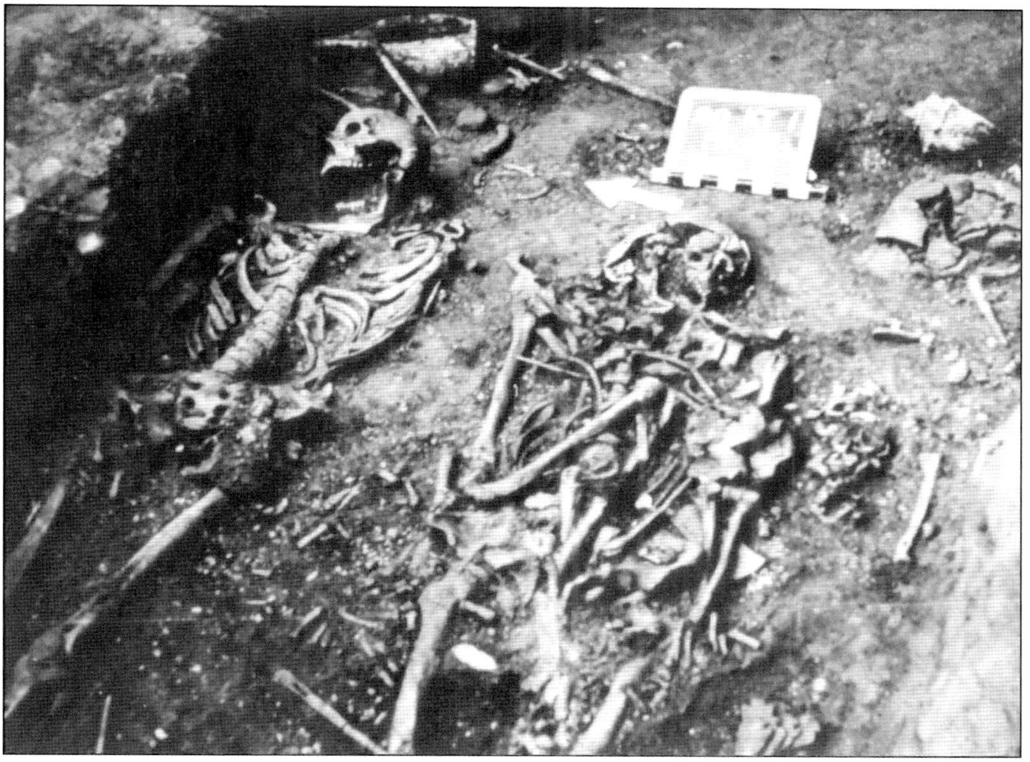

Workers found Indian artifacts and remains during the excavation for storm-sewer lines on White and Franklin Streets in 1962. Human remains, cups, plates, shells, eagle claws, pipes, and bear's teeth were some of the findings. It was such a remarkable discovery that construction of the sewer lines had to be put on hold.

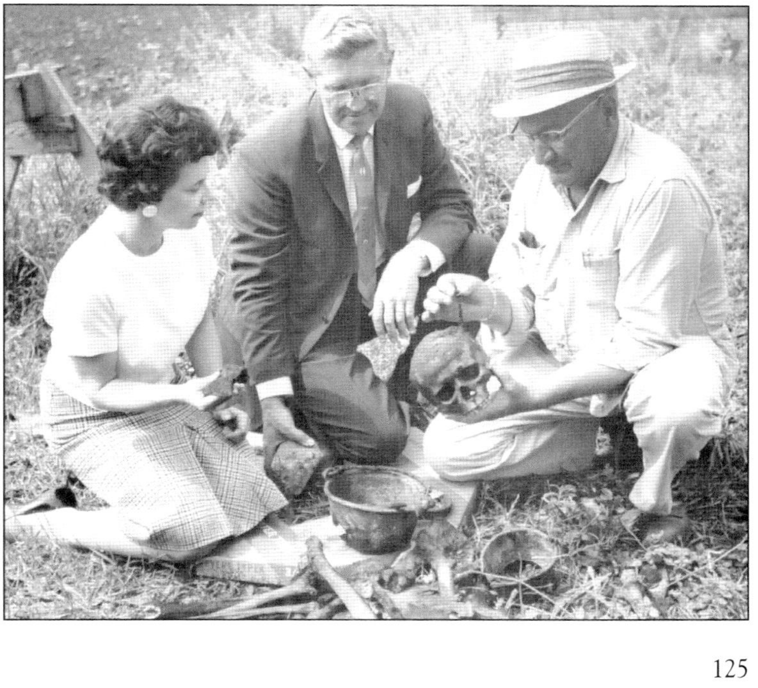

Dr Flanders (right), a University of Michigan professor, looks over the artifacts from the storm-sewer excavation. He took over the project and studied the Indian artifacts. Thousands of years ago, the Hopewell Indians lived in the area; in more recent times, in the 1700s to 1800s, the Ottawa Indians lived in Grandville.

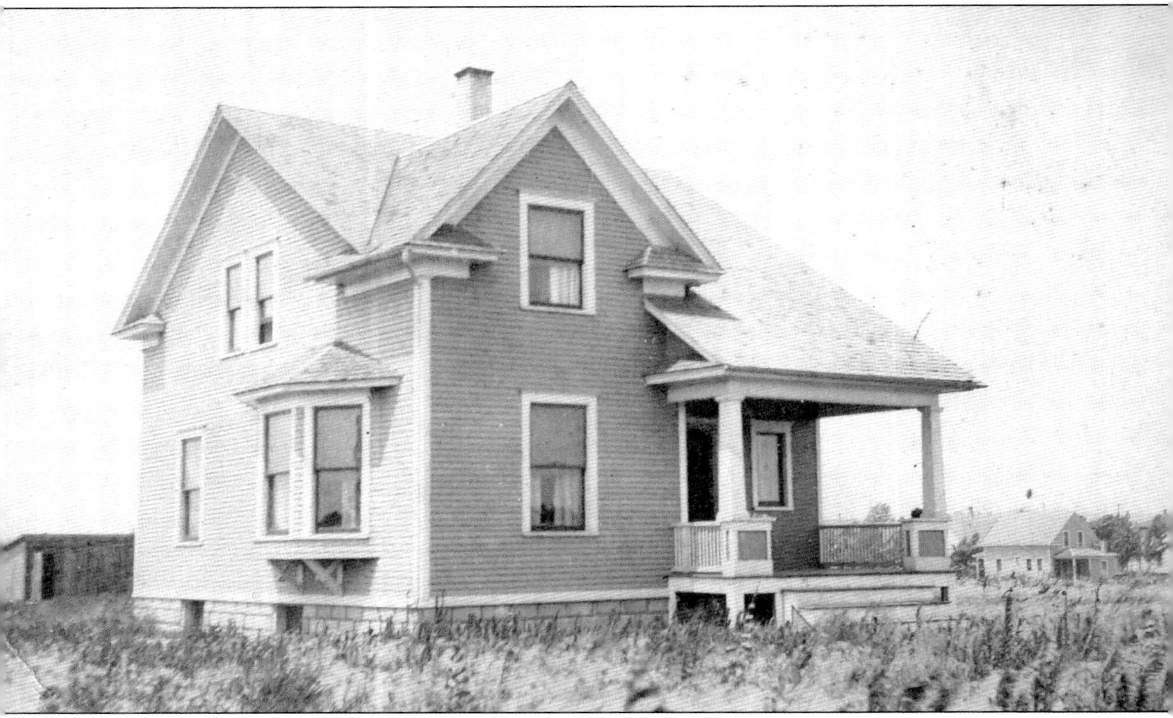

The following letter was sent with this photograph on July 13, 1913: "Dear Mom, Here is our new home we bought in Grandville. How do you like the looks of it? The house faces the east and this photograph shows the south side of it. I got my oil stove today at the hardware store here. It cost $10.95 storeroom price. It is a peach! The one in the catalog was only 14 inches high. This one has legs. It has a fine oven with a blue flame. We are sure looking forward to seeing you soon. Lovingly to all, Al."

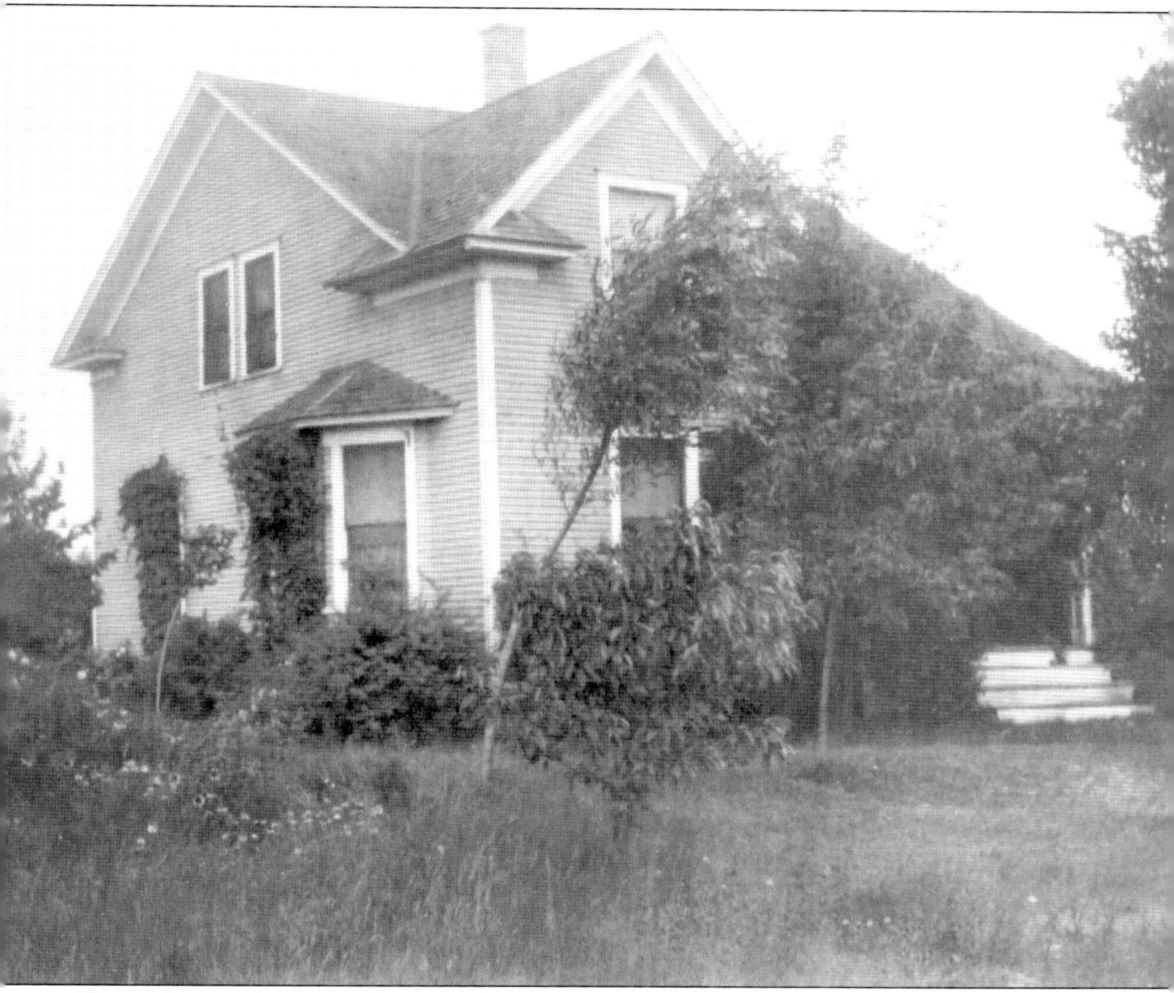

Here is the same house in July 1928. The couple that lived here must have loved their house and their community, or they would have never stayed. People do stay in Grandville. It is a caring city that is easy to fall in love with. It has a small-town feel of the past while being a forward-thinking city of the future. There is not a better place to call home!

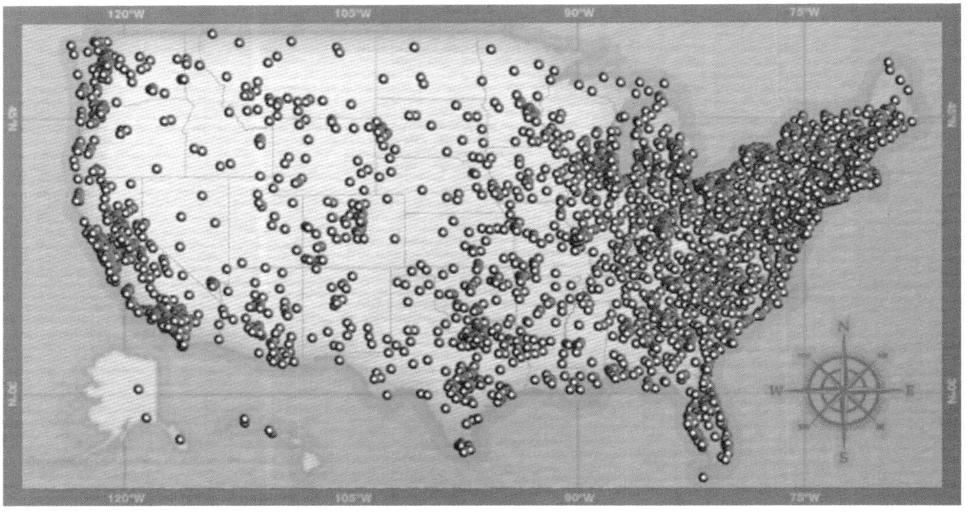

Consistent with our mission to preserve history on a local level, this book was printed in South Carolina on American-made paper and manufactured entirely in the United States. Products carrying the accredited Forest Stewardship Council (FSC) label are printed on 100 percent FSC-certified paper.

MADE IN THE USA